TOP 10 PARIS

MIKE GERRARD & DONNA DAILEY

EYEWITNESS TRAVEL

Left **Glass Pyramid, Musée du Louvre** Right **Crypt vaults, Sacré-Coeur**

LONDON, NEW YORK,
MELBOURNE, MUNICH AND DELHI
www.dk.com

Produced by Book Creation Services Ltd, London
Reproduced by Colourscan, Singapore
Printed and bound in China by Leo Paper Products Ltd

First American Edition, 2002
09 10 9 8 7 6 5 4 3 2 1

Published in the United States by
DK Publishing
375 Hudson Street, New York,
New York 10014

Reprinted with revisions 2003, 2004, 2005, 2006, 2007, 2008, 2009

ISSN 1479-344X
ISBN: 978-0-75663-255-7

Within each Top 10 list in this book, no hierarchy of quality or popularity is implied. All 10 are, in the editor's opinion, of roughly equal merit.

Floors are referred to throughout in accordance with French usage; i.e. the "first floor" is the floor above ground level.

Contents

Paris Top 10

The information in this DK Eyewitness Top 10 Travel Guide is checked annually.
Every effort has been made to ensure that this book is as up-to-date as possible at the time of going to press. Some details, however, such as telephone numbers, opening hours, prices, gallery hanging arrangements and travel information are liable to change. The publishers cannot accept responsibility for any consequences arising from the use of this book, nor for any material on third party websites, and cannot guarantee that any website address in this book will be a suitable source of travel information. We value the views and suggestions of our readers very highly. Please write to: Publisher, DK Eyewitness Travel Guides, Dorling Kindersley, 80 Strand, London, Great Britain WC2R 0RL.

Cover: All photographs specially commissioned except: Front – **4Corners Images**: SIME /Giovanni Simeone main; **DK Images**: Max Alexander clb. Spine – **DK Images**: Robert O'Dea b. Back – **DK Images**: cra; Max Alexander ca; Eric Meacher cla.

Left **Rose window, Notre-Dame** Right **Stone carvings, Arc de Triomphe**

Around Town

Streetsmart

Left **Bois de Boulogne** Right **Montmartre**

PARIS TOP 10

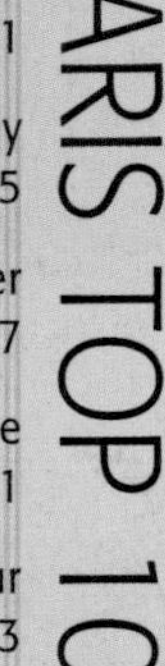

TOP 10 Paris Highlights

From Notre-Dame to the Eiffel Tower, Paris holds some of the world's most famous sights and these ten attractions should be top of the list for any first-time visitor. With the exception of the overtly modern Pompidou Centre, they have been landmarks of this elegant and romantic capital for centuries and remain awe-inspiring sights, no matter how often you visit the city.

1 Musée du Louvre

The world's largest museum unsurprisingly also contains one of the world's most important collections of art and antiquities. To complete the superlatives, the building was once France's largest royal palace *(see pp8–11)*.

2 Musée d'Orsay

This remarkable conversion has turned a former railway station into one of the world's leading art galleries *(above)* and is, for many, reason alone to visit Paris *(see pp12–15)*.

3 Eiffel Tower

Some six million visitors a year ascend to the top of this most famous Paris landmark for the spectacular views. It was erected for the Universal Exhibition of 1889 *(see pp16–17)*.

4 Notre-Dame

This great Gothic cathedral, founded on the site of a Roman temple, was completed in 1334 and is a repository of French art and history. It also represents the geographical heart of France *(see pp18–21)*.

5 Sacré-Coeur

The terrace in front of this monumental white-domed basilica in Montmartre affords one of the finest free views over Paris *(see pp22–3)*.

6 Arc de Triomphe

Napoleon's triumphal arch, celebrating battle victories, stands proudly at the top of the Champs-Elysées and, along with the Eiffel Tower, is one of the city's most enduring images *(see pp24–5)*.

metière de
ontmartre
5
Montmartre
BD DE CLICHY
BOULEVARD DE ROCHECHOUART
Pigalle
BD DE MAGENTA
RUE DU FAUBOURG ST DENIS
RUE LA FAYETTE
RUE DU FAUBOURG ST MARTIN
BOULEVARD DE LA VILLETTE
RUE LA FAYETTE
BLVD MONTMARTRE
BLVD POISSONNIERE
BD DE STRASBOURG
BD DE MAGENTA
RUE DU FAUBOURG DU TEMPLE
BD ST MARTIN
PLACE DE LA REPUBLIQUE
Belleville
RUE REAUMUR
RUE DE TURBIGO
AVE DE LA REPUBLIQUE
BOULEVARD DE SEBASTOPOL
BOULEVARD VOLTAIRE
RUE RIVOLI
Les Halles
RUE BEAUBOURG
rdin des
ileries
1
7
ILERIES
RUE DE
QUAI DU LOUVRE
RUE DU RENARD
Marais
BD BEAUMARCHAIS
VOLTAIRE
RIVOLI
9
QUAI DES GRANDS AUGUSTINS
Ile de la Cité
QUAI DE L'HOTEL DE VILLE
DE RENNES
BOULEVARD
4
Ile St-Louis
PLACE DE LA BASTILLE
BD HENRI IV
QUAI DE LA TOURNELLE
ST GERMAIN
BD BOURDON
BD DE LA BASTILLE
SAINT MICHEL
RUE ST JACQUES
Latin Quarter
RUE MONGE
La Seine
AVE LEDRU ROLLIN
Jardin du Luxembourg
8
QUAI ST BERNARD
BOULEVARD
Jardin des Plantes
1 miles 0 km 1

7 Centre Georges Pompidou

Home to the Paris Museum of Modern Art, the design of the Pompidou Centre makes it a distinctive exhibition in itself. The Centre also has extensive research facilities *(see pp26–7)*.

8 Panthéon

The great and the good of France are buried in the Panthéon *(above)*, including Voltaire and Victor Hugo *(see pp28–9)*.

9 Sainte-Chapelle

Called "a gateway to heaven", this splendid medieval church *(left)* was built to house the relics collected by St Louis on his many Crusades *(see pp30–31)*.

10 Hôtel des Invalides

The glowing golden dome of the Hôtel des Invalides church *(right)* is unmistakable across the rooftops of Paris *(see pp32–3)*.

For guided tours in Paris **See p165**

Musée du Louvre

One of the world's most impressive museums, the Louvre contains more than 350,000 priceless objects. Built as a fortress by King Philippe-Auguste in 1190, Charles V (1364–80) was the first king to make it his home. In the 16th century François I replaced it with a Renaissance-style palace and founded the royal art collection with 12 paintings looted from Italy. Revolutionaries opened the collection to the public in 1793. Shortly after, Napoleon renovated the Louvre as a museum.

Musée du Louvre façade

Try out Le Café Marly in the Richelieu Wing or the fast-food hall in Carrousel du Louvre. For a special option make a reservation at the Grand Louvre restaurant below the pyramid.

Beat the queues and buy tickets from the machines at the Carrousel du Louvre entrance (99 rue de Rivoli, 75001).

Musée du Louvre, 75001
- *Map L2*
- *01 40 20 50 50*
- *www.louvre.fr*
- *Open 9am–6pm Mon, Thu, Sat & Sun, 9am–10pm Wed & Fri; closed Tue & public hols*
- *Admission €9 (subject to change); reduced price of €6 after 6pm Wed & Fri; free 1st Sun of month; under 18s free; under 26s free Fri after 6pm*
- *Partial disabled access*

Top 10 Exhibits

1. Venus de Milo
2. Mona Lisa
3. Glass Pyramid
4. Marly Horses
5. The Raft of the Medusa
6. The Winged Victory of Samothrace
7. The Lacemaker
8. Slaves
9. Medieval Moats
10. Perrault's Colonnade

1 Venus de Milo

The positioning of this statue (unless moved for renovation), dramatically lit at the end of a hallway, enhances its beauty. It dates from the end of the 2nd century BC and was discovered on the Greek island of Milos in 1820.

2 Mona Lisa

Arguably the most famous painting in the world, Leonardo's portrait of the woman with the enigmatic smile *(see p11)* was encased in glass after a knife attack. Visit early or late in the day.

3 Glass Pyramid

The unmistakable pyramid, designed by I.M. Pei, became the Louvre's new entrance in 1989. Stainless steel tubes form the 21-m-high (69-ft) frame *(below)*.

4 Marly Horses

Coustou's rearing horses being restrained by horse-tamers were sculpted in 1745 for Louis XIV's Château de Marly. Replicas stand near the Place de la Concorde.

For more Paris museums **See pp34–5**

5 The Raft of the Medusa

A shipwreck three years earlier inspired this early Romantic painting *(right)* by Théodore Géricault (1791–1824) in 1819. The work depicts a moment when the survivors spot a sail on the horizon.

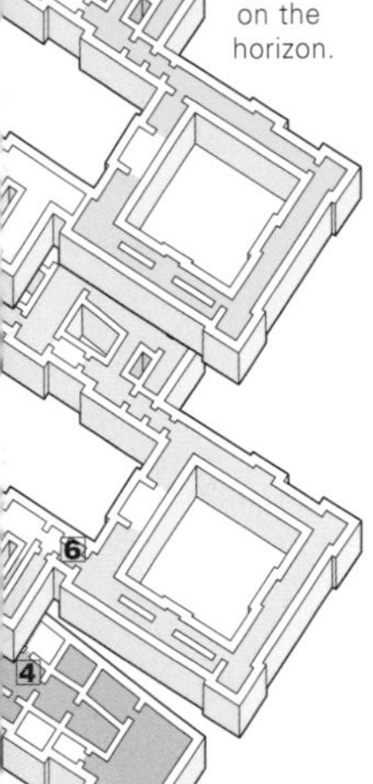

Key

Ground Floor

First Floor

Second Floor

6 The Winged Victory of Samothrace

This Hellenistic treasure (3rd–2nd century BC) stands atop a stone ship radiating grace and power. It commemorates a naval triumph at Rhodes.

7 The Lacemaker

Jan Vermeer's masterpiece *(below)*, painted around 1665 gives a simple but beautiful rendering of everyday life and is the highlight of the Louvre's Dutch collection.

8 Slaves

Michelangelo sculpted these two slaves (1513–20) for the tomb of Pope Julius II in Rome. He purposely left parts unfinished to symbolize the figures emerging from "prisons" of stone.

9 Medieval Moats

An excavation in the 1980s uncovered the remains of the medieval fortress. You can see the base of the towers and the drawbridge support.

10 Perrault's Colonnade

The majestic east façade by Claude Perrault (1613–88), with its columns *(below)*, was part of an extension plan commissioned by Louis XIV.

Gallery Guide

The main entrance is beneath the glass pyramid, but you can also enter through the Carrousel du Louvre shopping mall at 99 rue de Rivoli. From the ticket hall, corridors radiate out to each of the three wings – the Sully, Denon and Richelieu – set around several courtyards. The works are displayed on four floors, with paintings and sculpture collections arranged by country of origin. There are separate areas for *objets d'art*, antiquities, prints and drawings.

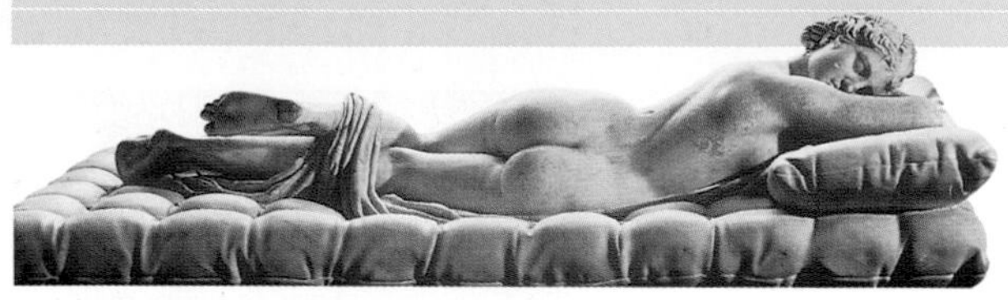

Above **Sleeping Hermaphrodite, Greek Antiquities**

TOP 10 Louvre Collections

1 French Paintings

This superb collection ranges from the 14th century to 1848 and includes works by such artists as Jean Watteau, Georges de la Tour and JH Fragonard.

2 French Sculpture

Highlights include the Tomb of Philippe Pot by Antoine le Moiturier, the Marly Horses *(see p8)* and the works by Pierre Puget in the glass-covered courtyards.

Collections floorplan

3 Egyptian Antiquities

The finest collection outside Cairo, featuring a Sphinx in the crypt, the Seated Scribe of Sakkara, huge sarcophagi, mummified animals, funerary objects and intricate carvings depicting everyday life in Ancient Egypt.

Akhenaton and Nefertiti, Egypt

4 Greek Antiquities

The wondrous art of Ancient Greece here ranges from a Cycladic idol from the third millennium BC to Classical Greek marble statues (*c*.5th century BC) to Hellenistic works (late 3rd–2nd century BC).

5 Oriental Antiquities

A stunning collection includes a re-created temple of an Assyrian king and the Codex of Hammurabi (18th century BC), mankind's oldest written laws.

6 Italian Paintings

French royalty adored the art of Italy and amassed much of this collection (1200–1800). There are many works by da Vinci including the *Mona Lisa*.

7 Italian Sculpture

Highlights of this collection, dating from the early Renaissance, include a 15th-century *Madonna and Child* by Donatello and Michelangelo's *Slaves (see p9)*.

8 Dutch Paintings

Rembrandt works take pride of place in this section, along with domestic scenes by Vermeer and portraits by Frans Hals.

9 Objets d'Art

This collection of ceramics, jewellery and other items spans many countries and centuries.

10 Islamic Art

An exquisite collection ranging from the 7th century to the Ottoman Empire (14th–19th centuries). Closed for renovation.

For more Paris museums **See pp34–5**

Leonardo da Vinci and the Mona Lisa

***Mona Lisa*, Leonardo da Vinci's enigmatic portrait**

Born in Vinci to a wealthy family, Leonardo da Vinci (1452–1519) first took up an apprenticeship under the Florentine artist Andrea del Verrocchio, then served the Duke of Milan as an architect and military engineer, during which time he painted the acclaimed Last Supper *mural (1495). On his return to Florence, to work as architect to Cesare Borgia, he painted his most celebrated portrait, the* Mona Lisa *(1503–06). It is also known as* La Gioconda, *allegedly the name of the model's aristocratic husband, although recent speculation suggests that da Vinci himself could be the subject. The masterpiece, particularly the sitter's mysterious smile, shows mastery of two techniques:* chiaroscuro, *the contrast of light and shadow, and* sfumato, *subtle transitions between colours. It was the artist's own favourite painting and he took it with him everywhere. In 1516 François I brought them both to France, giving da Vinci the use of Château de Cloux, near Amboise in the Loire Valley, where he died three years later. The* Mona Lisa *is the Renaissance master's only known surviving work of portraiture.*

Top 10 Louvre Residents

1. Charles V (1364–80)
2. Henri II (1547–49)
3. Catherine de' Medici (1519–89)
4. Henri IV (1589–1610)
5. Louis XIII (1610–43)
6. Louis XIV (1643–1715)
7. Anne of Austria (1601–66)
8. Guillaume Coustou, sculptor (1677–1746)
9. Edmé Bouchardon, sculptor (1698–1762)
10. François Boucher, artist (1703–70)

Leonardo da Vinci

A Renaissance man extraordinaire, Leonardo was not only an artist but a sculptor, engineer, architect and scientist. His many achievements included the study of anatomy and aerodynamics.

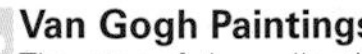

TOP 10 Musée d'Orsay

This wonderful collection covers a variety of art forms from the 1848–1914 period, including a superb Impressionists section. Its setting, in a converted railway station, is equally impressive. Built in 1900, in time for the Paris Exposition, the station was in use until 1939, when it was closed and largely ignored, bar its use as the location for Orson Welles' 1962 film, The Trial. *It was later used as a theatre and as auction rooms, and in the mid-1970s was considered for demolition. In 1977, the Paris authorities decided to save the imposing station building by converting it into this striking museum.*

Musée d'Orsay façade

The busy museum restaurant serves lunch and dinner on Thursdays. For a snack or a drink try the upper level café (Des Hauteurs) or the self-service mezzanine café just above.

Regular music concerts are held. Call 01 40 49 47 50 for details.

1 rue de la Légion-d'Honneur, 75007
• Map J2
• 01 40 49 48 14
• www.musee-orsay.fr
• Open 9:30am–6pm Tue–Sun (Thu till 9:45pm); closed 1 Jan, 1 May, 25 Dec
• Admission €8 (€5.50 18–25s, under 18s free); combined ticket for museum and temporary exhibitions €9.00 (€7.00 18–25s). Tickets can be bought online.

Top 10 Features

1. The Building
2. Van Gogh Paintings
3. Le Déjeuner sur l'Herbe
4. Olympia
5. Blue Waterlilies
6. Degas' Statues of Dancers
7. Jane Avril Dancing
8. Dancing at the Moulin de la Galette
9. La Belle Angèle
10. Café des Hauteurs

1 The Building

The former railway station which houses this museum is almost as stunning as the exhibits. The light and spacious feel when one first steps inside, after admiring the magnificent old façade, takes one's breath away.

2 Van Gogh Paintings

The star of the collection is Vincent Van Gogh (1853–90) and the most striking of the canvases on display is the 1889 work showing the artist's *Bedroom at Arles (below)*. Also on display are self-portraits, painted with the artist's familiar intensity (Rooms 35, 49, 50).

3 Le Déjeuner sur l'Herbe

Edouard Manet's (1832–83) controversial painting (1863) was first shown in an "Exhibition of Rejected Works". Its bold portrayal of a classically nude woman *(below)* enjoying the company of 19th-century men in suits brought about a wave of criticism (Room 19).

For more Paris museums **See pp34–5**

4 Olympia

Another Manet portrayal (1865) of a naked courtesan, receiving flowers sent by an admirer, was also regarded as indecent and shocked the public and critics, but it was a great influence on later artists (Room 14).

5 Blue Waterlilies

Claude Monet (1840–1926) painted this stunning canvas (1919) on one of his favourite themes. His love of waterlilies led him to create his own garden at Giverney to enable him to paint them in a natural setting. This experimental work *(below)* inspired many abstract painters later in the 20th century (Room 16).

6 Degas' Statues of Dancers

Edgar Degas' (1834–1917) sculpted dancers range from the innocent to the erotic. The striking *Young Dancer of Fourteen* (1881) is the only one exhibited in the artist's lifetime *(left)* (Room 31).

7 Jane Avril Dancing

Toulouse-Lautrec's (1864–1901) paintings define Paris's *belle époque*. Jane Avril was a Moulin Rouge dancer and featured in several of his works, like this 1895 canvas *(below)* (Room 47).

8 Dancing at the Moulin de la Galette

One of the best-known paintings of the Impressionist era (1876), the exuberance of Renoir's (1841–1919) work captures the look and mood of Montmartre (Room 32).

9 La Belle Angèle

This portrait of a Brittany beauty (1889) by Paul Gauguin (1848–1903) shows the influence of Japanese art on the artist. It was bought by Degas, to finance Gauguin's first trip to Polynesia (Room 43).

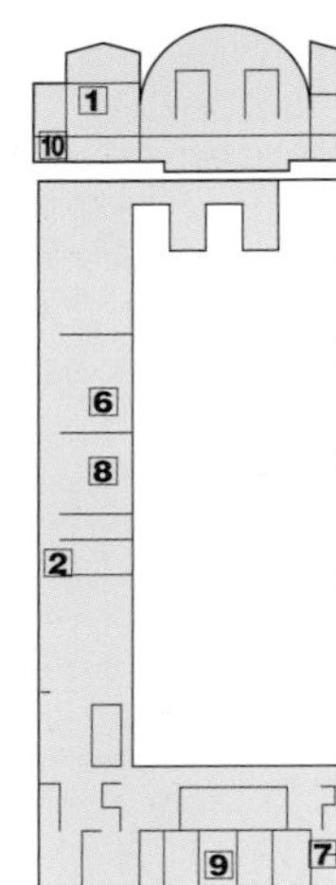

Musée d'Orsay Upper Level

10 Café des Hauteurs

As a rest from all the art, the Musée d'Orsay's café is delightfully situated behind one of the former station's huge clocks, making a break here an experience in itself. The food is good too.

Gallery Guide

As soon as you enter the gallery, collect a map of its layout. Escalators near the entrance lead to all three floors. The ground floor houses fine works from the early to mid-19th century, as well as striking Oriental works, decorative arts and a book shop. The middle level includes Naturalist and Symbolist paintings and sculpture terraces. The upper level is home to the Impressionist and Post-Impressionist galleries, which contain the collection's most popular paintings.

For more Paris art galleries **See pp36–7**

Left *Blue Dancers* (1890), Degas Right *La Belle Angèle* (1889), Gauguin

Musée d'Orsay Collections

1 The Impressionists

One of the best Impressionist collections in the world. Admirers of Manet, Monet and Renoir will not be disappointed.

2 The Post-Impressionists

The artists who moved on to a newer interpretation of Impressionism are equally well represented, including Matisse, Toulouse-Lautrec and the towering figure of Van Gogh.

3 School of Pont-Aven

Paul Gauguin *(see p13)* was at the centre of the group of artists associated with Pont-Aven in Brittany. His work here includes the carved door panels known as the *House of Pleasure* (1901).

4 Art Nouveau

Art Nouveau is synonymous with Paris, with many metro stations retaining entrances built in that style. Pendants and bottles by René-Jules Lalique (1860–1945) are among the examples.

5 Symbolism

This vast collection includes works by Gustav Klimt (1862–1918), Edvard Munch (1863–1944) and James Whistler's (1834–1903) 1871 portrait of his mother.

6 Romanticism

The Romantics wanted to heighten awareness of the spiritual world. One striking work is *The Tiger Hunt* (1854) by Eugène Delacroix (1798–1863).

Floorplan: the collections

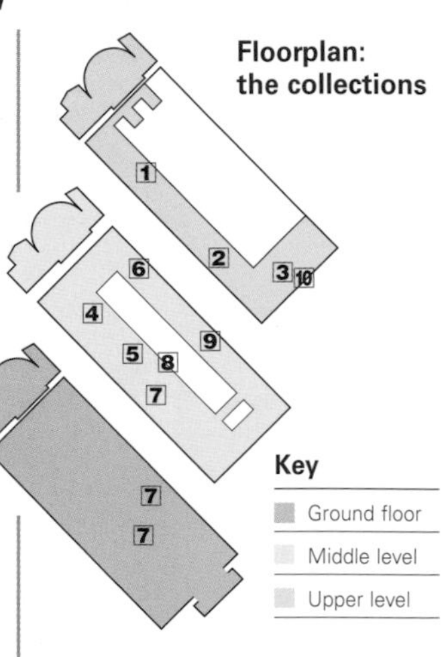

7 Sculpture

The collection includes pieces by Rodin *(see p111)* and satirical carvings of politicians by Honoré Daumier (1808–79).

8 Naturalism

Naturalist painters intensified nature in their work. *Haymaking* (1877) by Jules Bastien-Lepage (1848–84) is a fine example.

9 Nabis

The Nabis Movement moved art into a more decorative form. Pierre Bonnard (1867–1947) is one of its exponents.

10 Photography Collection

Some 10,000 early photographs include work by Bonnard, Degas and photographer Julia Margaret Cameron (1815–79).

Top 10 Impressionists

1. Claude Monet (1840–1926)
2. Edouard Manet (1832–83)
3. Auguste Renoir (1841–1919)
4. Edgar Degas (1834–1917
5. Camille Pissarro (1830–1903)
6. Alfred Sisley (1839–99)
7. James Whistler (1834–1903)
8. Walter Sickert (1860–1942)
9. Mary Cassatt (1845–1926)
10. Berthe Morisot (1841–95)

(Prices for Impressionist paintings at auction are considered a financial barometer for the art world. One of Monet's Waterlily paintings fetched US$22.6 million.)

The Impressionist Movement

Regarded as the starting point of modern art, the Impressionist Movement is probably the best-known and best-loved art movement in the world – certainly if prices at auction and the crowds in the Musée d'Orsay's galleries are anything to go by. The movement started in France, and almost all its leading figures were French, including the Parisian-born British artist Alfred Sisley. Impressionism was a reaction against the formality and Classicism insisted upon by the Académie des Beaux-Arts in Paris, who were very much the art establishment and decided what would or would not be exhibited at the all-important Paris Salon. The term "impressionism" was actually coined by a critic of the style, who dismissed the 1872 Monet painting Impression: Sunrise *in a magazine. The artists themselves then adopted the term. The style profoundly influenced painters such as Van Gogh and was to have a lasting influence on 19th- and 20th-century art.*

***Cathedral at Rouen* (1892–3), Claude Monet**

Dancing at the Moulin de la Galette (1876), Renoir

TOP 10 Eiffel Tower

The most distinctive symbol of Paris, the Eiffel Tower (Tour Eiffel) was much maligned by critics when it rose on the city's skyline in 1889 as part of the Universal Exhibition, but its graceful symmetry soon made it the star attraction. At 320 m (1,050 ft) high, it was the world's tallest building until it was surpassed by New York's Empire State Building in 1931. Despite its delicate appearance, it weighs 10,100 metric tons and engineer Gustave Eiffel's construction was so sound that it never sways more than 7 cm (2.5 in) in strong winds.

Eiffel Tower from the Trocadéro

In addition to the restaurants on levels 1 and 2, vendors sell snacks at the base.

Try and visit the tower at night, when it is beautifully floodlit and the queues are shorter.

Champ-de-Mars, 7e • Map B4 • 01 44 11 23 23 • www.tour-eiffel.fr • Open: Lift 9:30am–11:45pm daily (last adm for top: 10:30pm) (mid-Jun–1 Sep: 9am–12:45am; last adm for top: 11pm); Stairs 9:30am–6:30pm daily (mid-Jul–1 Sep: 9am–12:45am; last adm midnight) • Admission: €4.00 (stairs); €4.50–€11.50 (lift, depending on level) • Disabled access first and second levels only

Top 10 Features

1. Viewing Gallery
2. Ironwork
3. Lighting
4. View from the Trocadéro
5. Cineiffel
6. First Level
7. Second Level
8. Hydraulic Lift Mechanism
9. Bust of Gustave Eiffel
10. Champ de Mars

1 Viewing Gallery

At 276 m (906 ft), the view is stupendous from the third-level viewing gallery, stretching for 80 km (50 miles) on a clear day. You can also see Gustave Eiffel's sitting room on this level.

2 Ironwork

The complex pattern of the girders, held together by 2.5 million rivets, stabilizes the tower in high winds. The 18,000 metal parts can expand up to 15 cm (6 in) on hot days.

For more on the Eiffel Tower Quarter **See pp110–17**

3 Lighting

A 292,000-watt lighting system makes the Eiffel Tower the most spectacular night-time sight in Paris. Illuminated for 10 minutes every hour, it forms a golden filigree against the dark sky.

4 View from the Trocadéro

Day or night, the best approach for a first-time view of the tower is from the Trocadéro *(see p136)*, which affords a monumental vista from the terrace across the Seine.

5 Cineiffel

Located on the first level, this small museum tells the history of the tower through an audio-visual show. It includes footage of famous visitors to the tower, from Charlie Chaplin to Adolf Hitler.

6 First Level

You can walk the 360 steps to the 57 m (187 ft) high first level, or jump the lift queue by booking a table at the Altitude 95 restaurant *(see p117)*. Mail your postcards at the post office.

7 Second Level

At 115 m (377 ft) high, this is the location of the Jules Verne Restaurant, one of the finest in Paris for both food and views *(see p117)*. The walk up from the first level is 700 steps.

8 Hydraulic Lift Mechanism

The 1889 lift mechanism is still in operation and travels some 100,000 km (62,000 miles) a year. The lifts have limited capacity, so on busy days allow two hours to the top.

9 Bust of Gustave Eiffel

This bust of the tower's creator, by Antoine Bourdelle, was placed below his remarkable achievement, by the north pillar, in 1930.

10 Champ-de-Mars

The long gardens of this former parade ground *(right)* stretch from the base of the tower to the École Militaire (military school).

Caricature of Gustave Eiffel with his tower

The Life of Gustave Eiffel

Born in Dijon, Gustave Eiffel (1832–1923) was an engineer and builder who made his name building bridges and viaducts. Eiffel was famous for the graceful designs and master craftsmanship of his wrought-iron constructions. He once remarked that his famous tower was "formed by the wind itself". In 1890 he became immersed in the study of aerodynamics, and kept an office in the tower until his death, using it for experiments. In 1889, when the Eiffel Tower was erected, its creator was awarded the Légion d'Honneur for the achievement.

TOP 10 Notre-Dame

The heart of the country, both geographically and spiritually, the Cathedral of Notre-Dame (Our Lady) stands majestic on the Ile de la Cité. After Pope Alexander III laid the foundation stone in 1163, an army of craftsmen toiled for 170 years to realize Bishop Maurice de Sully's magnificent design. Almost destroyed during the Revolution, the Gothic masterpiece was restored in 1841–64 by architect Viollet-le-Duc. Some 130 m (430 ft) in length with a high-vaulted nave and double side aisles, it also contains France's largest organ.

3 Flying Buttresses

The striking buttresses supporting the cathedral's east façade are by Jean Ravy and have a span of 15 m (50 ft). The best view is from Square Jean XXIII.

Notre-Dame seen from the River Seine

There are cafés opposite the Square Jean XXIII.

Free organ recitals on Sunday afternoons.

6 Parvis Notre-Dame-Place Jean-Paul II, 75004 • Map N4 • 01 53 10 07 00 (towers); 01 42 34 56 10 (cathedral) • Open: cathedral 8am–6:45pm daily (to 7:15pm Sat–Sun); towers Apr–Sep: 10am–6:30pm daily (to 11pm Sat–Sun Jun–Aug); Oct–Mar: 10am–5:30pm daily • Adm: €7.50, (€4.80 18–25s, under-18s free, free 1st Sun of month)

Top 10 Features

1. West Front
2. Portal of the Virgin
3. Flying Buttresses
4. The Towers
5. Galerie des Chimières
6. The Spire
7. Rose Windows
8. Statue of the Virgin and Child
9. Carved Choir Stalls
10. Treasury

1 West Front

The glorious entrance to the cathedral *(right)* is through three elaborately carved portals. Biblical scenes, painted in the Middle Ages, represent the life of the Virgin, the Last Judgment and the Life of St Anne. Above is the Gallery of Kings of Judaea and Israel.

2 Portal of the Virgin

The splendid stone tympanum *(left)* was carved in the 13th century and shows the Virgin Mary's death and glorious coronation in heaven. However, the Virgin and Child carving seen between the doors is a modern work of art.

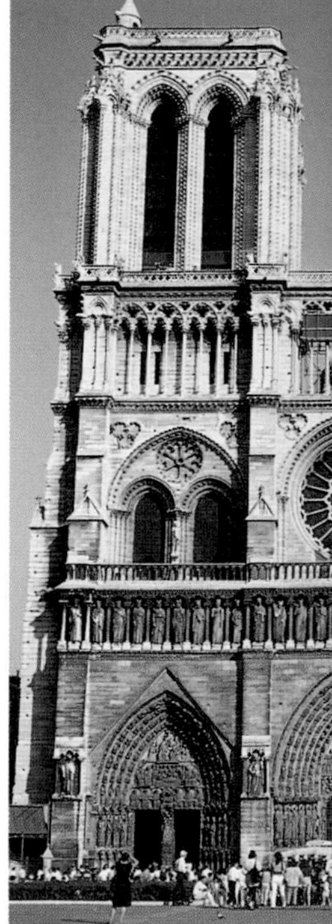

4 The Towers

The twin towers are 69 m (226 ft) high: visitors can climb the 387 steps of the north tower for splendid vistas over Paris. The south tower houses the Emmanuel Bell, weighing 13 tonnes.

For more Paris churches **See pp40–41**

5 Galerie des Chimères

Lurking between the towers are the famous gargoyles *(chimères)*, placed here by Viollet-le-Duc to ward off evil.

6 The Spire

The 90-m (295-ft) spire was added by Viollet-le-Duc. Next to the Apostles statues on the roof is one of the architect, admiring his work.

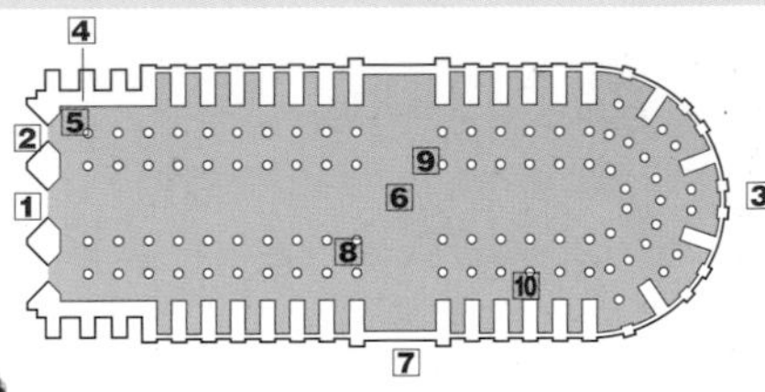

Floorplan of the Cathedral

7 Rose Windows

Three great rose windows adorn the north, south and west façades, but only the north window *(below)* retains its 13th-century stained glass, depicting the Virgin surrounded by figures from the Old Testament. The south window shows Christ encircled by the Apostles.

8 Statue of the Virgin and Child

Also known as Notre-Dame de Paris (Our Lady of Paris), this beautiful 14th-century statue was brought to the cathedral from the chapel of St Aignan. It stands against the southeast pillar of the transept, at the entrance to the chancel.

9 Choir Stalls

More than half of the original stalls commissioned by Louis XIV survive. Among the beautifully carved work on the 78 stalls are scenes from the Life of the Virgin.

10 Treasury

Ancient manuscripts, reliquaries and religious garments are housed in the sacristy. The crown of thorns and a piece of the True Cross are on public view every Good Friday.

Cathedral Guide

Enter through the West Front. The stairs to the towers are outside to your left. Ahead, the central nave soars to a height of 35 m (115 ft), while 37 side chapels line the walls. These contain the "May" paintings by Charles le Brun, donated by the goldsmiths' guild each May in the 17th–18th centuries. The fine transept across the nave is the best place to admire the three rose windows. Remnants of the 14th-century stone screen can be seen on the north and south bays of the chancel. Nicolas Coustou's *Pietà* stands behind the high altar, flanked by statues of Louis XIII by Coustou and Louis XIV by Antoine Coysevox.

Left **Joan of Arc** Centre **Empress Josephine** Right **King Charles I**

Top 10 Famous Visitors to Notre-Dame

1 Joan of Arc

The French patriot Jeanne d'Arc (1412–31), who defended her country against the invading English, had a posthumous trial here in 1455, despite having been burnt at the stake 24 years earlier. At the re-trial she was found to be innocent of heresy.

2 François II and Mary Stuart

Mary Stuart (1542–87) (Mary Queen of Scots) had been raised in France and married the Dauphin in 1558. He ascended the throne as François II in 1559 and the king and queen were crowned in Notre-Dame.

3 Napoleon

The coronation of Napoleon (1769–1821) in Notre-Dame in 1804 saw the eager general seize the crown from Pope Pius VII and crown himself emperor and his wife Josephine, empress.

4 Josephine

Josephine's (1763–1814) reign as Empress of France lasted only five years; Napoleon divorced her in 1809.

5 Pope Pius VII

In 1809 Pope Pius VII (1742–1823), who oversaw the Notre-Dame coronation, was taken captive when the emperor declared the Papal States to be part of France. The pope was imprisoned at Fontainebleau, outside Paris, for a time.

6 Philip the Fair

In 1302 the first States General parliament was formally opened at Notre-Dame by Philip IV (1268–1314), otherwise known as Philip the Fair. He greatly increased the governing power of the French royalty.

7 Henry VI of England

Henry VI (1421–71) became King of England at the age of one. Like his father, Henry V, he also claimed France and was crowned in Notre-Dame in 1430.

8 Marguerite of Valois

In August 1572, Marguerite (1553–1589), sister of the French king Charles IX, stood in the Notre-Dame chancel during her marriage to Henri of Navarre (1553–1610), while he stood alone by the door.

9 Henri of Navarre

As a Protestant Huguenot, Henri's marriage to the Catholic Marguerite resulted in uprising and massacres. In 1589 he became Henri IV, the first Bourbon king of France, and converted to Catholicism, declaring that "Paris is well worth a mass".

10 Charles de Gaulle

On 26 August 1944, Charles de Gaulle entered Paris and attended a Te Deum mass to celebrate the liberation of Paris, despite the fact that hostile snipers were still at large both inside and outside the cathedral.

For more historic events in Paris **See pp44–5**

Top 10 Events in Notre-Dame History

1. Construction on the cathedral begins (1163)
2. St Louis places the Crown of Thorns here temporarily (1239)
3. Construction is completed (1334)
4. Re-trial of Joan of Arc (1455)
5. Crowning of Emperor Napoleon (1804)
6. Publication of Hugo's novel *The Hunchback of Notre-Dame* (1831)
7. Completion of 23-year restoration programme (1864)
8. Assassination attempt on Charles de Gaulle (1944)
9. De Gaulle's Requiem Mass is held (1970)
10. De Gaulle Special Memorial Service (1996)

The Man Who Saved Notre-Dame

Novelist Victor Hugo

By 1831, when Victor Hugo's novel Notre-Dame de Paris (The Hunchback of Notre-Dame) *was published, the cathedral was in a sorry state of decay. Even for the crowning of Emperor Napoleon in 1804, the setting for such ceremonious state occasions was crumbling and had to be disguised with wall hangings and ornamentation. During the Revolution, the cathedral was even sold to a scrap dealer, but was never actually demolished. Hugo was determined to save the country's spiritual heart and helped mount a successful campaign to restore Notre-Dame before it was too late; the man chosen to design and oversee the restoration was Eugène Emmanuel Viollet-le-Duc (1814–1879). Paris-born, Viollet-le-Duc had already proved his skill in restoration work, as evidenced by the cathedrals in Amiens and Laon, and on the spectacular walled city of Carcassone in southern France. Work began in 1841 and continued for 23 years until the building was finished more or less as we see it today. Viollet-le-Duc later went on to restore the chapel of Ste-Chapelle* (see pp30–31).

The Hunchback of Notre-Dame

Hugo's 1831 novel tells the story of Quasimodo, a hunchbacked bell-ringer at Notre-Dame, who falls in love with gypsy girl Esmeralda.

For more novels set in Paris **See pp46–7**

TOP 10 Sacré-Coeur

One of the most photographed images of the city, the spectacular white outline of Sacré-Coeur (Sacred Heart) watches over Paris from its highest point. The basilica was built as a memorial to the 58,000 French soldiers killed during the Franco-Prussian War (1870–71) and took 46 years to build, finally completed in 1923 at a cost of 40 million francs (6 million euros). Priests still pray for the souls of the dead here 24 hours a day. Although the interior is less impressive than many other churches in the city, people flock here for the panoramic views – at sunset, in particular, there are few sights in Paris more memorable.

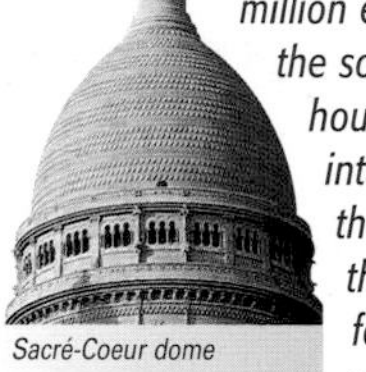

Sacré-Coeur dome

Avoid the crowds and head to 23 rue des Abbesses and grab a bite at the St Jean or head to place du Tertre for cheap crêpes and ice cream.

An evocative sung Mass takes place on Sundays at 11am.

Parvis du Sacré-Coeur, 75018 • Map F1 • 01 53 41 89 00 • www.sacre-coeur-montmartre.com • Open 6am–11pm, last entry 10:15pm (basilica), 9:30am–5:30pm (dome and crypt) daily • Admission €5.00 (dome and crypt only) • No disabled access

Top 10 Features

1. Great Mosaic of Christ
2. Crypt Vaults
3. Bronze Doors
4. Dome
5. Statue of Christ
6. Bell Tower
7. Equestrian Statues
8. Stained-Glass Gallery
9. Façade
10. The Funicular

1 Great Mosaic of Christ

A glittering Byzantine mosaic of Christ *(right)*, created by Luc Olivier Merson between 1912–22, decorates the vault over the chancel. It represents France's devotion to the Sacred Heart.

2 Crypt Vaults

The most interesting feature of the interior is the arched vaults of the crypt. A chapel contains the heart of Alexandre Legentil, one of the advocates of Sacré-Coeur.

3 Bronze Doors

The doors of the portico entrance are beautifully decorated with bronze relief sculptures depicting the Last Supper *(right)* and other scenes from the life of Christ.

For more Paris churches **See pp40–41**

4 The Dome
The distinctive egg-shaped dome of the basilica is the second-highest viewpoint in Paris after the Eiffel Tower. Reached via a spiral staircase, vistas can stretch as far as 48 km (30 miles) on a clear day.

5 Statue of Christ
The basilica's most important statue shows Christ giving a blessing. It is symbolically placed in a niche over the main entrance, above the two equestrian statues.

6 Bell Tower
The beautiful *campanile*, designed by Lucien Magne and added in 1904, is 80 m (262 ft) high. One of the heaviest bells in the world, the 19-ton La Savoyarde hangs in the belfry. Cast in Annecy in 1895, it was donated by the dioceses of Savoy.

7 Equestrian Statues
Two striking bronze statues of French saints stand on the portico above the main entrance, cast by H Lefèbvre *(below)*. One is of Joan of Arc, the other of Saint Louis.

8 Stained-Glass Gallery
One level of the great dome is encircled by stained-glass windows. From here there is a grand view over the whole interior.

The Franco-Prussian War

In 1870, as Prussia made moves to take over Germany, France was also threatened by its military power. Two Catholic businessmen in Paris vowed to build a church dedicated to the Sacred Heart if France were spared the Prussian onslaught. France declared war on Prussia in July, but she was ill-prepared and in September Napoleon III was captured. Parisians held fast, however, defending their city with home-made weapons and eating dogs, cats and rats. But by January 1871 they surrendered.

Captured French soldier taking leave of his wife

9 Façade
Architect Paul Abadie (1812–1884) employed a mix of domes, turrets and Classical features in his design. The Château-Landon stone secretes calcite when wet and bleaches the façade white.

10 The Funicular
To avoid the steep climb up to Sacré-Coeur, take the *funiculaire* cable railway and enjoy the views at leisure. It runs from the end of rue Foyatier, near Square Willette.

Top 10 Arc de Triomphe

The best day to visit the world's most familiar triumphal arch is 2 December, the date that marks Napoleon's victory at the Battle of Austerlitz in 1805, when the sun sets in line with the Champs-Elysées and the Arc de Triomphe, creating a spectacular halo around the building. Work began on the 50-m (164-ft) arch in 1806 but was not completed until 1836, due, in part, to Napoleon's fall from power. Four years later, Napoleon's funeral procession passed beneath it, on its way to his burial in Les Invalides (see pp32–3). *Today the arch is a focal point for rallies and public events.*

Arc de Triomphe pediment

Try to get here early, as the morning light shows the golden tone of the stone-work at its best.

Enjoy a coffee and the old-world charm of Le Fouquet (99 Ave des Champs-Elysées) – expensive, but worth the treat.

• Place du Général-de-Gaulle, 75008 • 01 55 37 73 77 (enquiries), 01 55 37 73 78 (tours) • http://arc-de-triomphe.monuments-nationaux.fr • Map B2 • Open Apr–Sep: 10am–11pm daily; Oct–Mar: 10am–0:30pm daily; closed 1 Jan, 1 May, 8 May (am), 14 Jul (am), 11 Nov, 25 Dec and for major events • Admission €9.00

Top 10 Features

1. Viewing Platform
2. Tomb of the Unknown Soldier
3. Museum
4. Departure of the Volunteers in 1792
5. Frieze
6. Triumph of Napoleon
7. Battle of Austerlitz
8. Battle of Aboukir
9. General Marceau's Funeral
10. Thirty Shields

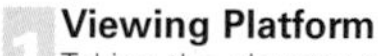

1 Viewing Platform

Taking the elevator or climbing the 284 steps to the top of the Arc de Triomphe *(below)* gives visitors a sublime and unique view of Paris. To the east is the Champs-Elysées *(see p103)*, one of the world's most famous avenues, and to the west, slightly out of line, is the Grande Arche of La Défense *(see p151)*.

2 Tomb of the Unknown Soldier

In the centre of the arch flickers the eternal flame on the Tomb of the Unknown Soldier, a victim of World War I buried on 11 November 1920. It is symbolically re-ignited every day at 6:30pm.

For more historic buildings in Paris **See pp42–3**

3 Museum

Within the arch is a small but interesting museum which tells the history of its construction and gives details of various celebrations and funerals that the arch has seen over the years. The more recent of these are shown in a short video.

6 Triumph of Napoleon

As you look at the arch from the Champs-Elysées, the relief on the left base shows the *Triumph of Napoleon*. This celebrates the Treaty of Vienna peace agreement signed in 1810, when Napoleon's empire was in its heyday.

7 Battle of Austerlitz

Another battle victory is shown on a frieze *(above)* on the arch's northern side. It depicts Napoleon's heavily outnumbered troops breaking the ice on Lake Satschan in Austria, a tactic which drowned thousands of enemy troops and helped France to victory.

8 Battle of Aboukir

Above the *Triumph of Napoleon* carving is this scene showing Napoleonic victory over the Turks in 1799. The same victory was commemorated on canvas in 1806 by the French painter Antoine Gros and is now on display at the palace of Versailles *(see p151)*.

9 General Marceau's Funeral

Marceau died in battle against the Austrian army in 1796, after a famous victory against them only the previous year. His funeral is depicted in this frieze *(right)*, located above the *Departure of the Volunteers in 1792* sculpture.

4 Departure of the Volunteers in 1792

One of the most striking sculptures is on the front right base *(right)*. It shows French citizens going to defend their nation against Austria and Prussia.

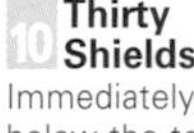

10 Thirty Shields

Immediately below the top of the arch runs a row of 30 shields, each carrying the name of a Napoleonic victory.

5 Frieze

A frieze running around the arch shows French troops departing for battle (east) and their victorious return (west).

The Great Axis

The Arc de Triomphe is at the centre of three arches and together they create a grand vision of which even Napoleon would have been proud. The emperor was responsible for the first two, placing the Arc de Triomphe directly in line with the Arc de Triomphe du Carrousel in front of the Louvre *(see pp8–11)*, which also celebrates the 1805 victory. As late as 1989, the trio was completed with the erection of the Grande Arche at La Défense. The 8km-long (5-mile) *Grand Axe* (Great Axis) runs from here to the Glass Pyramid at the Louvre.

Centre Georges Pompidou

Today one of the world's most famous pieces of modern architecture, the Pompidou Centre opened in 1977, when architects Richard Rogers and Renzo Piano startled everyone by turning the building "inside out", with brightly coloured pipes displayed on the façade. Designed as a cross-cultural arts complex, it houses the excellent Musée National d'Art Moderne (Modern Art Museum) as well as a cinema, library, shops and performance space. The outside forecourt is a popular gathering-spot for tourists and locals alike.

Centre Georges Pompidou façade

The centre's café is pleasant and has free WiFi access. For something grander, head to Georges, the roof-top brasserie.

Buy your tickets online to avoid the queues.

• Place Georges Pompidou 75004 • Map P2 • www.centrepompidou.fr • 01 44 78 12 33 • Open 11am–10pm Wed– Mon (until 11pm Thu); closed 1 May • Adm (museum) €10–12; Brancusi's Studio free (open 2–6pm Wed–Mon), free first Sun of the month.

Top 10 Features

1. Escalator
2. Top-Floor View
3. Buskers
4. Place Igor Stravinsky Fountains
5. Pipes
6. Bookshop
7. Brancusi's Studio
8. Man with a Guitar
9. Sorrow of the King
10. La Baigneuse

1 Escalator

One of the building's most striking and popular features is the external escalator *(right)*, which climbs, snake-like, up the front of the centre in its plexi-glass tube. The view gets better and better as you rise high above the activity in the Centre's forecourt, before arriving at the top for the best view of all.

2 Top-Floor View

The view from the top of the Pompidou Centre is spectacular. The Eiffel Tower is visible, as is Montmartre in the north and the Tour Montparnasse to the south. On clear days views can stretch as far as La Défense *(see p151)*.

3 Buskers

Visitors and locals gather in the open space in front of the Centre, especially on sunny days, to enjoy the variety of street performers, ranging from enigmatic mime artistes to the extrovert dazzle of fire-eaters.

4 Stravinsky Fountain

This colourful fountain in Place Igor Stravinsky was designed by Niki de Saint-Phalle and Jean Tinguely as part of the Pompidou Centre development. Inspired by composer Stravinsky's ballet *The Firebird* (1910), the bird spins and sprays water!

9 Sorrow of the King

French artist Matisse (1869–1964) was one of the proponents of the Fauvist Movement, noted for its bold use of colour. This collage *(below)* was created in 1952.

10 La Baigneuse

Joan Miró (1893–1983) was born in Barcelona but moved to Paris in 1920. His simplistic yet evocative *La Baigneuse (The Swimmer)* (1924) depicts a woman lost in serpentine waves.

5 Pipes

Part of the shock factor of the Pompidou Centre is that the utility pipes are outside the building. Not only that, they are vividly coloured: bright green for water, yellow for electricity and blue for air-conditioning.

6 Bookshop

The ground-floor bookshop sells a range of postcards, posters of major works in the Modern Art Museum and books on artists associated with Paris.

7 Brancusi's Studio

The studio of revolutionary Romanian sculptor Constantin Brancusi (1876–1957) is to the north of the centre, displaying his abstract works.

8 Man with a Guitar

Within the Modern Art Museum, this 1914 work by artist Georges Braque (1882–1963) is one of the most striking of the Cubist Movement.

Centre Guide

The Pompidou Centre can be as confusing inside as it appears on the outside. At busy periods, separate queues are created for the different attractions, so be sure to join the right one. The entrance to the Modern Art Museum is on the fourth floor and to the cinema is on the first floor. Large signs usually indicate the whereabouts of temporary exhibitions.

The Panthéon

Today Paris's beautiful Panthéon building is a fitting final resting place for the city's great citizens. However, it was originally built as a church, on the instigation of Louis XV to celebrate his recovery from a serious bout of gout in 1744. Dedicated to Sainte Geneviève, the structure was finished in 1790 and was intended to look like the Pantheon in Rome, hence the name; in fact it more closely resembles St Paul's Cathedral in London. During the Revolution it was turned into a mausoleum for the city's great achievers, but Napoleon gave it back to the church in 1806. It was later desecularized, handed back to the church once more, before finally becoming a public building in 1885.

Panthéon façade

Crêpes à Gogo (12 rue Soufflot, open 7am–11pm) is an ideal pit stop for a crêpe, coffee and an ice-cream.

Ticket sales stop 45 minutes before closing time, so arrive on time.

- *Place du Panthéon, 75005* • *Map N6*
- *01 44 32 18 00*
- *Open Apr–Sep 10am–6:30pm daily; Oct–Mar 10am–6pm daily. Closed 1 Jan, 1 May, 25 Dec.*
- *Admission €7.50 (under 25s €4.80, under 18s free)*
- *Disabled access to main floor only*

Top 10 Features

1. Dome
2. Dome Galleries
3. Crypt
4. Frescoes of Sainte Geneviève
5. Foucault's Pendulum
6. Monument to Diderot
7. Façade
8. Pediment Relief
9. Tomb of Voltaire
10. Tomb of Victor Hugo

1 Dome

Inspired by Sir Christopher Wren's design of St Paul's Cathedral in London, as well as by the Dôme Church at Les Invalides *(see p32)*, this iron-framed dome *(below left)* is made up of three layers. At the top a narrow opening only lets in a tiny amount of natural light, in keeping with the building's sombre purpose.

2 Dome Galleries

A staircase leads to the galleries immediately below the dome, affording spectacular 360-degree panoramic views of Paris. The pillars surrounding the galleries are both decorative and functional, providing essential support for the dome.

3 Crypt

The crypt is eerily impressive in its scale compared to most tiny, dark church crypts. Here lie the tombs and memorials to French citizens deemed worthy of burial here, including the prolific French writer Emile Zola *(see p17)*.

For more Paris burial sites **See p156**

4 Frescoes of Sainte Geneviève

Delicate murals by 19th-century artist Pierre Puvis de Chavannes, on the south wall of the nave, tell the story of Sainte Geneviève, the patron saint of Paris. In 451 she is believed to have saved the city from invasion by the barbaric Attila the Hun and his hordes due to the power of her prayers.

6 Monument to Diderot

French philosopher Denis Diderot (1713–84) is honoured by this grand 1925 monument by Alphonse Terroir.

7 Façade

The Panthéon's façade was inspired by Roman design. The 22 Corinthian columns support both the portico roof and *bas-reliefs*.

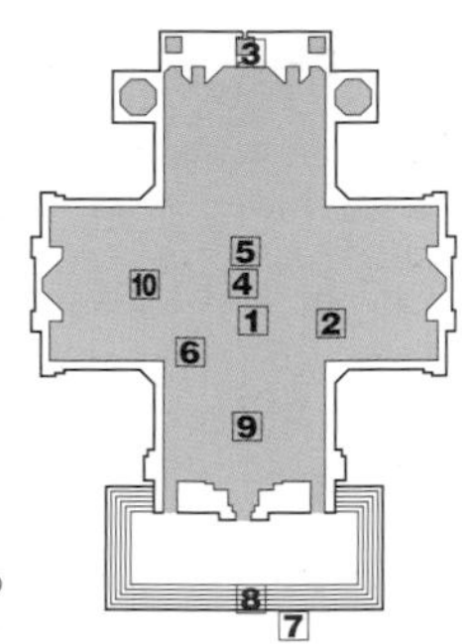

Panthéon Floorplan

9 Tomb of Voltaire

A statue of the great writer, wit and philosopher Voltaire (1694–1788) stands in front of his tomb.

10 Tomb of Victor Hugo

The body of the French author *(see p46)* was carried to the Panthéon in a pauper's hearse, at his own request.

5 Foucault's Pendulum

The landmark discovery of the earth's rotation was made from the Panthéon. In 1851 French physicist Jean Foucault (1819–68) suspended a weight from the dome. The weight swung back and forth, and as its position moved in relation to the floor below, so Foucault was able to prove his theory.

8 Pediment Relief

The *bas-relief* above the entrance *(below)* shows a female figure, representing France, handing out laurels to the great men of the nation – the same way that Greeks and Romans honoured their heroes.

Louis Braille

One of the most influential citizens to be buried in the Panthéon is Louis Braille. Born in France in 1809, Braille became blind at the age of three; at nine he attended the National Institute for the Young Blind in Paris and proved to be a gifted student. He continued at the Institute as a teacher and, in 1829, had the idea of adapting a coding system in use by the army, by turning words and letters into raised dots on card. Reading braille transformed the lives of blind people forever. Its inventor died in 1852.

TOP 10 Sainte-Chapelle

This Gothic masterpiece, built by Louis IX (1214–70) as a shrine for his holy relics of the passion and completed in 1248, is considered the most beautiful church in Paris, not least for its 15 stained-glass windows soaring 15 m (50 ft) to a star-covered vaulted roof. The church was damaged during the Revolution but restored in the mid-19th century.

Sainte-Chapelle façade

For a little 1920s-style elegance, stop for coffee at the Brasserie des Deux Palais on the corner of Boulevard du Palais and rue de Lutèce.

A pair of binoculars comes in handy if you want to see the uppermost panels.

- *6 blvd du Palais, 75001*
- *Map N3*
- *01 53 40 60 97*
- *Open Mar–Oct: 9:30am–6pm; Nov–Feb: 9am–5pm; closed 1 Jan, 1 May, 25 Dec*
- *Admission €7.50 (free 1st Sun of month Nov–Mar); €10.00 joint adm to Conciergerie* (see p69). *Ticket sales stop 30 mins before closing.*
- *Restricted disabled access*
- *http://sainte-chapelle.monuments-nationaux.fr*

Top 10 Features

1. Upper Chapel Entrance
2. Rose Window
3. Window of Christ's Passion
4. Apostle Statues
5. Window of the Relics
6. The Spire
7. Main Portal
8. St Louis' Oratory
9. Seats of the Royal Family
10. Evening Concerts

1 Upper Chapel Entrance

As you emerge, via a spiral staircase, into this airy space *(right)*, the effect of light and colour is breathtaking. The 13th-century stained-glass windows, the oldest extant in Paris, separated by stone columns *(below)*, depict Biblical scenes from *Genesis* through to the Crucifixion. To "read" the windows, start in the lower left panel and follow each row left to right, from bottom to top.

2 Rose Window

The Flamboyant-style rose window, depicting St John's vision of the Apocalypse in 86 panels, was replaced by Charles VIII in 1485. The green and yellow hues are at their brightest at sunset.

For more Paris churches **See pp40–41**

5 Window of the Relics

Another striking window *(below)*, this tells the story of St Helena and the True Cross and of St Louis bringing his many relics to Sainte-Chapelle.

6 The Spire

The open lattice-work and pencil-thin shape give the 75-m (245-ft) *flèche* (spire) a delicate appearance. Three earlier church spires burned down – this one was erected in 1853.

Relics of the Passion

The devout Louis IX, later St Louis, was the only French king to be canonized. While on his first Crusade in 1239, he purchased the alleged Crown of Thorns from the Emperor of Constantinople. He subsequently acquired other relics, including pieces of the True Cross, nails from the Crucifixion and a few drops of Christ's blood, paying almost three times more for them than for the construction of Sainte-Chapelle itself. The relics now reside in Notre-Dame.

7 Main Portal

Like the Upper Chapel, the main portal has two tiers. Its pinnacles are decorated with a crown of thorns as a symbol of the relics within.

3 Window of Christ's Passion

Located above the apse, this stained-glass depiction of the Crucifixion is the chapel's most beautiful window.

4 Apostle Statues

Beautifully carved medieval statues of 12 apostles stand on pillars along the walls. Badly damaged in the Revolution, most have been restored: the bearded apostle *(right)*, fifth on the left, is the only original statue.

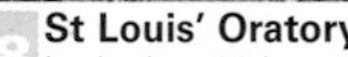

8 St Louis' Oratory

In the late 14th century Louis XI added an oratory where he could attend Mass unobserved, watching through a small grille in the wall. The chapel originally adjoined the Conciergerie, the former royal palace son the Ile de la Cité *(see p69)*.

9 Seats of the Royal Family

During Mass, the royal family sat in niches located in the fourth bays on both sides of the chapel, away from the congregation.

10 Evening Concerts

Sainte-Chapelle has excellent acoustics. From March to November classical concerts are held here several evenings a week.

Hôtel des Invalides

The "invalides" for whom this imposing Hôtel was built were wounded soldiers of the late 17th century. Louis XIV had the building constructed between 1671–8, and there are still old soldiers housed here, although only a dozen or so compared to the 6,000 who first moved in. They share their home with the greatest French soldier of them all, Napoleon Bonaparte, whose body rests in a crypt directly below the golden dome of the Dôme Church. Other buildings accommodate military offices, the Musée de l'Armée and smaller military museums.

Musée de l'Armée façade

Le Café du Musée, between the Varenne metro station and the Musée Rodin ***(see p111)*** **is a lovely spot for a drink.**

A ticket provides access to all attractions.

- *129 rue de Grenelle, 75007*
- *Map D4*
- *01 44 42 38 77*
- *www.invalides.org*
- *Open Apr–Sep: 10am–6pm daily, until 9pm Tue (Oct–Mar: until 5pm); closed first Mon of month (except Jul–Sep), 1 Jan, 1 May, 1 Nov, 25 Dec*
- *Admission €8 adults; €6 concessions; free under 18s* • *Limited disabled access*

Top 10 Features

1. Napoleon's Tomb
2. Golden Dome
3. Musée de l'Armée
4. Dôme Church Ceiling
5. Hôtel des Invalides
6. Church Tombs
7. St-Louis-des-Invalides
8. Invalides Gardens
9. Musée de l'Ordre de la Libération
10. Musée des Plans-Reliefs

2 Golden Dome

The second church at the Hôtel was begun in 1677 and took 27 years to build. Its magnificent dome stands 107 m (351 ft) high and glistens as much now as it did when Louis XIV, the Sun King, had it first gilded in 1715.

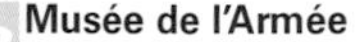

1 Napoleon's Tomb

Napoleon's body was brought here from St Helena in 1840, some 19 years after he died. He rests in splendid grandeur in a cocoon of six coffins *(left)*, almost situated "on the banks of the Seine" as was his personal wish.

3 Musée de l'Armée

The Army Museum is one of the largest collections of militaria in the world. Enthusiasts will be absorbed for hours, and even the casual visitor will be fascinated. The "Department Moderne", which traces military history from Louis XIV to Napoleon III, has been revamped and is especially worth a visit *(see p114)*.

For the Invalides Quarter **See pp110–17**

4 Dôme Church Ceiling

The colourful, circular painting on the interior of the dome above the crypt is the *Saint Louis in Glory* painted in 1692 by the French artist, Charles de la Fosse. Near the centre is St Louis, who represents Louis XIV, presenting his sword to Christ in the presence of the Virgin and angels.

Hôtel des Invalides Floorplan

9 Musée de l'Ordre de la Libération

The Order of Liberation, France's highest military honour, was created by Général de Gaulle in 1940 to acknowledge contributions during World War II. The museum details the history of the honour and the wartime Free French movement.

5 Hôtel des Invalides

One of the loveliest sights in Paris *(above)*, the Classical façade of the Hôtel is four floors high and 196 m (645 ft) end to end. Features include the dormer windows with their variously shaped shield surrounds.

7 St-Louis-des-Invalides

Adjoining the Dôme Church is the Invalides complex's original church. It is worth seeing for its 17th-century organ, on which the first performance of Berlioz's *Requiem* was given.

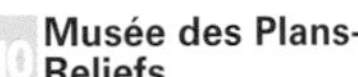

10 Musée des Plans-Reliefs

Maps and models of French forts and fortified towns are displayed here and some of them are beautifully detailed, such as the oldest model on display, of Perpignan in 1686.

6 Church Tombs

Encircling the Dôme Church are the imposing tombs of great French military men, such as Marshal Foch and Marshal Vauban, who revolutionized military fortifications and siege tactics.

8 Invalides Gardens

The approach to the Hôtel is across public gardens and then through a gate into the Invalides Gardens themselves. Designed in 1704, their paths are lined by 17th-and 18th-century cannons.

Hôtel Guide

Approach the Hôtel des Invalides from the Seine for the best view, and then walk around to the south side (by the Dôme Church) to reach the ticket office. You will need a ticket for the museums and to see Napoleon's Tomb. If time is short, concentrate on the Musée de l'Armée, before walking through to the front of the buildings and reaching the impressive cobbled courtyard directly in front of the Dôme Church.

Left **Mona Lisa, Musée du Louvre** Centre **Musée Carnavalet** Right **Cannons, Musée de l'Armée**

Top 10 Museums

1 Musée du Louvre

French and Italian sculpture, Greek and Roman antiquities and paintings from the 12th to 19th centuries are just some of the highlights of the world's largest museum *(see pp8–11)*.

2 Musée Carnavalet

Housed in a grand Marais mansion, this museum presents Parisian decorative arts through the ages. The collection includes painting, sculpture and antique furniture, re-creating private residences of the 16th and 17th centuries. There is also a collection of mementoes from the Revolution. Classical music concerts are occasionally held here *(see p85)*.

3 Musée des Arts Décoratifs

Set over nine floors in the west wing of the Louvre, this decorative arts museum showcases furniture and tableware from the 12th to the early 21st centuries. The breathtaking anthology of pieces includes everything from Gothic panelling and Renaissance porcelain, to 1970s carpets and chairs by Philippe Starck. Also in the museum is the Musée de la Mode et du Textile, which produces fashion exhibitions and the Musée de la Publicité, which has exhibitions on advertising *(see p95)*.

4 Musée National du Moyen-Age

This splendid museum dedicated to the art of the Middle Ages is known by several names, including the Musée de Cluny after the beautiful mansion in which it is housed, and the Thermes de Cluny after the Roman baths adjoining the museum. Highlights include the famous "Lady and the Unicorn" tapestries, medieval stained glass and exquisite gold crowns and jewellery *(see p120)*.

Muséum National d'Histoire Naturelle garden

5 Muséum National d'Histoire Naturelle

Paris's Natural History Museum in the Jardin des Plantes contains a fascinating collection of animal skeletons, plant fossils, minerals and gemstones. Its highlight is the magnificent Grande Galerie de l'Evolution, which depicts the varying interaction between man and nature during the evolution of the planet *(see p60, p129)*.

6 Musée du Quai Branly

In a city dominated by western art, this impressive museum housing 300,000 artefacts tips the balance in favour of arts from Africa, Asia, Oceania and the Americas. Must-sees include the African instruments. The striking Jean Nouvel-designed building is an attraction in itself. *(see p112).*

7 Musée de l'Armée

France's proud military history is on display in this museum, housed in a wing of the Hôtel des Invalides. Exhibits include military art and artifacts from ancient times through to the 20th century, with a large modern exhibit devoted to World War II. Napoleon's campaign tent, his stuffed dog, and suits of armour and weapons from medieval times are among the many highlights *(see p114).*

8 Musée Cognacq-Jay

The Hôtel Donon is a fine setting for this superb collection of 18th-century art, furniture, porcelain and other decorative arts, amassed by the wealthy founders of the Samaritaine department store. Paintings by Rembrandt, Gainsborough and other masters alone are worth the visit *(see p85).*

Venus with Doves, Musée Cognacq-Jay

9 Cité de l'Architecture et du Patrimoine

In the east wing of the Palais Chaillot, the Cité de l'Architecture showcases French architectural heritage and has become one of the world's great (and largest) architectural centres. The unmissable Galeries des Moulages houses three-dimensional models of great French cathedrals *(see pp135–6).*

10 Musée de Montmartre

Montmartre has long been home to the artists of Paris and several of them have lived in this old house, including Renoir, Dufy and Utrillo. Artifacts from the 19th century are on display, to help conjure up the era, along with posters, maps and documents on the house's history. The garden also gives good views of the surrounding district *(see p141).*

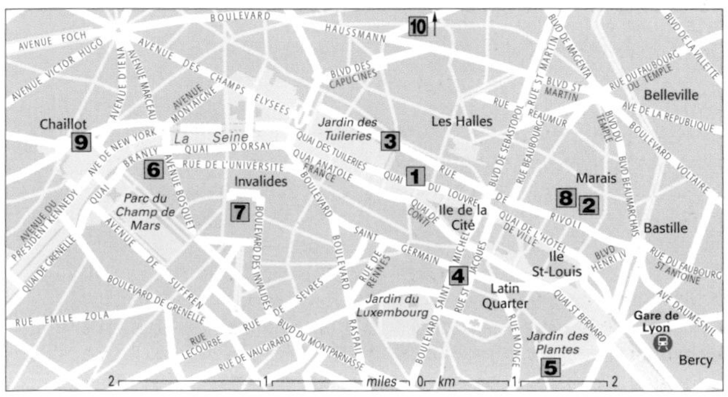

For Paris art galleries **See pp36–7**

Left **Bedroom at Arles (1889), Van Gogh, Musée d'Orsay** Right **Jeu de Paume**

Top 10 Art Galleries

1 Musée d'Orsay

See pp12–15.

2 Musée Picasso

A favourite of Parisians and visitors alike. The beautifully restored Hôtel Salé *(see p90)* in the Marais is a splendid setting for this extensive collection of paintings, sculptures, drawings and other works by Pablo Picasso (1881–1973), including works from his Cubist period. Large sculptures also adorn the garden and courtyard. Some of the artist's personal art collection of works by his contemporaries is also on display *(see p85)*.

3 Musée Rodin

On a sunny day, head straight for the gardens of the Musée Rodin, in the Hôtel des Invalides complex, where you can enjoy some of the French sculptor's most famous works, including *The Thinker* and *The Burghers of Calais*, while strolling among the shady trees and rose bushes. Then pay a visit inside the beautiful 18th-century mansion, the Hôtel Biron, where Auguste Rodin (1840–1917) lived and worked for nine years, until his death. An extensive collection of his works from throughout his career is on display *(see p111)*.

4 Musée National d'Art Moderne

The revolutionary Pompidou Centre is the perfect home for the city's outstanding Modern Art Museum. It features some 1,400 works on two levels, one focusing on the artists and movements of the first half of the 20th century, the other featuring art from the 1960s to the present day. Temporary exhibitions are held throughout the year *(see pp26–7)*. *Pl Georges Pompidou, 75004 • Map P2 • Open 11am–9pm, Wed–Mon • Admission charge*

5 Jeu de Paume

This gallery is one of the finest exhibition spaces in the city, being set within a 19th-century real tennis court *(jeu de paume)*. It is a showcase for outstanding photography, film and video. *1 pl de la Concorde, 75008 • Map D3 • Open noon– 9pm Tue, noon–7pm Wed–Fri, 10am– 7pm Sat–Sun • Admission charge*

Musée National d'Art Moderne

For more on Paris artists **See p144**

6 L'Orangerie

The prime exhibits here are eight of Monet's huge waterlily canvases *(see p13)* and the gallery, located in a corner of the Tuileries, has recently been renovated to improve their display. The Walter-Guillaume collection covers works by Renoir, Picasso, Modigliani and other modern masters from 1870–1930. *Jardin des Tuileries, 75001 • Map D3 • www.musee-orangerie.fr • Open 12:30–7pm Wed–Mon (9pm Fri) • Admission charge*

7 Espace Montmartre Salvador Dalí

This underground museum with its black walls, lighting effects and soundtrack features some of Dalí's lesser-known works, including bronzes and book illustrations *(see p141)*.

Lip Sofa, Salvador Dalí

8 Musée Marmottan-Claude Monet

The Impressionist paintings of Claude Monet are the star attraction at this museum, featuring some 165 works donated by his son and perhaps the finest collection of his works in the world. They include a series of his late waterlily paintings. Other Impressionist and Realist painters are also represented, and there is a fine collection of illuminated medieval manuscripts *(see p153)*.

9 Musée Maillol

Works of the French artist Aristide Maillol, including his drawings, engravings, paintings and plastercasts, are the focal point of this museum which was created by his model, Dina Vierny. Works by Rodin and Picasso are also on display *(see p121)*.

10 Maison Européenne de la Photographie

If you're a photography fan, don't miss this splendid gallery in the Marais. Its exhibitions range from portraits to documentary work, retrospectives to contemporary photographers *(see p87)*.

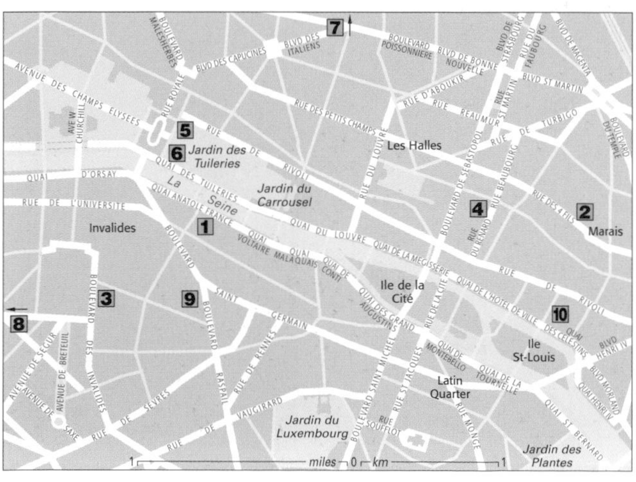

Left **Jardin du Luxembourg** Centre **Jardin des Plantes** Right **Bois de Boulogne**

TOP 10 Parks and Gardens

1 Jardin du Luxembourg

Parisians love this centrally located park, set around the Palais du Luxembourg. The sweeping terrace is a great place for people-watching, while locals sunbathe around the Octagonal Lake or sail toy boats in the water. Statues are dotted throughout the grounds, and there is a café *(see p119)*.

2 Jardin des Tuileries

These formal gardens were laid out in the 17th century as part of the old Palais de Tuileries and stretch along the Seine between the Louvre and the Place de la Concorde. The walkways are lined with lime and chestnut trees, and there is a series of bronze figures by Aristide Maillol *(see p95)*.

3 Jardin des Plantes

Established as a medicinal herb garden for the king in 1626, these vast botanical gardens are a wonderfully tranquil spot. Paths are lined with statuary and mature trees, including the oldest in Paris, an *Acacia robinia* dating from 1636. There is also an alpine garden *(see p129)*.

4 Bois de Boulogne

At the weekends, Parisians head for this vast park on the western edge of the city, with a boating lake and paths for cycling, jogging and strolling. There are three formal gardens, lakes and waterfalls, and even two horse-racing tracks. A good spot for a break from the city bustle *(see p152)*.

5 Bois de Vincennes

Another great escape from the city, this park is to the east of Paris what the Bois de Boulogne is to the west. A former royal hunting ground, it was landscaped in the 1860s. Now it features ornamental lakes and waterfalls, a zoo, a funfair and horse-racing tracks *(see p151)*.

6 Parc Monceau

The most fashionable green space in Paris, full of well-heeled residents of the nearby mansions and apartments. The lush landscaping dates from the 18th century, and some architectural follies, such as the Classical colonnade, survive *(see p153)*.

Bois de Boulogne

7 Jardins du Palais Royal
These lovely gardens were once part of the Palais Royal, which now houses the State Council. They are surrounded by arcades which date from the late 18th century, and by an impressive modern pillar arrangement.
Pl du Palais Royal, 75001 • Map L1

8 Versailles
There are gardens galore at this famous royal palace, from the formal French gardens with their geometric paths and shrubberies, to the wandering paths through the rural-style English garden north of the Petit Trianon. In summer, you can row boats on the lovely cross-shaped Grand Canal *(see p151)*.

9 Parc Montsouris
Located south of Montparnasse, this is the second-largest park in central Paris and very popular with city residents. It was laid out in the English style atop an old granite quarry by landscape architect Adolphe Alphand between 1865 and 1878. Hemingway *(see p47)* and other writers and artists frequented the park in the mid-20th century. It has a jogging path, lake and a bandstand. *Blvd Jourdan, 75014 • Metro Cité Universitaire*

10 Parc des Buttes Chaumont
City-planner Baron Haussmann created this wonderful retreat northeast of the city centre in 1867, from what was formerly a rubbish dump *(see p61)*. His architects built artificial cliffs, waterfalls, streams, and a lake complete with an island crowned by a Roman-style temple. There's also boating available, a café and views of Sacré-Coeur *(see pp22–3)*. *Rue Manin, 75019 • Metro Buttes-Chaumont*

Top 10 Fountains

1 Agam Fountain
Jewish architect Yaacov Agam designed this fountain of water and lights. *La Défense • RER La Défense*

2 Four Seasons Fountain
Paris looks down on figures representing the Seine and Marne rivers, designed in 1739 by sculptor Edme Bouchardon. *Rue de Grenelle • Map C4*

3 Fontaine des Innocents
Carved by Jean Goujon in 1547, this is Paris's only Renaissance fountain. *Square des Innocents • Map N2*

4 Medici Fountain
This ornate 17th-century fountain with a pond was built for Marie de Médicis. *Jardin du Luxembourg • Map L6*

5 Molière Fountain
This 19th-century fountain honours the French playwright. *Rue de Richelieu • Map E3*

6 Observatory Fountain
Four bronze statues representing the continents hold aloft a globe. *Jardin du Luxembourg • Map L6*

7 Châtelet Fountain
The two sphinxes of this 1808 fountain commemorate Napoleon's victory in Egypt. *Pl du Châtelet • Map N2*

8 Fontaine de Stravinsky
Birds squirt water from this colourful fountain *(see p27)*.

9 Trocadéro Fountains
Spouting towards the Eiffel Tower, these fountains are illuminated at night *(see p17)*.

10 Versailles Fountains
The fountains at Versailles *(see p154)* flow to music on summer Sunday afternoons.

Left **Notre-Dame** Centre **Sacré-Coeur** Right **Sainte-Chapelle**

TOP 10 Places of Worship

1 Notre-Dame

See pp18–21.

2 Sacré-Coeur

See pp22–3.

3 Sainte-Chapelle

Although the chapel is no longer used for worship, the soaring stained-glass windows encourage reverence *(see pp30–31)*.

4 Eglise du Dôme

The final resting place of Napoleon Bonaparte is the beautiful Dôme Church in the Hôtel des Invalides complex – an elaborate monument to French Classical style. Built as the chapel for the resident soldiers of the Invalides, its ornate high altar is in stark contrast to the solemn marble chapels surrounding the crypt, which hold the tombs of French military leaders. Its golden dome can be seen for miles around *(see pp32–3)*.

Baptism of Christ, La Madeleine

5 Panthéon

Patterned after the Pantheon in Rome, this domed late 18th-century church only served as a house of worship for two years, before becoming a monument and burial place for the great and the good of the Revolution era. Later distinguished citizens are also buried here *(see pp28–9)*.

6 St-Eustache

For centuries, this monumental Gothic edifice was the "market church" serving the traders of Les Halles. Taking more than 100 years to build, it was finally completed in 1637 and its cavernous interior displays the architectural style of the early Renaissance. Popular Sunday afternoon organ recitals and other classical concerts take place in this wonderfully atmospheric setting *(see p75)*.

7 La Madeleine

Designed in the style of a Greek temple in 1764, this prominent church in Paris's financial district, on the edge of the Opéra Quarter, is one of the city's most distinctive sights, spectacularly surrounded by 52 Corinthian columns. The church was consecrated to Mary Magdalene in 1845. The bronze doors, which include *bas-reliefs* depicting the Ten Commandments, and the *Last Judgment* on the south pediment are exterior highlights, while the ornate marble and gold interior has many fine statues, including François Rude's *Baptism of Christ*. Organ recitals are often held in the church. *Pl de la Madeleine, 75008 • Map D3 • Open 9am–7pm daily (services vary) • Free*

8 Grande Synagogue de la Victoire

Built in the late 19th century, this elaborate synagogue is the second-largest in Europe. Its façade design represents the Tablets though, sadly, the building is not open to the public. Other smaller synagogues can be found in the Marais, which has a large Jewish community, including one at 10 rue Pavée, built in 1913 by Hector Guimard, the architect who designed the city's Art Nouveau metro stations. ⊗ *44 rue de la Victoire, 75008* • *Map E2*

9 Mosquée de Paris

The city's Grande Mosque was built during the 1920s as a tribute to North African Muslims who gave military support to France during World War I. It features beautiful Moorish architecture, executed by craftsmen brought over from North Africa, and a peaceful interior courtyard *(see p129)*.

10 St-Sulpice

Outstanding frescoes in the Chapel of the Angels by Eugène Delacroix are the highlight of this 17th-century church's otherwise sober interior. With more than 6,500 pipes, its organ, designed by Jean-François Chalgrin in 1776, is one of the largest in the world. The novelist Victor Hugo married Adèle Foucher here in 1822 *(see p119)*.

St-Sulpice façade

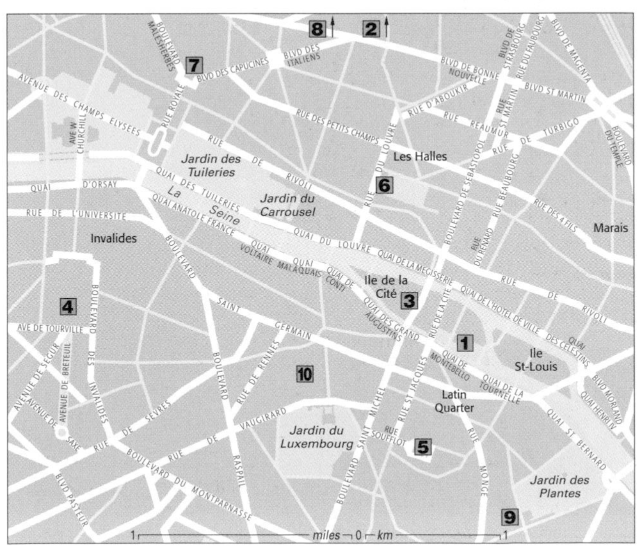

Left **Conciergerie** Right **Hôtel de Ville**

Top 10 Historic Buildings

1 Hôtel des Invalides
See pp32–3.

2 Versailles
Louis XIV turned his father's old hunting lodge into the largest palace in Europe and moved his court here in 1678. It was the royal residence for more than a century until Louis XVI and his queen Marie-Antoinette fled during the Revolution *(see p151)*.

3 Conciergerie
Originally home to the caretaker and guards of the Palais de Justice, the Conciergerie was turned into a jail at the end of the 14th century. It took its place in history during the Revolution, when more than 4,000 citizens (including Marie-Antoinette) were held prisoner here, half of whom were guillotined. It remained a prison until 1914 *(see p69)*.

4 Palais de Justice
The enormous building that now houses the French law courts and judiciary dates back to Roman times and was the royal palace until the 14th century, when Charles V moved the court to the Marais. During the Revolution, thousands were sentenced to death in the Première Chambre Civile, allegedly the former bedroom of Louis IX *(see p70)*.

Palais de Justice

5 Hôtel Dieu
The Hôtel Dieu, now the hospital for central Paris, was built on the site of a foundling home in 1866–78; the original 12th-century building on the Ile de la Cité was demolished during the urban renewal schemes of the 19th century. A monument in the courtyard commemorates a courageous battle here in 1944 when Paris police held out against the German Nazis. *1 pl du Parvis Notre-Dame, 75001 • Map N4*

6 Palais de l'Elysée
This imposing palace has been the official residence of the President of the French Republic since 1873. It was built as a private mansion in 1718 and subsequently owned by Madame de Pompadour, mistress of Louis XV, who extended the English-style gardens to the Champs-Elysées. Napoleon signed his abdication here in 1815 *(see p105)*.

7 Hôtel de Ville
Paris's city hall sports an elaborate façade, with ornate stonework, statues and a turreted roof. It is a 19th-century reconstruction of the original town hall, which was burned down in the Paris Commune of 1871 *(see*

p45). Though the pedestrianized square in front is pleasant now, it was once the site of gruesome executions: Ravaillac, assassin of Henri IV, was quartered alive here in 1610. *4 pl de l'Hôtel de Ville, 75001 • Map P3 • 01 42 76 40 40 • Open for tours only (booking essential: 01 42 76 54 04) • Free*

8 Palais-Royal

This former royal palace now houses State offices. Built by Cardinal Richelieu in 1632, it passed to the crown on his death 10 years later and was the childhood home of Louis XIV. The dukes of Orléans acquired it in the 18th century. *Pl du Palais Royal, 75005 • Map L1 • Closed to the public*

9 La Sorbonne

The city's great university had humble beginnings in 1253 as a college for 16 poor students to study theology, but France's first print-ing house was also established here in 1469. After suppression during the Revolution it became the University of Paris *(see p119)*.

10 Palais du Luxembourg

Marie de Médicis had architect Salomon de Brosse model this palace after her childhood home, the Pitti Palace in Florence. Shortly after its completion she was exiled by her son, Louis XIII. It was seized from the crown during the Revolution to become a prison. The building now houses the French Senate. Nearby is the Musée du Luxembourg. *15 rue de Vaugirard, 75006 • Map L6 • 01 44 54 19 49 • Open for reserved tours only; gardens open dawn-dusk • Admission charge*

Palais du Luxembourg

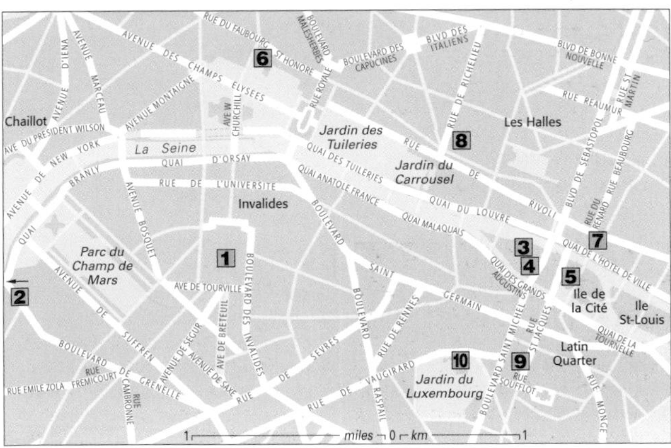

Left **Charlemagne crowned as Holy Roman Emperor** Right **Paris Commune burning of the city**

TOP 10 Historical Events in Paris

1 Arrival of the Parisii

Though the remains of Neolithic settlements have been found dating back to 4500 BC, the first inhabitants are considered to be a Celtic tribe called the Parisii, who settled on the Ile de la Cité in the 3rd century BC. Hunters and fishermen, they named the village Lutetia, meaning "boatyard on a river". The tribe minted their own gold coins and a pagan altar was found beneath Notre-Dame.

2 Roman Settlement

The Romans conquered the Parisii in 52 BC and destroyed their city. After rebuilding it as their administrative centre, they founded their own town on the Left Bank. The baths in the Hôtel de Cluny *(see p34)* and the amphitheatre in rue Monge are the only remains. In AD 360 the Roman prefect was declared emperor and Lutetia was renamed Paris, after its original inhabitants.

3 Founding of France

Roman rule weakened under Barbarian attacks. In 450 the prayers of a young nun, Geneviève, were credited with saving the city from invasion by Attila the Hun and she became patron saint of Paris. But in 476 the Franks captured the city. They converted it to Christianity and made Paris the capital of their new kingdom, France.

4 Charlemagne, Holy Roman Emperor

In 751 the Carolingian dynasty became rulers of France when Pepin the Short ascended the throne. His heir Charlemagne was crowned Holy Roman Emperor in 800 and moved the capital to Aix-La-Chapelle. Paris fell into decline until nobleman Hugues Capet became king in 987, moving the capital back to his home city.

5 Bourbon Dynasty

Henri III named his son-in-law, Henri of Navarre, as his heir, but when the king was assassinated in 1589, Catholics refused to accept a Protestant monarch. After a four-year war, Henri converted to Catholicism and entered Paris as the first Bourbon king. He, too, was assassinated in 1610, leaving his young son Louis XIII to usher in *Le Grand Siècle* (Grand Century), as the 17th century later came to be known.

Succession of Louis XIII

6 French Revolution

Following decades of excess by the monarchy and the gulf between rich and poor, Paris erupted with the storming of the Bastille prison in 1789 *(see box)*.

7 Napoleon's Coronation

As Paris rose from the ashes of the Revolution, a young general from Corsica, Napoleon Bonaparte, saved the city from a royalist revolt, then led military victories in Italy and Egypt. He crowned himself Emperor of France in Notre-Dame in 1804 *(see p20)*.

8 The Second Empire

In 1851, Napoleon's nephew, Louis-Napoleon, seized power as Emperor Napoleon III. He appointed Baron Haussmann to oversee massive building works that transformed Paris into the most glorious city in Europe. The wide boulevards, many public buildings, parks, sewer system and the first department stores date from 1852 to 1870.

9 The Paris Commune

Following France's defeat in the Franco-Prussian War in 1871 *(see p23)*, many citizens rejected the harsh terms of the surrender and a left-wing group revolted, setting up the Paris Commune. But, after 72 days, government troops marched on the city. In a week of street fighting (21–28 May), much of the city burned and thousands of rebellious citizens were killed.

10 Liberation of Paris

The Occupation of France by Germany during World War II were some of Paris's darkest days, but the city was also the centre for the French Resistance. Allied forces liberated Paris on 25 August 1944; just two days earlier, the German commander Von Choltitz had ignored Adolf Hitler's order to burn the city.

Top 10 Events in the French Revolution

1 14 July 1789
Storming of the Bastille prison, a symbol of repression, launches the Revolution.

2 4 August 1789
The abolition of feudalism, and the right of everyone to be a free citizen is declared.

3 26 August 1789
Formal declaration of the Rights of Man and the Citizen, which incorporated the ideals of equality and dignity, later incorporated into the 1791 Constitution.

4 October 1789
Citizens march on Versailles and the royal family returns to Paris as prisoners in the Tuileries Palace *(see p95)*.

5 20 June 1791
The royal family try to escape but are spotted in Varenne and return as captives.

6 10 August 1792
A mob storms the Tuileries and the royals are imprisoned in the Temple.

7 21 September 1792
The monarchy is formally abolished and the First Republic is proclaimed.

8 1792–4
"The Terror" reigns, under the radical Commune led by Robespierre, Danton and Marat. Thousands are executed by guillotine.

9 21 January 1793
Louis XVI is found guilty of treason and executed. His queen Marie-Antoinette follows him to the guillotine on 16 October.

10 28 July 1794
Robespierre is guillotined, ending the Terror, and the Revolution draws to a close.

Left **Plaque on Victor Hugo's house** Right **Film still from A Tale of Two Cities**

Top 10 Historical Novels set in Paris

1 Les Misérables

The 1862 novel by Victor Hugo (1802–85) is an all-too-vivid portrayal of the poor and the dispossessed in early 19th-century Paris. At its centre is the tale of nobleman Jean Valjean, unfairly victimized by an unjust system. The younger character of Marius is based around Hugo's own experiences as an impoverished student.

2 The Hunchback of Notre-Dame

Better known by its English title, which inspired a film of the same name, Victor Hugo's Gothic novel was published in France in 1831 as *Notre-Dame de Paris*. Set in the Middle Ages, it tells the strange and moving story of a hunchback bell-ringer Quasimodo and his love for Esmeralda *(see p21)*.

3 A Tale of Two Cities

The finest chronicler of 19th-century London life, Charles Dickens (1812–70) broke with tradition to set his 1859 novel in Paris, against the background of the French Revolution *(see p45)*. His description of conditions in the Bastille prison makes for grim reading.

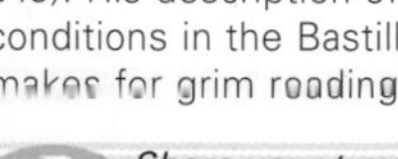

4 Le Père Goriot

Honoré de Balzac (1799–1850) chronicled Paris life masterfully in his 80-volume *La comédie humaine* series, and this 1853 novel is certainly among the finest. Balzac's house at 47 rue Raynouard in the 16th *arrondissement*, where he lived from 1840–47, is open to the public *(see p137)*.

5 Sentimental Education

Gustave Flaubert (1821–80) studied law in Paris but illness disrupted his chosen career and he devoted himself to literature. This work (*L'education sentimentale* in French), first published in 1870 in two volumes, stands alongside his greatest novel, *Madame Bovary* (1857), and marks the move from Romanticism to Realism in French literature.

Guy de Maupassant

6 Bel-Ami

Guy de Maupassant (1850–93) published this, one of his best novels, in 1885, criticizing the get-rich-quick Parisian business world of the *belle époque* (Beautiful Age). Maupassant is known as one of the world's greatest short-story writers, and he is buried in the cemetery at Montparnasse *(see p152)*.

7 A la Recherche du Temps Perdu

The master work of Marcel Proust (1871–1922) was written in 13 volumes, the first novel appearing in 1913. Proust lived on boulevard Haussmann, and his epic tale is the fictionalized story of his own life, and of Paris during the *belle époque*. Proust is buried in Père Lachaise cemetery in eastern Paris *(see p153)*.

8 Nana

Perhaps the greatest Parisian chronicler of them all, Emile Zola (1840–1902) was born, lived and died in the city, although he spent part of his youth in Aix-en-Provence in southern France. *Nana* was published in 1880 and tells a shocking tale of sexual decadence, through the eyes of the central character, a dancer and prostitute.

9 L'Assommoir

Published in 1887, Zola's *L'Assommoir* (The Drunkard) shows a side of Paris that many at the time would have preferred to ignore – the alcoholism of the working classes. It is one of the author's series of 20 linked books known as the *Rougon-Macquart* sequence, which depict life in every quarter of society, through the eyes of two branches of the same family.

10 Thérèse Raquin

Here Zola focuses on the secret passions that lurk behind a single Paris shopfront, opening up to reveal a tale of obsessive lust that ultimately leads to a brutal murder. It was published in 1867 and, only his second novel, shows the author's astonishing maturity and unflinching examination of all aspects of 19th-century life.

Top 10 Foreign Writers who Lived in Paris

1 Ernest Hemingway

The US author (1899–1961) wrote *A Moveable Feast* as an affectionate portrait of his time in Paris from 1921–1926.

2 F Scott Fitzgerald

Like Hemingway, US writer Fitzgerald (1896–1940) lived in Montparnasse and frequented the bar La Coupole *(see p125)*.

3 George Orwell

The English novelist (1903–50) tells of his shocking experiences living in poverty in *Down and Out in Paris and London* (1933).

4 Samuel Beckett

Born in Ireland in 1906, the playwright lived in Paris from 1928 until his death in 1989.

5 Anaïs Nin

US novelist Nin (1903–77) met her lover, fellow American Henry Miller, in Paris. Her *Diaries* tell of her time here.

6 Albert Camus

Algerian born Camus (1913–60) moved to Paris in 1935 and lived here until his death.

7 Henry Miller

Miller (1891–1980) showed the seedier side of Paris in his novel *Tropic of Cancer* (1934).

8 Diana Mitford

Controversial fascist sympathiser and authoress, Mitford (1910-2003) spent her dotage in Paris.

9 Edmund White

Prolific novelist White (b.1940) is the author of *The Flaneur, a Stroll Through the Paradoxes of Paris.*

10 Milan Kundera

Czech born Kundera (b.1929) moved to Paris in 1978 where he wrote *The Unbearable Lightness of Being.*

For literary haunts **See p125**

Left **Palais de Chaillot** Centre **Liberty Flame** Right **Pont Alexandre III**

Top 10 Riverfront Views

1 Eiffel Tower

Although the top of the Eiffel Tower can be seen above rooftops across the city, one of the best views of this Paris landmark is from the Seine. The Pont d'Iéna lies at the foot of the tower, bridging the river to link it to the Trocadéro Gardens. The tower, illuminated at night, is a highlight of a dinner cruise on the Seine *(see pp16–17)*.

Eiffel Tower

2 Palais de Chaillot

The curved arms of the Palais de Chaillot encircling the Trocadéro Gardens can be seen from the Seine. In the centre of the gardens the magnificent fountains spout from the top of a long pool lined with statues, while two huge water cannons spray their charges back towards the river and the Eiffel Tower on the opposite bank *(see p135)*.

3 Liberty Flame

A replica of the Statue of Liberty's torch in New York was erected in 1987 by the *International Herald Tribune* to mark their centenary and honour the freedom fighters of the French Resistance during World War II. It is located on the right bank of the Pont de l'Alma, the bridge over the tunnel where Diana, Princess of Wales, was killed in an automobile crash in 1997. The Liberty Flame has now become her unofficial memorial and is often draped with notes and flowers laid in her honour.
Map C3

4 Grand Palais and Petit Palais

Gracing either side of the Pont Alexandre III are these two splendid exhibition halls, built for the Universal Exhibition in 1900. The iron Art Nouveau skeleton of the Grand Palais is topped by an enormous glass roof, which is most impressive when illuminated at night. The Petit Palais is smaller but similar in style, with a dome and many Classical features *(see p103)*.

5 Pont Alexandre III

The most beautiful bridge in Paris is the Pont Alexandre III, a riot of Art Nouveau decoration including cherubs, wreaths,

For Paris boat trips **See p164**

lamps and other elaborate statuary. Built for the Universal Exhibition of 1900, it leads to the Grand Palais and Petit Palais. There are wonderful views of the Invalides complex and the Champs-Elysées from the bridge *(see p104)*.

6 Dôme Church

An impressive view of the Eglise de Dôme in the Hôtel des Invalides complex can be had from the Pont Alexandre III. The golden dome beckons visitors down the long parkway lined with streetlamps and statues *(see pp32–3)*.

7 Musée du Louvre

This grand museum stretches along the river from the Pont Royal to the Pont des Arts. The wing that can be seen from the Seine was largely built during the reigns of Henri IV and Louis XIII in the late 16th and early 17th centuries *(see pp8–11)*.

8 Musée d'Orsay

The view of this modern art gallery from the Right Bank of the Seine is one of its finest angles, showing off the arched terminals and grand façade of this former railway station. Architect Victor Laloux designed it specifically to harmonize with the Louvre and Tuileries Quarter across the river *(see pp12–15)*.

9 Conciergerie

This huge and imposing building, which served as a notorious prison during the Revolution, commands the western end of the Ile de la Cité. Within its walls are some of the few remaining medieval features on the island, including the torture chamber, clock and twin towers which rise above the quai de l'Horloge *(see p69)*.

10 Notre-Dame

The great cathedral is never more majestic than when viewed from the Left Bank of the Seine. It rises on the eastern edge of the Ile de la Cité above the remains of the ancient tribes who first settled Paris in the 3rd century BC *(see pp18–21)*.

Notre-Dame

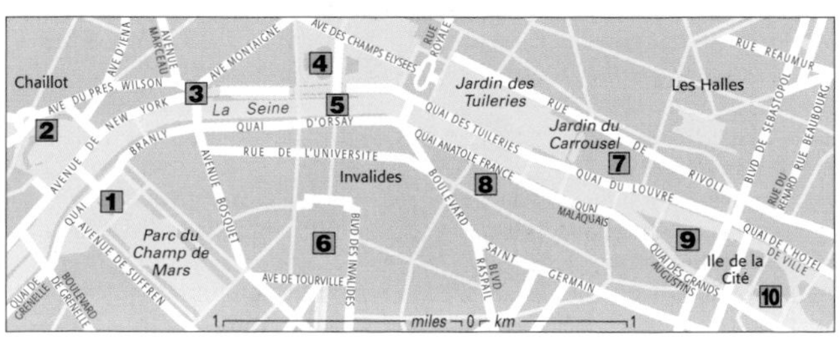

Left **The Passages** Right **Bois de Boulogne**

TOP 10 Walks in Paris

1 Jardin des Tuileries
A stroll through the beautiful Tuileries Gardens is one of the must-dos of Paris. Before the Revolution this was a prime spot for the aristocracy to show off their latest fashions, and it remains a great place for people-watching *(see p95)*.

2 The Left Bank
A very Parisian walk, particularly on a Sunday, is along the Left Bank (Rive Gauche) of the Seine. The riverside quays of the Latin Quarter have been lined with second-hand bookstalls *(bouquinistes)* for centuries. The books are mostly in French, but you'll also find stalls selling prints and postcards *(see p122)*.

3 Montmartre
The steep streets of the Butte are a good place to get some exercise after indulging in the irresistible French cuisine. Although this famous artists' quarter is more touristy than Bohemian these days, its old charms can still be found in the winding back streets and small squares *(see pp140–43)*.

4 The Marais
With inspiring art galleries, delectable delis, and shop after shop filled with contemporary fashions and *objets d'art*, a walk in the Marais is great fun, even if you only window-shop. The beautiful mansions are a great backdrop for your stroll and there are plenty of cafés and bars for sustenance *(see pp84–7)*.

5 Jardin des Plantes
In this historic botanical garden you can escape the bustle of the city and lose yourself on the shady tree-lined avenues, amid colourful flowerbeds, or the hothouses and exotic gardens. Or simply relax on the lawns *(see p129)*.

6 Jardin du Luxembourg
Napoleon designated this the "garden of children", and whether or not you have little ones in tow you'll enjoy a walk through this favourite haunt of the Latin Quarter. After you've seen the octagonal pond and the Medicis Fountain, seek out the miniature Statue of Liberty and the statues of French queens *(see p119)*.

Montmartre

7 The Passages
These covered arcades around the Grands Boulevards were built at the end of the 18th century to shelter elegant shoppers from bad weather. Now lined with speciality and antiques shops, they

For more on getting around Paris **See p164**

are wonderfully atmospheric places to explore. Most are in the 2nd *arrondissement*, and connecting passages Verdeau, Jouffroy and Panoramas together form the longest in Paris. ✎ *Map H5*

8 Ile St-Louis

Although you could walk end to end in about 10 minutes, the Seine's smaller island demands a more leisurely stroll. You'll discover superb little art galleries, trendy boutiques, and a village-like atmosphere within this up-market enclave *(see p68)*.

9 Bois de Boulogne

Come here at the weekend if you want to join the locals in the "great escape", and you'll have 865 ha (2,135 acres) from which to choose your path. The Bagatelle Gardens are a fine

Boulevard St-Germain

place for a walk in spring and summer, when a stunning array of roses and other flowers are in bloom *(see p152)*.

10 Boulevard St-Germain

There's no better way to enjoy the Latin Quarter than to do as the Parisians do – stroll the Boulevard St-Germain, preferably late on a Sunday morning. After your walk, honour the birthplace of café society with a coffee at either Les Deux Magots or Café de Flore, two of the city's most famous literary and intellectual haunts *(see p120)*.

Top 10 Outdoor Activities

1 Walking

Paris is a compact city so you can easily combine sightseeing with exercise.

2 Roller-blading

A fad which shows no sign of abating, skaters weave their way through traffic and pedestrians alike.

3 Cycling

Head for the Bois de Boulogne and Bois de Vincennes to escape the Paris traffic, or grab a Vélib' *(see p164)*.

4 Boating

Boating lakes in the Bois de Boulogne and Bois de Vincennes allow you to flex your rowing muscles.

5 Jogging

You can get your aerobic fix along the pathways of Paris's parks and gardens.

6 Tennis

You can play at any of the city's 170 courts. There is a small court fee.

7 Pétanque

This bowls-like game, where steel balls are tossed through the air, is said to be Paris's favourite sport.

8 Swimming

There are 34 public pools in Paris, but hours are restricted during school terms. Or try the pool at the Forum des Halles.

9 Football

France's football team has many young imitators in parks, gardens and streets.

10 Posing

A sport indulged in mainly by young men and women, it is best done at outdoor cafés to be sure of the biggest audience.

Left **Café de Flore** Centre **La Closerie des Lilas** Right **Café Marly**

TOP 10 Cafés and Bars

1 Café de Flore

A hang-out for artists and intellectuals since the 1920s, its regulars have included Salvador Dali and Albert Camus. During World War II Jean-Paul Sartre and Simone de Beauvoir "more or less set up house in the Flore". Although its prices have skyrocketed, its Art Deco decor hasn't changed and it's still a favourite with French filmmakers and literati *(see p125)*.

2 Les Deux Magots

Rival to the neighbouring Flore as the rendezvous for the 20th-century intellectual élite. Hemingway, Oscar Wilde, Djuna Barnes, André Breton and Paul Verlaine were all regulars, and Picasso met his muse Dora Maar here in 1937. Similarly pricey, with outside tables facing the boulevard and the square *(see p125)*.

3 Le Petit Vendôme

The search for the best sandwiches in Paris stops here, with bread from the award-winning Julien bakery and just the right slathering of butter with the ham or Cantal cheese. Good hot dishes too. *8 rue des Capucines, 75002 • Map E3 • 01 42 61 05 88 • Closed Sat–Sun • €€*

Les Deux Magots

4 Café Marly

Superbly situated in the Richelieu wing of the Louvre *(see p9)*, the café offers simple but expertly prepared brasserie fare (steaks, salads, salmon tartare, sandwiches) as well as delicious cakes and pastries. The dining room has plush decor and velvet armchairs, but the best spot is under the arcade overlooking the glass pyramid and the cour Napoléon. *93 rue de Rivoli, 75001 • Map L2*

5 Café de la Paix

A grand Parisian café with prices to match, but it's worth a visit to enjoy the frescoed walls and sumptuous surroundings, designed by Charles Garnier, architect of the Opera House across the square *(see p97)*. This is another Paris landmark with a string of famous past patrons, and arguably the best *mille-feuille* cakes in town. *12 blvd des Capucines, 75008 • Map E3*

6 La Closerie des Lilas

The main restaurant here is expensive, but the bar is a good spot to soak up the atmosphere of this historic site where artists and writers from Baudelaire to Archibald MacLeish have drunk since 1808. Look out for the famous names of visitors etched

For more places to eat in Paris **See pp64–5**

on the tables. The busy brasserie also has live piano music in the evenings and attracts a chic crowd *(see p157)*.

7 Le Fumoir

There are many reasons to drop into this café-bar-restaurant next to the Louvre whether it be to people watch from the terrace out front or hide out with a martini and game of backgammon in the comfy library at the back. The hot chocolate is heavenly, cocktails are expertly made and the bistro cooking shows Italian and Swedish influences. *6 rue de l'Amiral de Coligny, 75001 • Map F4 • 01 42 92 00 24 • €€€€*

Café de la Paix

8 Chez Jeannette

Though the owners haven't touched the scruffy vintage décor, this café near Gare de l'Est has now become one of the hottest hangouts in Paris with a crowd outside to prove it. Inside, the high ceilings, mirrors and old-fashioned booths, as well as reasonably priced food, create a lively atmosphere. *46 rue du Faubourg-Saint-Denis, 75010 • Map G2 • 01 47 70 30 89 • No disabled access • €€*

9 Le Café de l'Industrie

Unpretentious but stylish, the Bastille café with three large rooms is decorated with everything from spears, to old film star publicity stills. The simple food, such as onion soup, is good value. Live jazz nights help to make this a popular hang-out with the locals *(see p92)*.

10 Jacques Mélac Bar

A gregarious wine bar off the beaten track and full of character, with a rustic beamed ceiling hung with country hams and a vine growing around the walls. The moustached owner from Auvergne is an enthusiastic wine lover and aims to please with his reasonably priced cellar. A fun harvest festival is held in mid-September. *42 rue Léon-Frot, 75011 • Metro Charonne • Closed Aug*

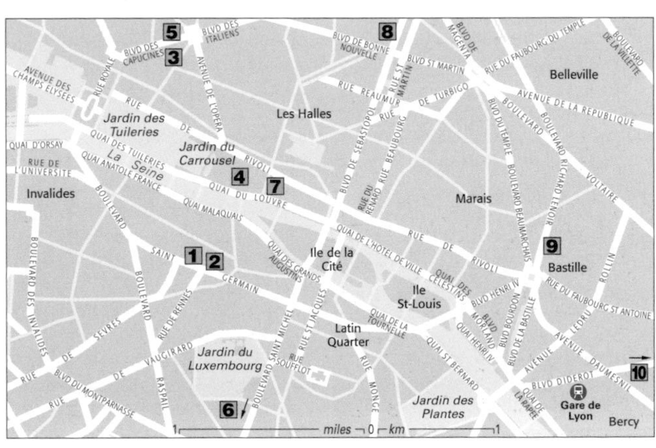

For price guides to Paris restaurants **See p73**

Left **Au Printemps** Right **Rue de Buci**

Top 10 Shops and Markets

1 Flower and Bird Markets

Dating from 1808, the colourful Marché aux Fleurs (flower market) on the Ile de la Cité is the oldest and one of the largest flower markets in Paris. Its blooms brighten up the area between the stark walls of the Conciergerie and Hôtel Dieu from Monday to Saturday – everything from orchids to orange trees. On Sundays it is joined by the Marché aux Oiseaux (bird market) with equally colourful, caged species. *Pl Louis-Lépine, 75002 • Map P4*

2 Au Printemps

One of Paris's two top department stores, Printemps opened in 1864. Its goods range from designer clothing and accessories, to middle-of-the-range labels and funky fashions, home decor and furniture. The sixth-floor tea room is crowned with a lovely Art Nouveau stained-glass cupola. *64 blvd Haussmann, 75009 • Map E2*

3 Galeries Lafayette

Printemp's great rival store opened in 1894 and is a monument to Parisian style, topped by a glorious steel-and-glass dome. Along with designer clothes, there's a fabulous food hall. The seventh floor has great views. *10 blvd Haussmann, 75009 • Map E2*

4 Marché Richard-Lenoir

Every Thursday and Sunday morning, this market stretches along the tree-lined boulevard that separates the Marais from the Bastille. Sunday is the best day, when locals come to socialize as well as shop for foods such as fish, meat, bread and cheese. Some stalls sell North African and other international fare. *Blvd Richard-Lenoir, 75011 • Map H5*

Marché aux Fleurs (flower market)

5 Place de la Madeleine

This is a gourmand's delight. Some of the most delectable speciality food shops in Paris are dotted around the edges of this square, including the famous Fauchon supermarket and the smaller Hédiard. There's Maille for mustard, Kaspia for caviar, Marquise de Sévigné for chocolates and La Maison de la Truffe for truffles *(see p98)*.

6 Rue de Buci

The artist Picasso reputedly did his shopping at this daily morning market in the heart of

St-Germain. The huge fruit and vegetable stalls are of high quality but of greater interest are the food shops opening on to the street, which sell specialist and regional fare. You can also buy prepared Italian dishes and delicious pastries. *Map L4*

7 Rue Mouffetard

One of the oldest street markets in Paris winds downhill through the Latin Quarter every Tuesday to Sunday morning. Although this formerly cheap and Bohemian market has been discovered as a tourist spot, it retains its charm, the narrow street lined with colourful food stalls and speciality shops. There are also good restaurants in the quieter side streets. *Map F6*

8 Le Bon Marché

Paris's first department store was founded on the Left Bank in 1852, its structure partially designed by Gustave Eiffel *(see p17)*. Today it's even more hip than its competitors, with an in-store boutique featuring avant-garde fashions and music. It also has designer clothes, its own line of menswear and the enormous La Grande Epicerie food hall. *22 rue de Sèvres, 75007 • Map D5*

Marché aux Puces du St-Ouen

9 Aligre Market

Away from the tourist bustle, this Bastille market, dubbed the "Notre-Dame of markets", retains an authentic Parisian atmosphere. Every morning North African traders hawk inexpensive produce in the open-air market, and there's an adjacent flea market and a covered market selling top-quality fare. *Pl d'Aligre, 75012 • Map H5*

10 Marché aux Puces de St-Ouen

Every Saturday to Monday the largest antiques market in the world comes alive. There are actually several markets here: the oldest, Marché Vernaison, is the most charming; Marché Malik sells vintage clothing. Others offer furniture, jewellery and paintings. *Porte de Clignancourt, 75018 • Metro Porte de Clignancourt*

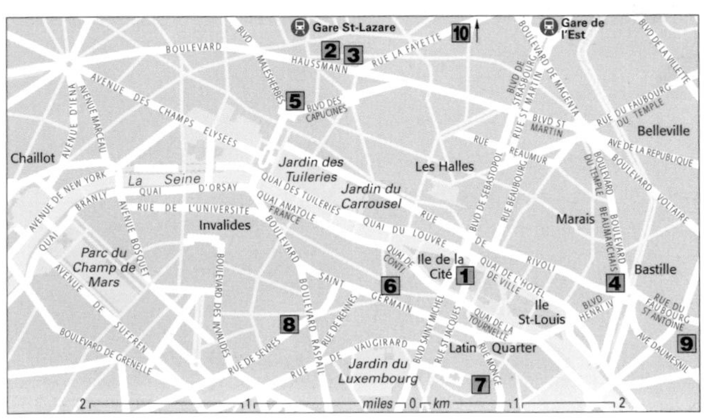

For more on shopping in Paris **See p169**

Left **Fête du Cinéma** Right **Tour de France**

Festivals and Events

1 Nuit Blanches

Paris held its first Nuit Blanche in 2002 and the all-night contemporary art event now attracts more than 1,500,000 people each year. Its goal is to give a fresh perspective on Paris with installations and exhibitions in several different neighbourhoods, and to make contemporary art more accessible to all. *First weekend Oct*

2 Fête du Cinéma

Film buffs should be sure to verify the exact dates of this annual event, held each June. For just three days, cinemagoers pay full price for the first film that they see, but can then see as many other films as they choose, for a few Euros each. *www.feteducinema.com*

3 Paris Jazz Festival

Paris is home to jazz all year round *(see pp62–3)*, but every summer there is a major jazz festival in the city. Acts from all over the world come to play in the Parc Floral de Paris in the Bois de Vincennes *(see p151)*, but there are many lesser venues involved as well. *Jun–end Jul • www.parcfloraldeparis.com*

4 Les Fêtes du Nuit

Classical music performances centred around the Bassin de Neptune Fountain at Versailles *(see p151)*. This is one of the best ways to appreciate the beauty and grandeur of the gardens. Book ahead to avoid disappointment. *End Aug–mid-Sep • www.chateauversaillesspectacles.fr*

5 Tour de France

Don't miss this summer highlight if you really want to understand the French passion for cycling. Towards the end of July each year, the world's greatest and most gruelling cycle race approaches Paris. The final stage is the Champs-Elysées, when thousands of fans pack the street to cheer the riders home and see who will win the Yellow Jersey. *www.letour.fr*

6 Festival d'Automne à Paris

This major festival promotes arts across the board in Paris, commissioning new works and encouraging all walks of life to see and enjoy performances of dance, music and drama. *Mid-Sep–Dec • www.festival-automne.com*

Paris Jazz Festival

7 **Fêtes des Vendanges**
Paris used to be one of the country's major wine producers, but these days only the vineyards at Montmartre remain *(see p142)*. These produce just under 600 litres (5 barrels) of wine each autumn, but great fun is had at the Fêtes des Vendanges when the wine is auctioned off for charity. *Oct: 2nd Fri (for three days)*

8 **Fête de la Musique**
To celebrate the summer equinox, professional and amateur musicians take to the streets of Paris. Major shows are held in Place de la République and other concert venues, but the most fun is to be had wandering through residential neighbourhoods and dropping into locals' bars. *21 Jun*

9 **Beaujolais Nouveau Day**
The arrival of the new vintage of Beaujolais Nouveau wine is celebrated throughout France, but especially in Paris. Bars, cafés, restaurants and wine shops all join in, hosting lively tastings and other events. Look for signs saying "*Le Beaujolais Nouveau est arrivé*" (Beaujolais Nouveau has arrived). *Nov: 3rd Thu*

10 **Mois de la Photo**
Paris reveres the art of photography and every alternate November (in even-numbered years) it hosts the "Month of the Photo". Galleries, museums, shops, cultural centres and many other venues all give space to exhibitions, workshops and lectures on all aspects of the art. For anyone interested in photography, it is the most exciting time to visit Paris. *Nov • www.mep-fr.org*

Top 10 Sports Events

1 **Tour de France**
This great cycle race reaches its climax in Paris.

2 **Prix de l'Arc de Triomphe**
This world-renowned horse race attracts the city's *crème de la crème.* *Longchamp racecourse • Oct: 1st Sun*

3 **French Tennis Open**
Forerunner to the Wimbledon Championships in London *Stade Roland Garros • end May–1st week Jun*

4 **International Show-Jumping**
Show-jumping fans and competitors descend on Paris. *Palais Omnisports de Paris-Bercy • mid-Mar*

5 **Six Nations Rugby**
The French team plays against England, Scotland, Ireland, Wales or Italy in this spring tournament. *Parc des Princes Stadium*

6 **Paris Marathon**
Runners start at the Champs-Elysées and end at avenue Foch. *Apr*

7 **Football Cup Final**
The biggest club event in French soccer. *Stade de France • mid-May*

8 **Prix de Diane-Hermès**
Parisian high society flocks to this up-market horse race *Chantilly • Jun: 2nd Sun*

9 **International Pétanque Tournament**
Players from all over the world compete in this bowls-like game. *Stade Suzanne Lenglen, 75015 • early Jul*

10 **Ice-Skating Grand Prix**
The Trophée Eric Bompard is the Parisian leg of the International Grand Prix. *Palais Omnisports de Paris-Bercy • Nov*

Left **The Lido** Centre **Le Crazy Horse Paris** Right **Théâtre de la Ville de Paris**

TOP 10 Entertainment Venues

1 Opéra National de Paris Garnier

Not just a night out, but a whole experience, opera has now returned to its original Paris base after the theatre had a spell as a dance-only venue. The vast stage can hold a cast of 450, and the building itself is an example of excessive opulence, complete with grand staircase, mirrors and marble *(see p97)*.

2 Folies-Bergère

The epitome of Parisian cabaret, the Folies were, for a time, no more than a troupe of high-kicking, bare-breasted dancers. Today, the musical shows have largely returned to the nostalgic days when Maurice Chevalier and Josephine Baker *(see p63)* performed here. *32 rue Richer, 75009 • Map F2 • 08 92 68 16 50 •*

3 The Lido

Home to the world famous troupe of long-legged dancers, the Bluebell Girls, the fabulous special effects include aerial ballets and an on-stage skating rink. There are many who regard this dinner-cabaret as an essential Parisian experience.

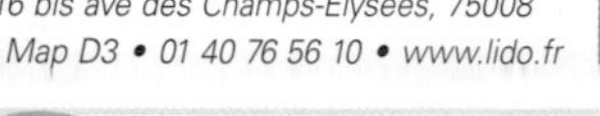

116 bis ave des Champs-Elysées, 75008 • Map D3 • 01 40 76 56 10 • www.lido.fr

Folies-Bergère

4 Moulin Rouge

The original home of the Can-Can, the theatre's dancers were immortalized on canvas by Toulouse-Lautrec during the *belle époque* and are on display in the Musée d'Orsay *(see p13)*. The show still has all the razzamatazz that has been dazzling audiences since 1889. The pre-show dinner is optional *(see p142)*.

5 Le Crazy Horse Paris

More risqué than the other big-name cabaret shows, the Saloon has a reputation for putting on the most professional as well as the sexiest productions. Striptease features, along with glamorous dancing girls and other cabaret acts. The computer-controlled lighting effects are spectacular.

12 ave George V, 75008 • Map C3 • 01 47 23 32 32 • www.lecrazyhorseparis.com

6 Le Cirque d'Hiver

Worth visiting for the freshly renovated façade alone, this whimsical 150-year-old building plays host to the traditional Cirque Bouglione, complete with trapeze artists and tame tigers. *110 rue Amelot, 75011 • Map H3 • 01 47 00 28 81 • www.cirquedhiver.com*

For more Paris cabarets and clubs **See p146**

7 Comédie Française

Paris's oldest theatre was founded in 1680 and is still the only one with its own repertory of actors, staging both classical and modern drama (in French). The current building dates from the 18th century. Around the corner from the main box office, a special window opens 45 minutes before curtain-up, selling reduced price tickets for under-27s and concessions. *1 pl Colette, 75001 • Map L1 • 08 25 10 16 80 (+33 (0) 1 44 58 15 15 from abroad) • www.comedie-francaise.fr*

8 Opéra National de Paris Bastille

Opened in 1992 as the largest opera house in the world, this modern building was heavily criticized, not least for its acoustics and poor facilities. However, this is still the best place to see opera in Paris. *Pl de la Bastille, 75012 • Map H5 • 08 92 89 90 90 (+33 (0) 172 29 35 35 from abroad) • www.operadeparis.fr*

9 Théâtre du Châtelet

The city's largest concert hall and fourth-largest auditorium was built in 1862. The repertoire covers classical music, ballet and opera, as well as popular Sunday morning chamber music concerts. *1 pl du Châtelet, 75004 • Map N2 • 01 40 28 28 00 • www.chatelet-theatre.com*

10 Théâtre de la Ville

Once known as the Sarah Bernhardt Theatre, in honour of the great Parisian actress who performed here and managed the theatre in the 19th century, today it puts on an eclectic range of modern dance, music shows and some classical theatre. *2 pl du Châtelet, 75004 • Map N2 • 01 42 74 22 77 • www.theatredelaville-paris.com*

Top 10 Films set in Paris

1 Les Enfants du Paradis

The city's underworld is shown in this 1944 classic.

2 Everyone Says I Love You

Woody Allen's 1996 movie included many scenes shot around Notre-Dame and the Left Bank.

3 A Bout de Souffle

French New Wave director Jean-Luc Godard's 1959 film stars Jean-Paul Belmondo as a car thief on the run.

4 French Can-Can

The Jean Renoir classic (1955) tells the story of how the famous dance was created in Montmartre clubs.

5 Last Tango in Paris

Controversial, erotic 1972 film starring Marlon Brando.

6 The Trial

Orson Welles used the then empty Gare d'Orsay (now the Musée d'Orsay) to create a convincingly huge and anonymous office for his 1962 version of Kafka's novel.

7 Subway

The metro was the star in this 1985 Luc Besson film about a man who seeks refuge at night in its stations.

8 Les 400 Coups

Gritty Paris streets feature in this 1959 François Truffaut film about a boy on the run.

9 Amélie

Jean-Pierre Jeunet's 2000 sensation about a girl's quest for love features numerous scenes in Montmartre.

10 Prêt-à-Porter

Robert Altman takes a satirical look at the Paris fashion industry in his 1995 film.

Left **Grande Galerie de l'Evolution** Right **Jardin d'Acclimation**

Children's Attractions

1 Disneyland Resort Paris
Formerly known as Euro-Disneyland, the French offspring of America's favourite theme park is a clone of its parent, and has now been joined by the Walt Disney Studios complex. Both have big queues, so arrive early. There are rides for children of all ages and most adults are equally enchanted *(see p151)*.

2 Parc de la Villette
One of the city's top children's attractions, with activities for all ages. The Cité des Sciences et de l'Industrie, a high-tech hands-on science museum, gets star billing, while the Cité des Enfants is a science and nature museum for younger children. Kids also love the Argonaute, a naval museum with a real submarine, the Géode with its IMAX screen and the Cité de la Musique, with musical activities for young people *(see p152)*.

Parc de la Villette

3 Eiffel Tower
A trip to the top is one of the most memorable activities for children in Paris *(see pp16–17)*.

4 Grande Galerie de l'Evolution
The most exciting and imaginatively designed display in the Natural History Museum is the Great Gallery of Evolution. Elephants, giraffes and other stuffed animals rise out of a re-created savannah, a huge whale skeleton hangs from the ceiling, while special lighting displays help tell the story of the development of life on earth. Nature workshops are also held for children under 12 *(see p129)*.

5 Musée de la Curiosité et de la Magie
Kids are enchanted by this museum of magic, located in the atmospheric cellars of the former home of the Marquis de Sade. Magicians conjure up hourly shows involving optical illusions, card tricks and lots of audience participation. The exhibits include fun-house mirrors and memorabilia from master magicians such as Houdini (1874–1926). *11 rue St-Paul, 75004 • Map R4 • 01 42 72 13 26 • Open 2–7pm Wed, Sat, Sun (daily during school holidays) • Admission charge • www.museedelamagie.com*

6 Parc Astérix

Dozens of attractions including Europe's longest roller coaster, an adventure playground and a replica of Albert Uderzo's original comic book village. *Plailly, 60128 • RER B to Roissy CDG1, then shuttle from bus stop A3 • 08 26 30 10 40 • Open Apr–mid-Oct: 10am–6pm Mon–Fri, 9:30am–7pm Sat–Sun • Admission charge • www.parcasterix.fr*

7 Jardin d'Acclimatation

An amusement park tucked away at the north end of the Bois de Boulogne *(see p152)*, with roller coasters, pony rides, puppet shows and two children's museums. On Wednesday and weekend afternoons, journey here on "le Petit Train", a steam train from Porte Maillot. *Bois de Boulogne, 75016 • Map A2 • Open 10am–7 pm daily (summer); 10am–6pm daily (winter) • Admission charge • www.jardindacclimatation.fr*

8 Grévin

This waxworks museum was founded in 1882. Kids will get most enjoyment from seeing celebrities from the world of pop music and film, although there are also wonderful tableaux from French history. *10 blvd Montmartre, 75009 • Map F2 • 01 47 70 85 05 • Open 10am–6:30pm Mon–Fri, 10am–7pm Sat, Sun & public hols • Admission charge • www.grevin.com*

9 Jardin du Luxembourg

The park has tennis courts, puppet shows, donkey rides and a good playground (for a fee). Perhaps most fun of all for the kids is the Parisian pastime of sailing miniature boats in the fountain. *Jardin du Luxembourg • Map E5 • Open daylight–dusk*

10 Parc des Buttes Chaumont

The highest park in Paris is great for a family picnic. Kids love the suspended bridges, waterfalls, donkey rides and puppet shows. *Parc des Buttes Chaumont, 75019 • Map H2 • Open 7am–11pm daily (9pm Oct–Apr) • Free*

Lift, Eiffel Tower

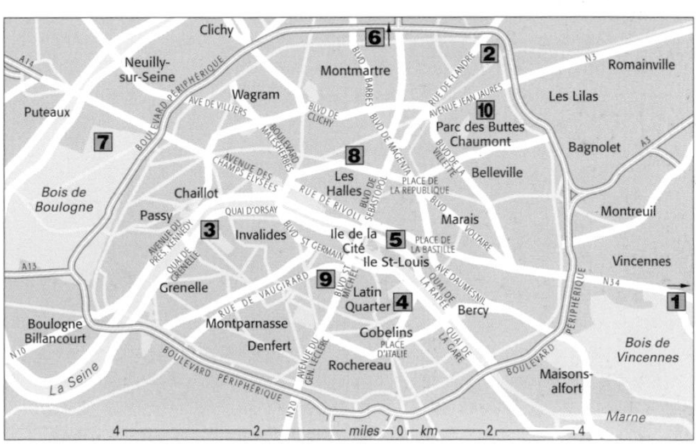

For family-friendly hotels **See p179**

Left **L'Arbuci** Centre **Au Duc des Lombards** Right **Le Bilboquet**

Top 10 Jazz Clubs

1 L'Arbuci

A well-established favourite, in the heart of St-Germain *(see pp118–21)*, attracting a good mix of regular locals and curious tourists. Eat in the pleasant brasserie upstairs, then head to the basement for some old-fashioned Dixie-style jazz.
25 rue de Buci, 75006 • Map L4

2 Au Duc des Lombards

The Left Bank may be the traditional home of jazz clubs but this sleek, modern club is firmly on the Right Bank, in the Les Halles district *(see pp74–7)*. The memorabilia of the "greats" who played here may have disappeared during refurbishment but the club's policy is still to bring in the best overseas jazz artists to play alongside home-grown talent. Good food is served day and night. *42 rue des Lombards, 75001 • Map N2*

3 Baiser Salé

Jazz, blues, Latin and African music are the mainstays at this tiny cellar club, which is low on space but high on volume. The Baiser was promoting World Music long before the phrase had been invented, and the eclectic approach has led to a relaxed and friendly atmosphere. It's cheaper than many clubs, too.
58 rue des Lombards, 75001 • Map N2

4 Le Bilboquet

There's a great sense of history in this revered jazz club. It first opened its doors in 1947, since which time legends including Miles Davis and Billie Holiday have performed here. Today, however, it's mostly local talent that you will see on stage. As well as music, there's also a relaxing bar and restaurant.
13 rue St-Benoît, 75006 • Map K4

5 Autour de Midi et de Minuit

Halfway up La Butte, this atmospheric joint has added some welcome buzz to the slopes of Montmartre. It's jazz all the way, mostly swing but some modern jazz as well, performed in a vaulted cellar below the excellent bistro. *11 rue Lepic, 75018 • Map E1*

Caveau de la Huchette

6 Jazz Club Lionel Hampton

The jazz club par excellence actually serves up a wider range of music than its name suggests. Check what's on as you might get blues, rock or even gospel music. There's a heavy emphasis

For more Paris entertainment **See pp58–9**

on visiting African-American musicians (Oscar Peterson has played here). A sophisticated experience. ✆ *Hôtel Le Méridien-Étoile, 81 blvd Gouvion-St-Cyr, 75017 • Map A2*

7 New Morning

An upstart by Paris standards, having opened in 1981. Its policy of embracing all kinds of music (jazz, blues, Latin, soul and the unclassifiable), not to mention inviting performers up from the floor, has led to a relaxed crowd of regulars. ✆ *7–9 rue des Petites-Ecuries, 75010 • Map F2*

8 Le Petit Journal Montparnasse

The club that barely sleeps – the doors close at 2am, but open up again four hours later. You can just drink, or have a meal while listening to the live music, which is mainly big band jazz but on some nights takes in salsa, blues or rock. ✆ *13 rue du Commandant-Mouchotte, 75014 • Map D6*

9 Le Petit Journal St-Michel

Younger brother of the Montparnasse original, this club opened in 1971 and concentrates more on New Orleans-style swinging jazz. A fun atmosphere in this Latin Quarter cellar, together with a pleasant dining room in which to have a meal, just off the main stage area. ✆ *71 blvd St-Michel, 75005 • Map M5*

10 Caveau de la Huchette

Don't be fooled by its tourist-trap setting in the heart of the Latin Quarter – this venue is worth every penny of the entrance price. The building was once home to Knights Templar, and jazz has been played under the medieval vaults since 1947. ✆ *5 rue de la Huchette, 75005 • Map N4*

Top 10 Musical Artistes in Paris

1 Edith Piaf

Discovered as a street singer in Paris, the diminutive Piaf (1915–63) became known as the "Little Sparrow".

2 Maurice Chevalier

The Parisian singer/actor (1888–1972) is, for many, *the* voice of France. In 1958 he won an Academy Award for his role in *Gigi*.

3 Django Reinhardt

Belgian gypsy guitarist Reinhardt (1910–53) first found fame in Paris in collaboration with Stephane Grappelli.

4 Lionel Hampton

US bandleader Hampton (*b.* 1909) regularly played in the Left Bank jazz clubs.

5 Sidney Bechet

US jazz virtuoso Bechet (1897–1959) settled in Paris in the 1940s and wrote his great tune "Les Oignons" in 1949.

6 Jacques Brel

Belgian singer/songwriter Brel (1929–78) moved to Paris in 1953, where audiences loved his melancholy songs.

7 Stephane Grappelli

Paris-born Grappelli (1908–97) studied classical violin, but later innovatively adapted the instrument to jazz.

8 Josephine Baker

The African-American dancer (1906–75) gained notoriety for dancing semi-nude at the Folies-Bergère.

9 Miles Davis

US trumpet-player Davis (1926–91) was a favourite in Paris for his "cool jazz" style.

10 Coleman Hawkins

US bebop saxophonist Hawkins (1904–69) played Paris many times in the 1930s.

Left **Guy Savoy** Centre **Le Jules Verne** Right **Taillevent**

TOP 10 Places to Eat

1 L'Astrance

There is probably no table in Paris that is more coveted than one in this sober 25-seat dining room, with a single set menu for €120 (without wine) or €190 (with matching wines), orchestrated by young culinary genius Pascal Barbot. Lunch is more affordable, starting at €70 per person. *4 rue Beethoven, 75016 • Map B4 • 01 40 50 84 40 • Closed Sat–Mon, Aug • No disabled access • €€€€€*

2 Guy Savoy

Artichoke and truffle soup is one of star chef Guy Savoy's signature dishes, in his chic and smart restaurant (jacket and ties required for male diners). One of the city's best dining experiences *(see p109)*. To sample Savoy's cooking at more affordable prices, also try the bistro-style Les Bookinistes in the St-Germain quarter *(see p127)*.

Brasserie Bofinger

3 Les Papilles

The setting – a wine shop lined with wooden tables – barely hints at this restaurant's remarkably sophisticated cooking, from a chef who once worked at Taillevent. Pick your wine straight off the shelves to accompany the bargain set menu *(see p127)*.

4 Taillevent

Taillevent's atmospheric oak-panelled dining room is frequented by a mix of businessmen and romantic couples. *Crépinette d'andouillette* (sausage pancake) with foie gras is one memorable dish and there's an exceptional wine list. You need to book well ahead to dine here *(see p109)*.

5 Le Jules Verne

Now in the perfectionist hands of world-famous chef Alain Ducasse, this restaurant on the second floor of the Eiffel Tower has entered the 21st century. Revamped with a futuristic brown decor and suitably luxurious menu, replete with truffles in winter. Service is excellent and the panoramic views are breathtaking, but book months in advance for a coveted window seat *(see p117)*.

6 Brasserie Bofinger

Paris's oldest brasserie, dating from 1864, is worth a visit for the original wood and glass decor and leather banquette seating. The menu offers staple bistro dishes such as oysters and pepper steak, briskly but politely served *(see p93)*.

7 Restaurant du Palais Royal

Under the arcades of the Palais Royal gardens is one of the most peaceful terraces in Paris, where you can feast on impeccable dishes such as squid ink and lobster risotto, and *rhum baba*. The red dining room feels particularly welcoming in colder weather *(see p99)*.

8 Le Scheffer

One bistro looks much like another, but inside this one in the Chaillot Quarter is a different story. The food is superb and the service is friendly. There's always a fun atmosphere and prices are reasonable. For all of these reasons, it's always wise to book ahead *(see p139)*.

9 Le Voltaire

A discreet Seine-side bistro, Le Voltaire attracts celebrities and politicians for its classic French cuisine, notably an exquisite *steak-frites*. *27 quai Voltaire, 75007 • Map E4 • 01 42 61 17 49 • Closed Sun–Mon, Aug • €€€€€*

10 L'Atelier de Joël Robuchon

Take a seat at the lacquered bar to experience a top French chef's take on contemporary cuisine. Signature dishes are the *merlan Colbert* (fried whiting), and carbonara with Alsatian cream and bacon. *5 rue de Montalembert, 75007 • Map E4 • 01 42 22 56 56 • €€€€€*

L'Atelier de Joël Robuchon

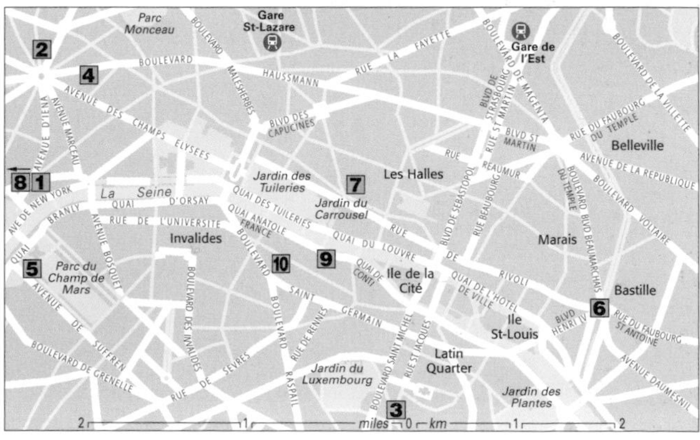

For a price guide to Paris restaurants **See p73**

AROUND TOWN

Left **Notre-Dame** Right **Salle des Gens d'Armes, Conciergerie**

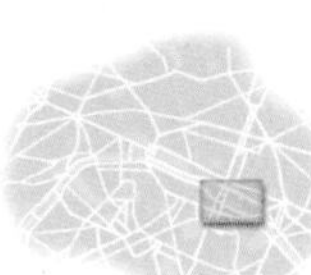

Ile de la Cité and Ile St-Louis

PARIS WAS BORN ON THE ILE DE LA CITÉ. *The first settlers came to this island on the Seine in 300 BC* (see p44) *and it has remained a focus of church and state power through the centuries, with the great cathedral of Notre-Dame and the law courts of the Palais de Justice commanding the island. This tiny land mass also has the honour of being the geographical heart of the country – all French distances are measured from Point Zéro, just outside Notre-Dame. While the Ile de la Cité seems overrun with tourists, the smaller Ile St-Louis, connected to its neighbour by a bridge, has a village-like feel and has been an exclusive residential enclave since the 17th century. Its main street is lined with shops, galleries and restaurants and is a wonderful place for a stroll.*

Top 10 Sights

1. Notre-Dame
2. Sainte-Chapelle
3. Conciergerie
4. Marché aux Fleurs
5. Crypte Archéologique
6. Pont Neuf
7. Palais de Justice
8. Place Dauphine
9. St Louis-en-l'Ile
10. Square du Vert-Galant

Angel detail, Sainte-Chapelle

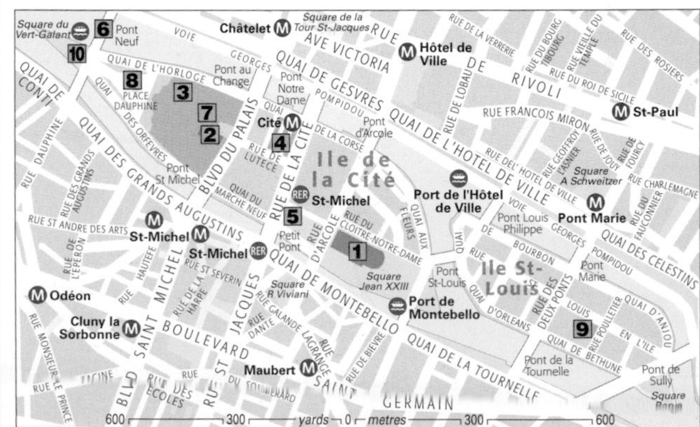

Sign up for DK's email newsletter on traveldk.com

1 Notre-Dame

See pp18–21.

2 Sainte-Chapelle

See pp30–31.

3 Conciergerie

This imposing Gothic palace, built by Philippe le Bel (the Fair) in 1301–15, has a rich history. Parts of it were turned into a prison, controlled by the concierge, or keeper of the king's mansion, hence the name. Ravaillac, assassin of Henri IV, was tortured here, but it was during the Revolution that the prison became a place of terror, when thousands were held here awaiting execution at the guillotine. Today you can see the Salle des Gardes and the magnificent vaulted Salle des Gens d'Armes (Hall of the Men-at Arms), the medieval kitchens, torture chamber, the Bonbec tower, and the prison. The cell where Marie-Antoinette was held and the history of other famous Revolution prisoners is on display. Outside, look for the square Tour de l'Horloge, erected in 1370, which houses the city's first public clock, still ticking away. *2 blvd du Palais, 75001 • Map N3 • Open Mar–Oct: 9:30am-6pm daily; Nov–Feb: 9am–5pm daily • Admission charge*

Sainte-Chapelle

4 Marché aux Fleurs

One of the last remaining flower markets in the city centre, the beautiful Marché aux Fleurs is also the oldest, dating from the early 19th century. It is held year-round, Monday to Saturday, in place Louis-Lépine, filling the north side of the Ile de la Cité with dazzling blooms from 8am to 7pm. There is also a bird market here on Sundays *(see p54)*. *Map N3*

5 Crypte Archéologique

Fascinating remnants of early Paris dating back to Gallo-Roman times were discovered in 1965 during an excavation of the square in front of Notre-Dame in order to build an underground car park. The archaeological crypt displays parts of 3rd-century Roman walls, rooms heated by hypocaust, as well as remains of medieval streets and foundations. The scale models showing the evolution of the city from its origins as a Celtic settlement are particularly interesting. *Place du Parvis-Notre-Dame, 75001 • Map P4 • Open 10am–6pm Tue–Sun • Admission charge*

Crypte Archéologique

The Guillotine

Dr Joseph Guillotine invented his "humanitarian" beheading machine at his home near the Odéon and it was first used in April 1792. During the Revolution some 2,600 prisoners were executed on the places du Carrousel, de la Concorde, de la Bastille and de la Nation, after awaiting their fate in the Conciergerie prison.

6 Pont Neuf

An incongruous name (New Bridge) for the oldest surviving bridge in Paris. Following its completion in 1607, Henri IV christened it by charging across on his steed; the bronze equestrian statue of the king was melted down during the Revolution but replaced in 1818. The city's first pedestrian bridge was unique for its time in that it had no houses built upon it. The bridge has 12 arches and a span of 275 m (912 ft) extending both sides of the island. *Map M3*

7 Palais de Justice

Stretching across the west end of the Ile de la Cité from north to south, the Palais de Justice, along with the Conciergerie, was once part of the Palais de la Cité, seat of Roman rule and the home of the French kings until 1358. It took its present name during the Revolution and the buildings now contain the city's law courts. You can watch the courts in session from Monday to Friday and wander through the public areas, with their many ornate features. The Cour du Mai (May Courtyard) is the area through which prisoners passed during the Revolution on their way to execution. *4 blvd du Palais, 75001 • Map M3 • Open 9am–6pm Mon–Fri, 9:30am–6pm Sat • Free*

8 Place Dauphine

In 1607 Henri IV transformed this former royal garden into a triangular square and named it after his son, the Dauphin and future King Louis XIII. Surrounding the square were uniformly built houses of brick and white stone; No. 14 is one of the few that retains its original features. One side was destroyed to make way for the expansion of the Palais de Justice. Today this quiet, charming spot is a good place to watch locals play *pétanque* *(see p51)*. *Map M3*

Pont Neuf and Square du Vert-Galant

Sculptured relief, Palais de Justice

9 St-Louis-en-l'Ile

This lovely Baroque church on Ile St-Louis was designed between 1664 and 1726 by the royal architect Louis Le Vau. The exterior features an iron clock (1741) at the entrance and an iron spire, while the interior, richly decorated with gilding and marble, has a statue of St Louis holding his Crusader's sword.
19 bis rue St-Louis-en-l'Ile, 75004 • Map Q5 • Open 9am–noon, 2–7pm, Tue–Sun

10 Square du Vert-Galant

The tranquil western tip of the Ile de la Cité, with its verdant chestnut trees, lies beneath the Pont Neuf – take the steps behind Henri IV's statue. This king had a notoriously amorous nature and the name of this peaceful square recalls his nickname, meaning "old flirt". From here there is a wonderful view of the Louvre *(see pp8–11)* and the Right Bank. It is also the departure point for cruises on the Seine on Les Vedettes du Pont-Neuf *(see p165)*. *Map M3*

A Day on the Islands

Morning

Arrive at **Notre-Dame** *(see pp18–21)* by 8am to beat the crowds and appreciate its magnificence, then head for the fragrant Marché aux Fleurs. As well as flowers, you can buy all kinds of garden accessories and seeds. Return to Notre-Dame if you want to ascend the towers, which open at 10am. Take a coffee break at **Le Flore en l'Ile** *(see p73)*, with its views of the cathedral.

The fascinating Crypte Archéologique is worth a half-hour visit, then spend the late morning at **Sainte-Chapelle** *(see pp30–31)*, when the sun beams through the stained-glass windows.

There are plenty of places for lunch, but on a sunny day try **La Rose de France** *(see p73)* with its terrace seating.

Afternoon

Spend a leisurely afternoon strolling the narrow streets of the Ile St-Louis, which are filled with characterful shops and galleries *(see p72)*.

Wind up with an afternoon treat by visiting **Berthillon,** considered the best ice-cream purveyor in France *(31 rue St-Louis-en-l'Ile • Open 10am–8pm Wed–Sun, closed mid-Jul-ug & school hols)*. With more than 70 flavours on offer, from plain vanilla to whisky, and including virtually any fruit you can think of, the hardest part will be choosing, although there is plenty of time to make your choice as there will inevitably be a queue, especially in summer.

Left **L'Epicerie** Centre **Librairie Ulysse** Right **Boulangerie des Deux Ponts**

Top 10 Shopping

1 L'Épicerie
This tiny shop packs in a great array of gourmet delights. Choose from delicacies like orange sauce to speciality vinegars and mustards, to chocolate "snails", all prettily packaged. *51 rue St-Louis-en-l'Ile, 75004 • Map Q5*

2 La Petite Scierie
This friendly, old-fashioned shop sells all types of foie gras and other duck preserves, straight from the farm. *60 rue St-Louis-en-l'Ile, 75004 • Map G5 • 01 55 42 14 88 • Closed Tue–Wed*

3 Librairie Ulysse
Today Paris, tomorrow the world. This eccentric travel bookshop will take you anywhere you want with thousands of titles in French and English – including many on Paris itself. *26 rue St-Louis-en-l'Ile, 75004 • Map Q5*

4 Calixte
The place to stock up for a picnic or the day's treats: superb croissants for the morning, pâtés and terrines and irresistible desserts for lunch. *64 rue St-Louis-en-l'Ile, 75004 • Map Q5*

5 Clair de Rêve
An interesting boutique that sells curiosities such as puppets and miniature theatres. It is an ideal place if you're looking for a present with a certain difference. *35 rue St-Louis-en-l'Ile, 75004 • Map Q5*

6 Alain Carion
A wealth of meteorites, fossils and minerals. Some specimens are put to good use in imaginative jewellery. *92 rue St-Louis-en-l'Ile, 75004 • Map Q5*

7 Pylones Boutique
Wild about rubber? That's the magic material for the whimsical jewellery and accessories here, along with novelty gifts. *57 rue St-Louis-en-l'Ile, 75004 • Map Q5*

8 Boulangerie des Deux Ponts
You won't be able to resist the bread baking in the wood-burning oven from this old-fashioned bakery. *35 rue des Deux-Ponts, 75004 • Map Q5*

9 Bamyan
A wonderful collection of ethnic goods including carvings, furniture, jewellery and other craft items from all over the world. *24 rue St-Louis-en-l'Ile, 75004 • Map Q5*

10 La Ferme Saint Aubin
Cheese in all shapes and sizes from all over France. An aromatic delight. *76 rue St-Louis-en-l'Ile, 75004 • Map Q5*

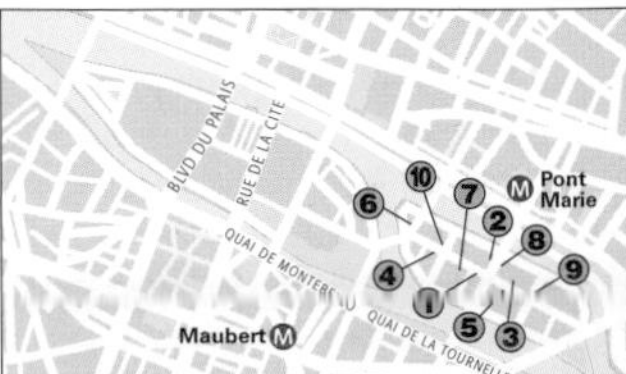

For more on shopping in Paris **See p169**

Price Categories

For a three-course meal for one with half a bottle of wine (or equivalent meal), taxes and extra charges		
	€	under €30
	€€	€30–€40
	€€€	€40–€50
	€€€€	€50–€60
	€€€€€	over €60

Left **La Rose de France** Right **Taverne Henry IV**

TOP 10 Places to Eat

1 Isami

One of the best Japanese restaurants in the city, but tiny so book ahead. Good choice of sushi. *4 quai d'Orléans, 75004 • Map P5 • 01 40 46 06 97 • Closed Sun, Mon, Aug (3 wks) • No disabled access • €€€€*

2 Le Fin Gourmet

Excellent bistro in a 17th-century building. Expect dishes such as scallops with shallots, or veal and baked apples. Bustling at lunchtime, candlelit and quieter in the evening. *42 rue St-Louis-en-l'Ile, 75004 • Map Q5 • 01 43 26 79 27• Closed Mon • No disabled access• €€€*

3 L'Orangerie

Perfect spot for a romantic dinner with candles, flowers and relaxing music. Try the leg of lamb. *28 rue St-Louis-en-l'Ile, 75004 • Map Q5 • 01 46 33 93 98 • Closed Sun, Mon, Aug • No disabled access • €€€€€*

4 La Charlotte de L'Isle

This tiny tea room with a witch-themed decor serves flavoured teas, rustic tarts and what is surely the most potent hot chocolate in town. *24 rue St-Louis-en-l'Ile, 75004 • Map G5 • 01 43 54 25 83 • Closed Mon–Wed, Aug • No disabled access*

5 Brasserie de l'Ile St-Louis

Wooden tables and a rustic look complement hearty Alsace fare such as Tripe in Reisling wine. *55 quai de Bourbon, 75004 • Map P4 • 01 43 54 02 59 • Closed Wed, Thu L, Aug • No disabled access • €€€*

6 La Rose de France

Lovely terrace and a cosy dining room. *24 pl Dauphine, 75001 • Map M3 • 01 43 54 10 12 • Closed Sat, Sun, Aug • €€*

7 Taverne Henry IV

A fine wine list and simple plates of *charcuterie* or cheese. *13 pl du Pont-Neuf, 75001 • Map M3 • 01 43 54 27 90 • Closed Sun • €€*

8 Mon Vieil Ami

A chic interior is the back-drop for dishes such as duck *en croûte* with *foie gras*. *69 rue St-Louis-en-l'Ile, 75004 • Map Q5 • 01 40 46 01 35 • Closed Mon, Tue, Jan, Aug • No disabled access • €€€€*

9 Le Flore en l'Ile

Go for the views as well as the food in this tearoom, open from breakfast until 2am. *42 quai d'Orléans, 75004 • Map P5 • 01 43 29 88 27 • No disabled access • €*

10 Berthillon

There is always a queue outside this legendary ice cream shop, except in August when it closes. *31 rue St-Louis-en-l'Ile, 75004 • Map G5 • 01 43 54 31 61 • Closed Mon–Tue, Aug*

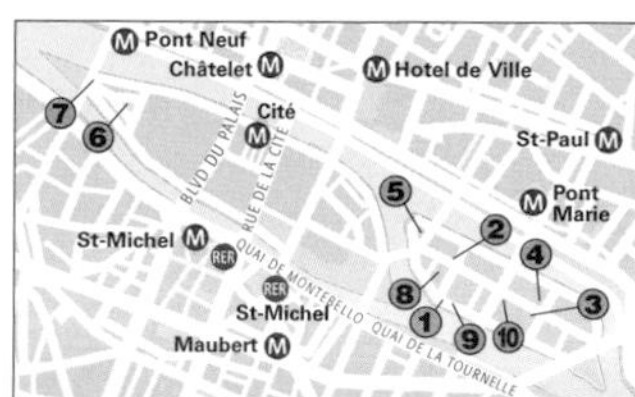

***Note:** Unless otherwise stated, all restaurants accept credit cards and serve vegetarian meals*

Left **Stravinsky fountains** Centre **Fashion in Les Halles** Right **Forum des Halles**

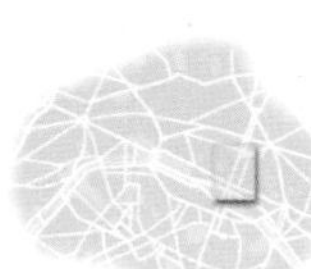

Beaubourg and Les Halles

THE SMALL BUT LIVELY BEAUBOURG QUARTER, *brimming with art galleries and cafés, has become a major tourist attraction since the construction of the Centre Georges Pompidou. This inside-out hulk of modern architecture has become the focus of the area and receives more annual visitors than either the Musée du Louvre or the Eiffel Tower. Les Halles was the marketplace of Paris for 800 years, its glass-covered pavilions packed with butchers, fishmongers and fruit and vegetable stalls; novelist Emile Zola called it "the belly of Paris". In 1969, the market was demolished and moved to the suburbs to alleviate traffic congestion. Sadly, the soulless underground shopping mall, Forum des Halles, replaced it, but there are still a few old-time bistros and specialist food shops that survive to recall its former character.*

La Défense du Temps

Top 10 Sights

1. Centre Georges Pompidou
2. Forum des Halles
3. St-Eustache
4. Bourse du Commerce
5. La Défense du Temps
6. Fontaine des Innocents
7. Eglise St-Merry
8. St-Germain l'Auxerrois
9. Musée de la Poupée
10. Tour St-Jacques

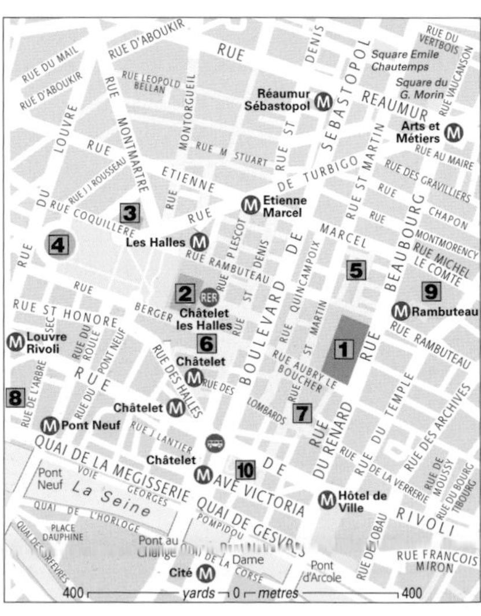

1 Centre Georges Pompidou

See pp26–7.

2 Forum des Halles

Ten years after the original market was demolished, the so-called "largest urban hole in Europe" was filled with this controversial shopping complex. This largely underground maze caters to the young, with music shops and boutiques. Outside, buskers, students and tourists mill about the steps and gardens (not a place to linger at night). Separate metal and glass buildings house the Pavillion des Arts and the Maison de la Poésie, centres for art and poetry respectively. Today, it's more of a sore spot than a hotspot and French architect David Mangin has been brought in to run a four-year renovation project, although a start-date has not yet been decided. *Map N2*

3 St-Eustache

With its majestic arches and pillars, St-Eustache is one of the most beautiful churches in Paris. Although Gothic in design, it took 105 years to build (1532–1637) and its interior decoration reflects the Renaissance style of this time. The church was modelled on Notre-Dame *(see pp18–21)*, with double side aisles and a ring of side chapels. The stained-glass windows made from sketches by Philippe de Champaigne (1631) and the ornate tomb of politician Jean-Baptiste Colbert (1619–83) are highlights. Don't miss the naive sculpture in Chapelle St-Joseph which recalls Les Halles' market days. *2 impasse St-Eustache, 75001 • Map M1 • Open 9:30am–7pm Mon–Fri, 10am–7pm Sat, 9:15am–7pm Sun • Free*

4 Bourse du Commerce

The circular building which houses the Commercial Exchange was erected as a grain market in 1767 and remodelled in the 19th century. It was first covered with a wooden dome, then by subsequent structures of iron and copper. Under today's glass dome, activity in the world trade market is covered at a leisurely pace compared to the way other world financial centres operate. *2 rue de Viarmes, 75001 • Map M1 • Open 9am–6pm Mon–Fri (identification papers are required to visit)*

St-Eustache

Georges Pompidou

Georges Pompidou (1911–74) had the unenviable task of following General de Gaulle as President of France, from 1969 until his death. During his tenure he initiated many architectural developments in Paris, including the controversial but ultimately successful Pompidou Centre, and the less popular scheme to demolish the Les Halles market.

5 Le Défenseur du Temps

The "Defender of Time", Paris's modern public clock, stands appropriately in the Quartier de l'Horloge (Clock Quarter) shopping area. This fantasy mechanical sculpture of brass and steel by Jacques Monastier is 4 m (13 ft) high and weighs one tonne. When the clock strikes the hour, the warrior fends off a savage bird, crab or dragon (representing air, water and earth) with his sword, with accompanying sound effects. At noon, 6pm and 10pm he vanquishes all three. It is currently awaiting repair but is still a must-see. ✎ *Rue Bernard-de-Clairvaux, 75003 • Map P2*

6 Fontaine des Innocents

The Square des Innocents is a Les Halles crossroads and a hang-out for street performers and students. It was built atop a cemetery in the 18th century, and two million remains were transferred to the Catacombs at Denfert-Rochereau. The splendid Renaissance fountain, the last of its era built in the city, was designed by Pierre Lescot and carved by sculptor Jean Goujon in 1547. It originally stood against a wall on rue St-Denis, and was later moved to the new square, when the fourth side was added *(see p39)*. ✎ *Rues St-Denis & Berger, 75001 • Map N2*

7 Eglise St-Merry

Formerly the parish church of the Lombard moneylenders, St-Merry was built between 1520 and 1612, and reflects the Flamboyant Gothic style. Its name is a corruption of St-Médéric, who was buried on this site in the early 8th century. The bell in the church's northwest turret, thought to be the oldest in Paris, dates from 1331 and hung in a chapel which once stood on the site. Other highlights include the decorative west front, the 17th-century organ loft, beautiful stained glass and carved wood panelling. ✎ *76 rue de la Verrerie, 75004 • Map P2 • Open noon–6:45pm daily • Free*

8 St-Germain l'Auxerrois

When the Valois kings moved to the Louvre palace in the 14th century *(see p8)*, this became the church of the royal

St-Germain l'Auxerrois

family. On 24 August 1572, the tolling of its bell was used as the signal for the St Bartholomew's Day Massacre, when thousands of Huguenots who had come to Paris for the wedding of Henri of Navarre to Marguerite of Valois were murdered *(see p20)*. The church features a range of architectural styles, from its Flamboyant Gothic façade to its Renaissance choir. Try and visit on Sunday afternoon when there are organ recitals. *2 pl du Louvre, 75001 • Map M2 • Open 8am–8pm daily • Free*

9 Musée de la Poupée

This delightful doll museum has a superb collection of 300 rare French dolls, including unglazed hand-painted porcelain dolls which were manufactured between 1850 and 1950. Many are imaginatively displayed in tableaux which portray various scenes, such as dolls having tea or playing with nursery toys. The museum also runs a doll hospital where doll doctor Véronique Derez works miracles on dolls of all ages. *Impasse Berthaud, 75003 • Map P2 • Open 10am–6pm Tue–Sun • Closed public hols • Admission charge*

10 Tour St-Jacques

The late Gothic tower, dating from 1523, is all that remains of the church of St-Jacques-la-Boucherie, once the largest medieval church in Paris and a starting point for pilgrims on their journey to Santiago de Compostela in Spain. In the 17th century the physicist Blaise Pascal used the tower for barometrical experiments. The church was pulled down after the Revolution. Today the tower is being restored (due to reopen mid-2009). *Pl du Châtelet, 75004 • Map N3 • Closed to public*

A Day in Les Halles

Morning

Tackle the **Centre Georges Pompidou** *(see pp26–7)* early, as the expansive modern art museum is worth a leisurely visit, and some of the excellent temporary exhibits may catch your eye. If you need refreshment after all that art, it has to be **Georges**, the brasserie at the top of the centre with good views and a choice of drinks, snacks or main meals.

On leaving the centre turn left to see the adjacent Stravinsky Fountain, then walk to the far end to visit the **Eglise St-Merry.**

Providing you have booked ahead, lunch at the 1912 bistro **Benoit** *(see p81)*, whose lunchtime menu is far cheaper than in the evening. After lunch have a peek at the **Défenseur du Temps clock**.

Afternoon

Pass the **Fontaine des Innocents** as you head for Les Halles, but first go into the church of **St-Eustache** *(see p75)* which was the place of worship of the market workers at the old Les Halles. You could then spend the rest of the afternoon shopping at the vast, if somewhat unprepossessing **Forum des Halles** *(see p75)*.

Stop for a drink at A La Tour de Montlhéry, more commonly known as **Chez Denise** *(see p81)*. It's packed at mealtimes, but by late afternoon you might be lucky enough to get a seat and be ready to try their famous Gâteau Marguerite with strawberries and cream.

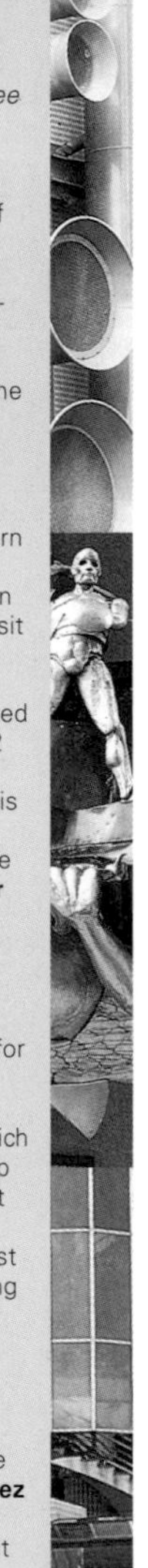

Left **Le Cochon à l'Oreille** Right **Sculpture outside St-Eustache church**

Top 10 Memories of Les Halles

1 Le Cochon à l'Oreille
Dating back to the early 20th century, this ornate working men's café/bar decorated with wall murals is where you'll see the last remaining market traders sipping their dawn drinks. *15 rue Montmartre, 75001 • Map F3*

2 Au Pied de Cochon
This 24-hour brasserie still serves dishes which used to appeal to the earthy tastes of market workers, including pigs' trotters *(see p81)*.

3 St-Eustache Sculpture
The naive sculpture by Raymond Mason in the church's Chapelle St-Joseph is a tribute to the beloved market. Its colourful figures depict *The Departure of Fruit and Vegetables from the Heart of Paris, 28 February 1969.*

4 Rue Montorgueil
The colourful market (Tuesday to Sunday) along this cobbled street is a reminder of the old Les Halles and is frequented by many Paris chefs. *Map N1*

5 Stöhrer
One of the loveliest old-fashioned patisseries in the city, founded in 1730 by a pastry chef who had worked for Louis XV. *51 rue Montorgueil, 75002 • Map N1*

6 Bistrot d'Eustache
A visit here is like stepping back into the jazz spots of Paris in the 1930–40s. It offers good, reasonably priced brasserie fare and live jazz on Friday and Saturday. *37 rue Berger, 75001 • Map N2*

7 La Fresque
This wonderful restaurant used to be a fishmongers. An original tiled fishing scene still decorates the back room. *100 rue Rambuteau, 75001 • Map N1*

8 Dehillerin
Since 1820, everyone from army cooks to gourmet chefs has come here for copper pots, cast-iron pans and cooking utensils. *18 rue Coquillière, 75001 • Map M1*

9 Duthilleul et Minart
For more than 100 years this shop has sold French work clothes and uniforms such as chef's hats and watchmaker's smocks. Good for unique gifts. *14 rue de Turbigo, 75001 • Map P1*

10 A La Cloche des Halles
This wine bar literally rings with history. The "cloche" is the bronze bell whose peal once signalled the beginning and end of the market day *(see p81)*.

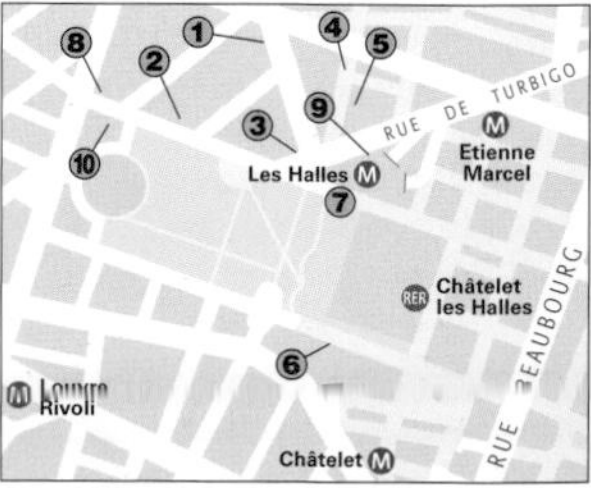

Left **Typical Paris beer bar** Centre **Le Sous-Bock** Right **Au Trappiste**

Top 10 Beer Bars

1 Le Sous-Bock

A good place for *moules* (mussels), with 400 types of beer to wash them down with. There are also 200 whiskies. *49 rue St-Honoré, 75001 • Map M2*

2 Quigley's Point

Right in front of Eglise St-Eustache, this friendly Irish pub serves beer from Holland, Germany, Ireland and Britain. *5 rue du Jour, 75001 • Map M1*

3 Hall's Beer Brewery

A rustic tavern, selling beers from all over the world. Traditional French food is served and there is even a beer-based cocktail menu. *68 rue St-Denis, 75001 • Map N2*

4 La Taverne des Halles

Decent pub food is served in this popular Belgian bar with a great selection of beer and wines. You can also watch football and rugby matches. *2 rue de la Cossonnerie, 75001 • Map N2*

5 The Frog and Rosbif

For homesick English or Anglophiles, this is the place to find real ale and pub grub like bangers and mash, play snooker, to read English newspapers and watch live football and rugby matches on the bar's satellite TV. *116 rue St-Denis, 75002 • Map F3*

6 McBrides

A popular place to watch football, this friendly Irish pub attracts homesick expats with its all-day fried breakfast. Enjoy live music on Sunday nights. *54 rue St-Denis, 75001 • Map F4 • 01 40 26 46 70*

7 Au Trappiste

Among the many beers on tap you can sample Jenlain, a French brew and Blanche Riva, a Belgian beer. Food is also served. *4 rue St-Denis, 75001 • Map F3*

8 Guinness Tavern

Fourteen beers are on tap in this Irish bar with live music every night and a bigger Irish concert once a month. The party really kicks in after 10pm. *31 bis rue des Lombards, 75004 • Map N2*

9 Café Oz

A range of Australian beers and wines combined with archetypal Outback decor makes this rowdy bar popular with antipodean ex-patriates and French patrons alike. *18 rue St-Denis, 75001 • Map F3*

10 La Taverne de Maître Kanter

Part of a chain of Alsatian-style taverns, this is a good place to relax over a pint of French beer. Food is also served. *16 rue Coquillière, 75001 • Map F3 • 01 42 36 74 24*

For more cafés and bars **See pp52–3**

Left **Forum des Halles**

TOP 10 Historical Events in Les Halles

1 Roman Era
A marketplace was first established on the Right Bank of the Seine in a place then called Les Champeaux.

2 10th Century
A larger market for meat, fruit and vegetables was at this time known to exist in the part of Paris which is now Les Halles.

3 1183
The market is enlarged by King Philippe Auguste, who built shelters for the market traders near St-Eustache church *(see p75)*. This date is generally accepted as the founding of Les Halles as the city's market.

4 1850s
Twelve huge iron structures are built to house the market. Napoleon III declares that Les Halles is essential to Paris life.

5 1965
Work begins on a modern wholesale market south of Paris, at Rungis.

6 1969
The market is closed and moved to Rungis, partly to ease the traffic congestion that was by now too much for the centre of the city.

7 1971
The old buildings are demolished and digging begins, to create for a time what is known as the *trou des Halles* (the hole of Les Halles).

8 Mid-1970s
As well as the shopping development, gardens are created and nearby buildings can be seen properly for the first time, including the church of St-Eustache.

9 1977
The Forum des Halles opens and ensures that the area remains as busy as ever, although the goods for sale (high fashion, CDs, fast food) have changed considerably since the market's early days.

10 1986
Second phase of the Forum des Halles opens, creating the biggest collection of shops under one roof in Paris, though many will always lament the passing of the original market.

St-Eustache

For more on shopping in Paris **See p169**

Price Categories

For a three-course meal for one with half a bottle of wine (or equivalent meal), taxes and extra charges		
	€	under €30
	€€	€30–€40
	€€€	€40–€50
	€€€€	€50–€60
	€€€€€	over €60

Above **Au Pied de Cochon**

Top 10 Places to Eat

1 Dans le Noir

For brave souls only, this pitch-black restaurant provides a unique dining experience. *51 rue Quincampoix, 75004 • Map F4 • 01 42 77 98 04 • No lunch weekdays • No disabled access • €€€*

2 Au Pied de Cochon

Long-time Les Halles favourite. If your taste is not for offal, there are options such as oysters and steak. Open 24 hours a day. *6 rue Coquillière, 75001 • Map M1 • 01 40 13 77 00 • €€€€*

3 Benoit

Try the lunchtime menu to cut costs at what is, justifiably the most expensive bistro in Paris. *20 rue St-Martin, 75004 • Map P1 • 01 42 72 25 76 • Closed Aug • No disabled access• €€€€€*

4 L'Ambassade d'Auvergne

Auvergne cooking, with lots of pork and cabbage dishes. Good for solo diners, as tables are shared. *22 rue du Grenier-St-Lazare, 75003 • Map P1 • 01 42 72 31 22 • Closed mid-Jul–mid-Aug • No disabled access • €€*

5 Tour de Montlhéry, Chez Denise

This bistro is an institution in Les Halles for its huge portions of meat. *5 rue des Prouvaires, 75001 • Map N2 • 01 42 36 21 82 • Closed Sat–Sun, mid-Jul–mid-Aug • €€€*

6 Le Grizzli

Charcuterie and pâtés are some of the simple dishes at this early 20th-century bistro. *7 rue St-Martin, 75004 • Map P1 • 01 48 87 77 56 • No disabled access • €€*

7 Café Beaubourg

The terrace here overlooks the Pompidou Centre. Flash-fried steak is a house special. *43 rue St-Merri, 75004 • Map P2 • 01 48 87 63 96 • No disabled access • €€*

8 La Cloche des Halles

Simple bar-bistro where you can dine on plates of cheese and cold meats. *28 rue Coquillière, 75001 • Map M1 • 01 42 36 93 89 • Closed Sun, 3 weeks in Aug • No credit cards •€*

9 Restaurant Georges

Sleek design and a spectacular view make this museum restaurant a great choice for a glamorous night out. *Centre Georges Pompidou, 19 rue Beaubourg, 75004 • Map G4 • 01 44 78 47 99 • Closed Tue • €€€€*

10 Le Hangar

Hidden down a street near the Pompidou this bistro is no secret to locals, who keep returning for the fabulous food, such as seared foie gras on olive-oil mash. Open for afternoon tea on Sundays. *12 Impasse Berthaud, 75003 • Map G4 • 01 42 74 55 44 • Closed Mon • €€€*

***Note:** Unless otherwise stated, all restaurants accept credit cards and serve vegetarian meals*

Left **Place des Vosges street sign** Centre **Place de la Bastille** Right **Maison de Victor Hugo**

Marais and the Bastille

FOR MANY, THE MARAIS IS THE MOST ENJOYABLE *quarter of Paris, with its mansions, museums and medieval lanes, but the district was little more than a muddy swamp until Henri IV built the place Royale (now place des Vosges) in 1605. Following its notoriety as the birthplace of the Revolution, the Bastille sank into oblivion, until artists and designers arrived in the 1990s. Its streets are now home to the city's liveliest nightspots.*

TOP 10 Sights

1. Musée Picasso
2. Musée Cognacq-Jay
3. Place des Vosges
4. Musée Carnavalet
5. Place de la Bastille
6. Marché d'Aligre
7. The Passages
8. Rue de Lappe
9. Maison Européenne de la Photographie
10. Maison de Victor Hugo

Bastille passage

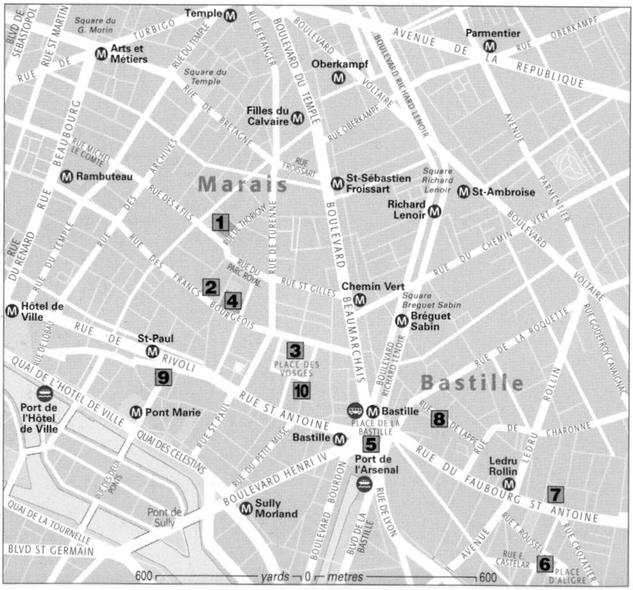

Preceding pages **Notre-Dame seen from the Seine**

1 Musée Picasso

When the Spanish-born artist Pablo Picasso died in 1973, his family donated thousands of his works to the French state in lieu of estate taxes. Thus Paris enjoys the largest collection of Picassos in the world. Housed in the Hôtel Salé *(see p90)*, the museum displays the range of his artistic development, from his Blue and Pink Periods to Cubism, and reveals his proficiency in an astonishing range of techniques and materials *(see p36)*. At the time of writing the museum is closed for a major refurbishment. *5 rue de Thorigny, 75003 • Map R2 • Closed for refurbishment until 2010/2011 • Admission charge (free first Sun of month) • www.musee-picasso.fr*

2 Musée Cognacq-Jay

This small but excellent museum portrays the sophisticated French lifestyle in the so-called Age of Enlightenment, which centred around Paris. The 18th-century art and furniture on display were once the private collection of Ernest Cognacq and his wife, Louise Jay, founders of the Samaritaine department store. It is superbly displayed in the Hôtel Donon, an elegant late 16th-century building with an 18th-century façade *(see p35)*. *8 rue Elzévir, 75003 • Map Q3 • Open 10am–6pm Tue–Sun • www.cognacq-jay.paris.fr*

3 Place des Vosges

Paris's oldest square is also one of the most beautiful in the world. The square was commissioned by Henri IV. Its 36 houses with red-gold brick and stone façades, slate roofs and dormer windows were laid out with striking symmetry in 1612. Originally built for silk workers, the likes of Cardinal Richelieu (1585–1642) and play-wright Molière (1622–73) quickly moved in and it remains an upper-class residential address. But everyone can enjoy a stroll around the area and the art galleries under the arcades. *Map R3*

4 Musée Carnavalet

Devoted to the history of Paris, this museum sprawls through two mansions, the 16th-century Carnavalet and 17th-century Le Peletier de Saint-Fargeau. The former was the home of Madame de Sévigné, the famous letter-writer, from 1677 to 1696 and a gallery here portrays her life. The extensive museum contains period rooms filled with art and portraits. Revolutionary artifacts and memorabilia of 18th-century philosophers Rousseau and Voltaire can be found *(see p34)*. *23 rue de Sévigné, 75003 • Map R3 • Open 10am–6pm Tue–Sun • www.carnavalet.paris.fr*

5 Place de la Bastille

Today this notorious square is surrounded by a busy traffic circle, which is not the best spot for contemplating its grim history. Originally the Bastille

Musée Cognacq-Jay

The Jewish Quarter

The Jewish Quarter, centred around rues des Rosiers and des Écouffes, was established in the 13th century and has attracted immigrants since the Revolution. Many Jews fled here to escape persecution in Eastern Europe, but were arrested during the Nazi Occupation. Since World War II, Sephardic Jews from North Africa have found new homes here.

was a fortress built by Charles V to defend the eastern edge of the city, but it soon became a jail for political prisoners. Angry citizens, rising up against the excesses of the monarchy, stormed the Bastille on 14 July 1789 *(see p45)*, setting off the French Revolution, and destroyed this hated symbol of oppression. In its place is the bronze Colonne de Juillet (July Column), 52 m (171 ft) high and crowned by the Angel of Liberty, which commemorates those who died in the revolutions of 1830 and 1848. Looming behind it is the Opéra Bastille, once the largest opera house in the world, which opened on the bicentennial of the Revolution in 1989. *Map H5*

6 Marché d'Aligre

Set around an old guardhouse and clocktower, the wonderful Aligre market is a melting pot of Parisians from all walks of life. It dates back to 1643 and was once as important as the more famous Les Halles *(see p75)*. In the gourmet covered market you'll see everything from rows of pheasants to a whole wild boar hanging from the stalls. North African traders give the outdoor produce market an ethnic flare. The flea market dates back to the days when nuns distributed second-hand clothing to the poor *(see p55)*.
pl d'Aligre • Map H5 • Open am daily

7 The Passages

The Bastille has been a quarter of working-class artisans and craft guilds since the 17th century and many furniture makers are still located in these small alleyways, called *passages*. The rue du Faubourg-St-Antoine is lined with shops displaying a striking array of both traditional period furniture and modern designs, but don't neglect to visit the narrow *passages*, such as the Passage de la Main D'Or, running off this and other streets

Maison de Victor Hugo

in the Bastille. Many artists and craftspeople have their ateliers (workshops) in these atmospheric alleys. *Map H5*

8 Rue de Lappe

Once famous for its 1930s dance halls *(bals musettes)*, rue de Lappe is still the Bastille's after-dark hotspot. This short, narrow street is filled with bars, clubs, restaurants and cafés, and positively throbs with music. Crowds of hip night-owls trawl the cobblestones looking for action, and spill into the adjoining rue de la Roquette and rue de Charonne where there are even more trendy bars and restaurants. *Map H5*

9 Maison Européenne de la Photographie

This excellent gallery showcasing contemporary European photography opened in 1996 in an early 18th-century mansion, Hôtel Hénault de Cantorbre. The restoration is a mix of historic features and modern spaces that show off its permanent collection and changing exhibitions, including multimedia works. *5–7 rue de Fourcy, 75004 • Map Q3 • Open 11am–8pm Wed–Sun • Admission charge (free Wed after 5pm &; for under 8s) • www.mep-fr.org*

10 Maison de Victor Hugo

French author Victor Hugo (1802–85) lived on the second floor of the Hôtel de Rohan-Guéménée, the largest house on the place des Vosges, from 1832 to 1848. He wrote most of *Les Misérables* here *(see p46)* and many other works. In 1903 the house became a museum of his life. *6 pl des Vosges, 75004 • Map R4 • Open 10am–6pm Tue–Sun • Closed public holidays • Admission charge for exhibitions • www.musee-hugo.paris.fr*

A Day in the Marais

Morning

Begin the morning at the **Musée Carnavalet** *(see p85)*, to beat the crowds and allow enough time to view the impressive collections. There is also a lovely garden courtyard. Afterwards, walk to the place des Vosges. Stand in the centre near the fountains to take in the whole square.

Have a coffee at Ma Bourgogne *(19 pl des Vosges • 01 42 78 44 64)*, right on the square. Afterwards, tour the **Maison de Victor Hugo,** then go to the southwest corner of the square, through a wooden door to the pretty garden of the **Hôtel de Sully** *(see p90)*. Then walk to place de la Bastille.

A good lunch choice is **Bofinger** *(see p93)*, with its ornate decor and true Parisian feel.

Afternoon

The **Place de la Bastille** *(see p85)* is something of a traffic nightmare, but take time to admire the statue in the centre and contemplate the events that happened here when this was the site of the city's dreaded prison. Walk around the square and along rue Faubourg-St-Antoine, a now fashionable shopping street. Turn off down some of the passageways to see the furniture-makers and craft workshops that have a long history in the area.

From here it's not far to **Le Baron Rouge** wine bar *(see p93)*, for a glass of wine and a light evening meal of cheese and *charcuterie* (cold meats).

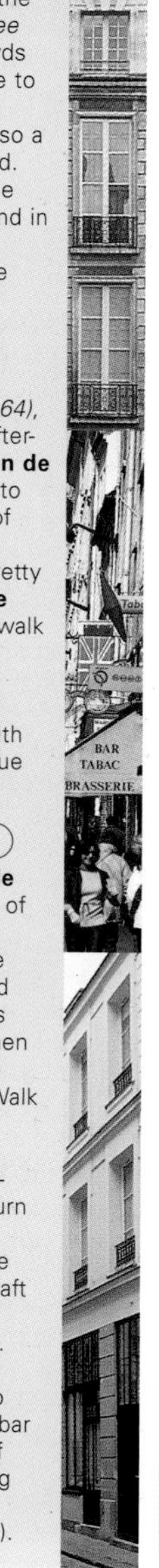

Left **Isabel Marant** Right **Issey Miyake Europe**

Top 10 Shops

1 Izraël

Also called the "World of Spices," this is a treasure trove of the world's best food and drink. Tiny but packed with meat, cheese, wine, rum, dates, honey, mustard… it has to be seen. *30 rue François-Miron, 75004 • Map P3*

2 BHV

The Bazar de l'Hôtel de Ville is an upmarket all-round shopper's paradise at which you can track down everything from DIY products to stylish underwear. *52–64 rue de Rivoli, 75004 • Map F4*

3 Issey Miyake Europe

Superstar Japanese designer sells his limited edition clothing in a chic shop that blends in well with the buildings on the square. *3 pl des Vosges, 75004 • Map R3*

4 Autour du Monde

Stylish clothes and objects for the home from French designer Bensimon. The canvas sneakers in pastel colours for kids and adults are a classic. *8, 12 rue des Francs Bourgeois, 75003 • Map G4 • 01 42 77 16 18*

5 Florence Finkelsztajn

This shop offers a range of cakes with freshly baked rye bread and a deli. *24 rue des Ecouffes, 75004 • Map Q3*

6 Buzz

For the ultimate in contemporary Parisian interior design, this trendy boutique is an unmissable delight. *8 rue Trésor, 75004 • Map Q3*

7 Isabel Marant

A designer better known to Parisians than overseas, her work is hip but elegant. *16 rue de Charonne, 75011 • Map H5*

8 Aladine

Fabulous displays of old kitchenware, boxes, jars, ashtrays… anything with a colourful old advertisement on it, from the 1960s back to whatever the owner can get her hands on. *12 rue Trousseau, 75011 • Map H5*

9 Au Levain du Marais

Exceptional baker producing traditional breads and pastries, and more unusual flavours such as a raisin rye bread. *32 rue de Turenne, 75003 • Map R3*

10 Emery & Cie

Stylish, coloured ceramics, tiles, lamps and other goods, run by an interior decorator. *18 passage de la Main d'Or, 75011 • Map H5*

For more on shopping in Paris **See p169**

Left **André Bissonet** Centre **La Petite Fabrique** Right **Librairie l'Arbre à Lettres**

TOP 10 Specialist Shops

1 The Red Wheelbarrow Bookstore

An English-language bookshop where you can pick up that translated French classic you may have been inspired to read. *22 rue St-Paul, 75004 • Map R4*

2 André Bissonet

A delightful hidden treasure is this shop/workshop where the owner lovingly restores antique musical instruments such as trumpets, harps and violins. *6 rue du Pas-de-la-Mule, 75003 • Map H5*

3 La Chaiserie du Faubourg

Bastille has always been the area for furniture makers, and this chair repair shop keeps the tradition alive. *26 rue de Charonne, 75011 • Map H5*

4 Pasta Linea

Visit for fresh pasta dishes made in-house from organic Italian flour. Not much seating, but the leafy Place des Vosges is nearby. *9 rue de Turenne, 75004 • Map G4*

5 The Filofax Centre

The name says it all, for the ubiquitous binder that palmtop organizers have not ousted completely. *32 rue des Francs-Bourgeois, 75013 • Map R3*

6 L'Art du Bureau

If your desk is your altar, you'll find everything you could possibly need here, and it's all in the most modern designs. In fact, this shop is worth visiting for the design aspects alone. *47 rue des Francs-Bourgeois, 75004 • Map R3*

7 Librairie l'Arbre à Lettres

Beautiful bookshop, though the content is on the serious side, concentrating on art, philosophy and politics. *56 rue du Faubourg-St-Antoine, 75012 • Map H5*

8 A l'Olivier

For 150 years this shop has specialized in all kinds of oil, from the finest olive oil to massage oil. *23 rue de Rivoli, 75004 • Map H5*

9 Papeterie Saint Sabin

Parisian stationery shops are a class apart, and here you will find stylish notebooks, pens, pads and other tasteful items. *16 rue St-Sabin, 75011 • Map H4*

10 A la Petite Fabrique

This shop doesn't just sell chocolate, you can watch it being made. More than 40 flavours and novelty chocolates in all shapes. *12 rue St-Sabin, 75011 • Map H4*

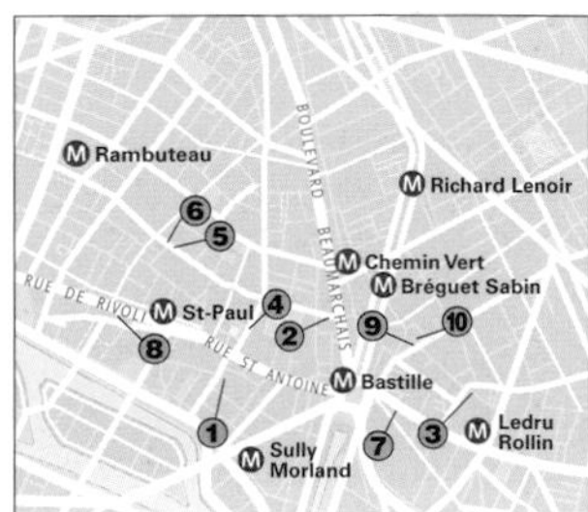

Left **Hôtel de Sens** Centre **Hôtel de Soubise** Right **Hôtel de Lamoignon**

Top 10 Mansions

1 Hôtel de Coulanges

This mansion boasts beautiful early 18th-century architecture, although the right wing dates from the early 1600s. *35 rue des Francs-Bourgeois, 75004 • Map Q2 • Open only for concerts*

2 Hôtel Salé

Built in 1656–9 for Aubert de Fontenay, a salt-tax collector, this mansion was restored in 1986 to provide a home for the Musée Picasso *(see p85)*.

3 Hôtel Guénégaud

Designed by the architect François Mansart in the mid-17th century, this splendid mansion houses a Hunting Museum. *60 rue des Archives, 75003 • Map P3 • Open 11am–6pm Tue–Sun • Admission charge*

4 Hôtel de Beauvais

The young Mozart performed at this 17th-century mansion. Notice the balcony decorated with goats' heads. *68 rue François-Miron, 75004 • Map P3 • Closed to the public*

5 Hôtel de Sully

This 17th-century mansion was home to the Duc de Sully, chief minister to Henri IV. It now forms part of the Jeu de Paume *(see p36)*. *62 rue St-Antoine, 75004 • Map R4 • Open noon–7pm Tue–Sun • Admission charge*

6 Hôtel de Sens

One of Paris's few medieval mansions. Henri IV's wife Marguerite de Valois *(see p20)* lived here after their divorce. Now a fine arts library. *1 rue Figuier, 75004 • Map Q4 • Closed to the public*

7 Hôtel de St-Aignan

The plain exterior hides an enormous mansion within. It is now the Museum of Jewish Art and History. *71 rue du Temple, 75003 • Map P2 • Open 11am– 6pm Mon–Fri, 10am–6pm Sun • Admission charge • www.mahj.org*

8 Hôtel de Soubise

Along with the adjacent Hôtel de Rohan, this 17th-century mansion houses the national archives. *60 rue des Francs-Bourgeois, 75003 • Map Q2 • Open 2–5:30pm Wed–Mon*

9 Hôtel de Lamoignon

Built in 1584 for the daughter of Henri II. *24 rue Pavée, 75004 • Map Q3 • Closed to the public*

10 Hôtel de Marle

This 16th-century mansion houses the Swedish Cultural Centre and café. *11 rue Payenne, 75003 • Map G4 • Open 10am–1pm, 2–6pm Tue–Fri (9pm Tue) • Admission charge*

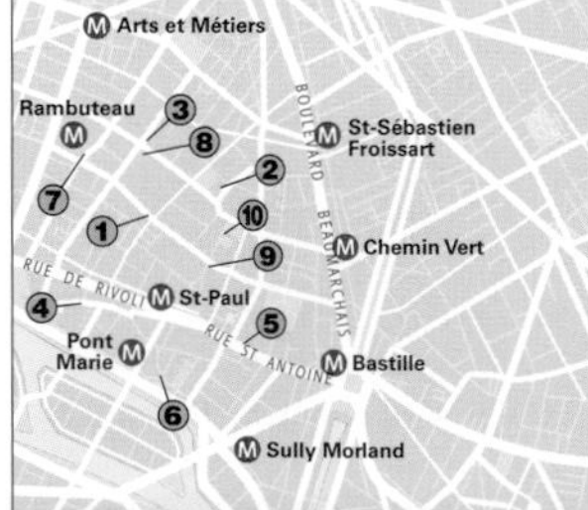

For more historic buildings in Paris **See pp42–3**

Left **Galerie Patrick Seguin** Centre **Galerie Lavignes-Bastille** Right **Galerie Durand-Dessert**

TOP 10 Galleries

1 Galerie Marian Goodman
Housed in a 17th-century mansion, this gallery is a slice of New York. Artists on show include Jeff Wall and video-maker Steve McQueen. *79 rue du Temple, 75003 • Map 2P • Open 11am–7pm Tue–Sat*

2 Galerie Akié Aricchi
Eclectic exhibitions covering photography, sculpture and paint, often with an Asian influence. *26 rue Keller, 75011 • Map H5 • Open 3–7pm Tue–Sat*

3 Galerie Gutharc-Ballin
Alain Gutharc devotes his space to the work of young artists, whether they be working in paint, photography, sculpture or mixed media. *7 rue St Claude, 75003 • Map H4 • Open 2–7pm Tue–Fri, 11am–1pm & 2–7pm Sat*

4 Galerie Daniel Templon
A favourite among the French contemporary art establishment, exhibiting big, international names as well as talented newcomers. *30 rue Beaubourg, 75003 • Map P2 • Open 10am–7pm Mon–Sat*

5 Galerie Karsten Greve
Retrospective style and leading contemporary photography, sculpture and painting can be found at this gallery. *5 rue Debelleyme, 75003 • Map R2 • Open 11am–7pm Tue–Sat*

6 Galerie Patrick Seguin
This off-shoot gallery features stylish 1930–50s furniture. *5 rue des Taillandiers, 75011 • Map H4 • Open 10am–7pm Tue–Sat*

7 Galerie Lavignes-Bastille
Modern posters, books and prints for sale as well as originals. *27 rue de Charonne, 75011 • Map H5 • Open 2–7pm Tue–Sat*

8 Galerie Liliane et Michel Durand-Dessert
Housed in a former factory, the gallery concentrates on contemporary art. *28 rue de Lappe, 75011 • Map H5 • Open 11am–7pm Tue–Sat*

9 Galerie Yvon Lambert
Changing exhibitions cover sculpture, photography and art. *108 rue Vieille du Temple, 75003 • Map Q1 • Open 10am–1pm, 2:30–7pm Tue–Fri, 10am–7pm Sat • www.yvon-lambert.com*

10 Galerie Nikki Diana Marquardt
A gallery of politically motivated artworks executed in all types of art media. *9 pl des Vosges, 75004 • Map R3 • Open 2–5pm Tue–Fri, noon–6pm Sat • http://galerienikkidianamarquardt.com*

Left **Barrio Latino** Right **Pop In**

TOP 10 Fashionable Hang-outs

1 Zéro Zéro

It doesn't get much cooler than this den-like bar with wood panelling and flowered wallpaper. Though not listed on the menu, cocktails are a speciality. *89 rue Amelot, 75011 • Map H4*

2 Andy Wahloo

Located in one of Henri IV's former mansions, pop art and oriental decor form a backdrop for some of the city's most fashionable soirées. *33 rue des Gravilliers, 75003 • Map Q1*

3 Barrio Latino

Vast club on three floors with a generally louche Latin atmosphere. *46–8 rue du Faubourg-St-Antoine, 75012 • Map H5*

4 Bataclan

The concert hall attracts international artists as well as household French names, while the adjoining bar provides beer and meals. *50 boulevard Voltaire, 75011 • Map H4*

5 Pop In

A shabby-chic bar cum nightclub with cheap drinks, friendly staff, a cool crowd and funky DJs. *105 rue Amelot, 75011 • Map H4*

6 Café de l'Industrie

This fashionable and sizeable café has three rooms where the walls are lined with paintings and old-fashioned artifacts. The food is cheap but pretty good, and the later it gets the better the buzz *(see p53)*. *16 rue St-Sabin, 75011 • Map H4*

7 Le Clown Bar

As its name suggests, clown-related clutter fills this fashionable, arty hangout. The wine list is excellent and the staff knowledgeable. *114 rue Amelot, 75011 • Map H4*

8 Le Fanfaron

This is a must for lovers of rare film music, the Rolling Stones and Iggy Pop, with hip tunes and the cheapest beer in Bastille. *6 rue de la Main d'Or, 75011 • Map H5*

9 Le Square Trousseau

This bistro was one of the first media watering holes when the Bastille became chic a few years ago. *1 rue Antoine-Vollon, 75012 • Map H5*

10 SanZSanS

Video screens show what's happening in this trendy, modern bar. *49 rue du Faubourg-St-Antoine, 75011 • Map H5*

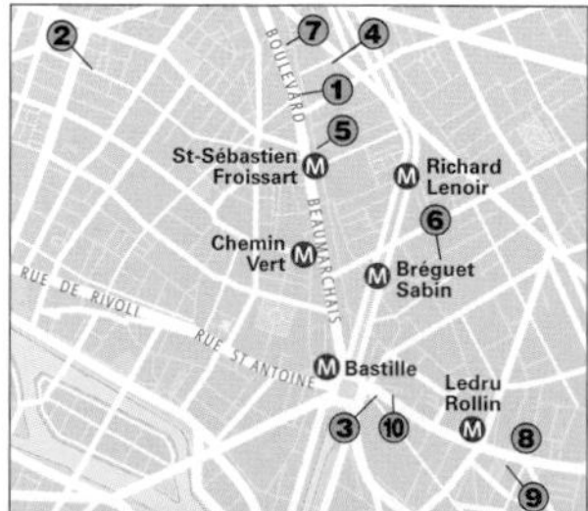

For more bars in Paris **See pp52–3**

Price Categories

For a three-course meal for one with half a bottle of wine (or equivalent meal), taxes and extra charges		
	€	under €30
	€€	30–€40
	€€€	€40–€50
	€€€€	€50–€60
	€€€€€	over €60

Left **Bofinger**

TOP 10 Places to Eat

1 L'Ambroisie
The finest service matching the finest of food. Renowned wine list, and the chocolate tart is out of this world. Reserve in advance. *9 pl des Vosges, 75004 • Map R3 • 01 42 78 51 45 • €€€€€*

2 Gli Angeli
One of Paris's best Italian restaurants. Their *carpaccio* is highly rated, as is the *tiramisù*. *5 rue St-Gilles, 75003 • Map R3 • 01 42 71 05 80 • No disabled access • €€€*

3 La Guirlande de Julie
Owned by Claude Terrail of the Tour d'Argent, this delightful restaurant offers *haute cuisine* at affordable prices. *25 pl des Vosges, 75003 • Map R3 • 01 48 87 94 07 • Closed Mon • €€€*

4 Au Vieux Chêne
Hidden down a side street, this atmospheric bistro is a treat. Expect updated French classics such as bacon-wrapped monkfish with white beans. *7 rue Dahomey, 75011 • 01 43 71 67 69 • Closed Sun, Aug • €€€*

5 La Gazzetta
Contemporary French dishes, such as venison, polenta, dried figs and dandelion leaves, in a relaxing neo-Art Deco setting. *29 rue de Cotte, 75012 • Map H5 • 01 43 47 47 05 • Open Tue–Sat, Sun L • €€*

6 Bofinger
Paris's oldest brasserie (1864) offers staple dishes such as oysters and peppered steak. *5-7 rue de la Bastille, 75004 • Map H5 • 01 42 72 87 82 • No disabled access• €€*

7 Le Baron Rouge
A true Parisian atmosphere and simple food, such as cold meats and cheese. *1 rue Théophile-Roussel, 75012 • Map H5 • 01 43 43 14 32 • Closed Mon • €*

8 Chez Paul
This old bistro has a fairly simple menu but it is always delicious. Book ahead. *13 rue de Charonne, 75011 • Map H5 • 01 47 00 34 57 • €€€*

9 Unico
Set in a former butcher's shop, this Argentinian restaurant mixes retro design with the best steaks in Paris. *15 rue Paul Bert, 75011 • Map H4 • 01 43 67 68 08 • €€€*

10 L'As du Fallafel
Undoubtedly the best fallafel joint. The "special" with fried aubergine and spicy sauce is a must. *34 rue des Rosiers, 75004 • Map Q3 • 01 48 87 63 60 • €€*

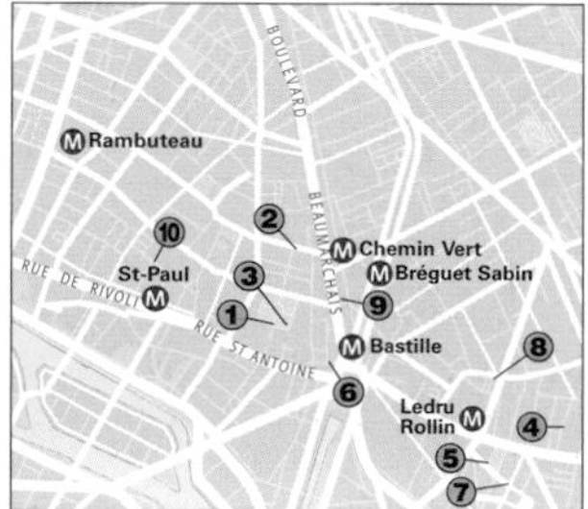

Note: *Unless otherwise stated, all restaurants accept credit cards and serve vegetarian meals*

Left **Louvre façade** Centre **Café Marly, Louvre** Right **Musée Nationale de la Mode et du Textile**

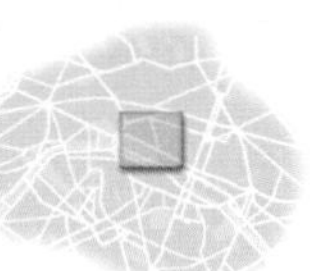

Tuileries and Opéra Quarters

THESE TWO QUARTERS were once the province of the rich and the royal. Adjoining the Tuileries Gardens is the largest museum in the world, the Louvre, while the grand opera house gives the second quarter its name. The Place de la Concorde is one of the most historic sites in the city.

TOP 10 Sights

1. Musée du Louvre
2. Rue de Rivoli
3. Place de la Concorde
4. Jardin des Tuileries
5. Musée des Arts Décoratifs
6. Art Nouveau Museum
7. Palais-Royal
8. Place Vendôme
9. Opéra de Paris Garnier
10. Place de la Madeleine

Opéra de Paris Garnier

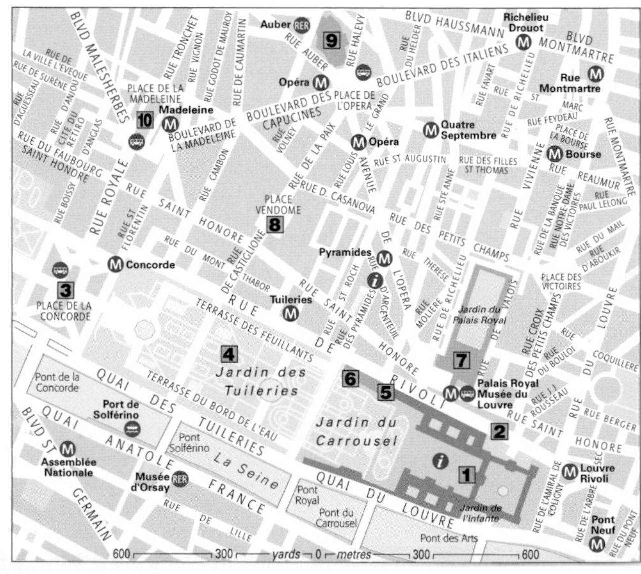

1 Musée du Louvre

See pp8–10.

2 Rue de Rivoli

Commissioned by Napoleon and named after his victory over the Austrians at Rivoli in 1797, this grand street links the Louvre with the Champs-Elysées *(see p103)*. It was intended as a backdrop for victory marches but was not finished until the 1850s, long after the emperor's death. Along one side, railings replaced the old Tuileries walls, opening up the view, while opposite, Neo-Classical apartments sit atop the long arcades. These are now filled with a mix of shops, selling luxury goods or tourist souvenirs. *Map M2*

3 Place de la Concorde

This historic octagonal square, covering more than 8 ha (20 acres), is bounded by the Tuileries Gardens on one side and marks the starting point of the Champs-Elysées on the other. It was built between 1755–75 to designs by architect Jacques-Ange Gabriel as the grand setting for a statue of Louis XV, but by 1792 it had become the place de la Révolution and its central monument was the guillotine. Louis XVI, Marie-Antoinette and more than 1,000 others were executed here *(see p70)*. In 1795, in the spirit of reconciliation, it received its present name. The central obelisk, 23 m (75 ft) tall and covered in hieroglyphics, is from a 3,300-year-old Luxor temple, and was a gift from Egypt, erected in 1833. Two fountains and eight statues representing French cities were also added. On the north side of the square are the mansions Hôtel de la Marine and Hôtel Crillon, also by Gabriel. *Map D3*

Arcades on rue de Rivoli

4 Jardin des Tuileries

These gardens *(see p38)* were first laid out as part of the old Tuileries Palace, which was built for Catherine de Médici in 1564 but burned down in 1871. André Le Nôtre redesigned them into formal French gardens in 1664. At the Louvre end is the Arc de Triomphe du Carrousel, erected by Napoleon in 1808. Here is also the entrance to the underground shopping centre, the Carrousel du Louvre. Nearby, sensuous nude sculptures by Aristide Maillol (1861–1944) adorn the ornamental pools and walkways. At the far end is the hexagonal pool, the Jeu de Paume gallery *(see p36)* and the Musée de l'Orangerie *(see p37)*, famous for its giant canvases of Monet waterlilies. *Map J2*

5 Musée des Arts Décoratifs

This huge collection covers the decorative arts from the Middle Ages through to the 20th century. With more than 100 rooms, the many highlights include the Medieval and Renaissance rooms, the Art Deco rooms, and a wonderful jewellery collection. Also in the same building are the Musée de la Mode and the Musée de la Publicité, which are open for temporary exhibitions and worth a visit. *107 rue de Rivoli, 75001 • Map M2 • Open 11am–6pm Tue–Fri (until 9pm Thu), 10am–6pm Sat & Sun • Admission charge • www.lesartsdecoratifs.fr*

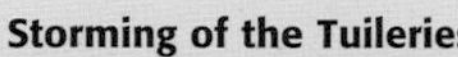

Storming of the Tuileries

Looking at the Tuileries Gardens now, where children play and lovers stroll, it is hard to imagine the scenes that took place here on 20 June 1792. The palace and gardens were invaded by French citizens seeking to overthrow the monarchy. This was finally achieved on 10 August, when the Tuileries Palace was sacked and Louis XVI overthrown.

6 Art Nouveau Museum

This small museum (part of Maxim's restaurant and downstairs nightclub) houses Pierre Cardin's impressive Art Nouveau collection – an elegant assembly of 550 works of art designed by big names such as Tiffany, Toulouse-Lautrec, Galle Massier and Marjorelle. A guided visit can be combined with lunch in the glamorous restaurant. *3 rue Royale, 75008 • Map D3 • Open 2pm–5:30pm Wed–Sun, guided tours 3:15pm, 4pm, 4:30pm, tour and lunch at Maxim's noon • Adm • www.maxims-musee-art-nouveau.com*

7 Palais-Royal

In the late 18th century this former royal palace and garden underwent extensive changes under the dukes of Orléans. The architect, Victor Louis, was commissioned to build 60 uniformly styled houses around three sides of the square and the adjacent theatre, which now houses the Comédie Française, France's national theatre *(see p59)*. Today the arcades house specialist shops, galleries and restaurants, and the courtyard is filled with striking modern works of art *(see p43)*. *Pl du Palais Royal, 75001 • Map L1 • Public access to gardens and arcades only*

8 Place Vendôme

Jules Hardouin-Mansart, the architect of Versailles *(see p151)*, designed the façades of this elegant royal square for Louis XIV in 1698. Originally intended for foreign embassies, bankers soon moved in and built lavish dwellings. It remains home to jewellers and financiers today.

Palais Royal courtyard

Opéra de Paris Garnier façade

The world-famous Ritz hotel was established here at the turn of the 20th century *(see p172)*. The central column, topped by a statue of Napoleon, is a replica of the one destroyed by the Commune in 1871. *Map E3*

9 Opéra National de Paris Garnier

Designed by Charles Garnier for Napoleon III in 1862, Paris' opulent opera house took 13 years to complete. A range of styles from Classical to Baroque incorporates stone friezes and columns, statues and a green, copper cupola. The ornate interior has a Grand Staircase, mosaic domed ceiling over the Grand Foyer and an auditorium with a ceiling by Marc Chagall. There's even an underground lake beneath the building – the inspiration for Gaston Leroux's Phantom of the Opera *(see p58)*. *Pl de l'Opéra, 75009 • Map E2 • 01 40 01 17 89 • Open 10am–5:30pm daily (closes at 1pm on day of matinee performances; closed some dates in Dec) • Admission charge • www.operadeparis.fr*

10 Place de la Madeleine

Surrounded by 52 Corinthian columns, the huge Classical-style La Madeleine church *(see p40)* commands this elegant square. On the east side a colourful flower market is held Tuesday to Saturday. The square is surrounded by some of the most up-market *épiceries* (food stores) and speciality shops in the city *(see p98)*. *Map D3*

A Day in the Tuileries

Morning

Visiting the **Louvre** *(see pp8–11)* takes planning, and you should get there at least 15 minutes before opening time (unless you've already bought your ticket). Spend the whole morning in the museum, and pick up a map as you enter so that you can be sure to see the main highlights. Have a morning coffee in the Café Marly just outside the museum.

From the Louvre, either visit the Carrousel du Louvre's underground shops or walk along **rue de Rivoli** towards **place de la Concorde** *(see p95)*. This end of the street is filled with souvenir shops but avoid the overpriced cafés and turn right to rue Mondavi for a good lunch at Lescure, a little rustic bistro *(7 rue de Mondovi • 01 42 60 18 91 • Closed Sat, Sun)*.

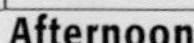

Afternoon

After being indoors all morning, get some fresh air in the **Jardin des Tuileries** *(see p95)* then walk down to **place de la Madeleine** to spend the afternoon browsing and shopping in its many excellent food stores or visit the **Art Nouveau Museum.** Later, take tea in the restaurant of one of the best shops, **Hédiard** *(see p98)*.

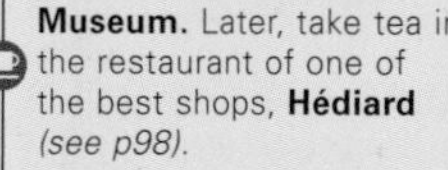

If you are on a budget however, and plan to visit the Louvre on Wednesday or Friday, reverse this itinerary, as admission to the Louvre is much cheaper after 6pm. With late-night opening you could spend more than three hours exploring the collection.

Left **Fauchon biscuits** Right **La Maison du Miel honey**

Top 10 Food Shops

1 Hédiard

Founded in 1854, this world food emporium features a cornucopia of fruits and vegetables, exotic spices and oils and a host of other gourmet delights. *21 pl de la Madeleine, 75008 • Map D3*

2 Fauchon

The king of Parisian *épiceries* (grocers). The mouth-watering window displays are works of art and tempt you inside for pastries, exotic fruits and some 20,000 other items. *26 & 28–30 pl de la Madeleine, 75008 • Map D3*

3 Au Verger de la Madeleine

Vintage wines are the speciality at this store. The owner will help you find a wine to match the year of any special occasion. *4 blvd Malesherbes, 75008 • Map D3*

4 Caviar Kaspia

The peak of indulgence. Caviars from around the world, plus smoked eels, salmon and other fishy fare. *17 pl de la Madeleine, 75008 • Map D3*

5 La Maison de la Truffe

France's finest black truffles are sold here during the winter truffle season, and you can get preserved truffles and other delicacies the rest of the year. *19 pl de la Madeleine, 75008 • Map D3*

6 La Maison du Miel

The "house of honey", family-owned since 1908, is the place to try speciality honeys, to spread on your toast or your body in the form of soaps and oils. *24 rue Vignon, 75009 • Map D3*

7 Boutique Maille

The retail outlet for one of France's finest mustard-makers. Try flavoured mustards such as Cognac or champagne. There are also lovely ceramic condiment jars. *6 pl de la Madeleine, 75008 • Map D3*

8 Marquise de Sévigné

A superb chocolate shop and salon, where you can have a tea, coffee or hot chocolate at the bar and sample the sweets too. *32 pl de la Madeleine, 75008 • Map D3*

9 Betjeman and Barton

This tea shop offers some 200 varieties from all over the world, as well as wacky teapots. *23 blvd Malesherbes, 75008 • Map D3*

10 Ladurée

A splendid *belle époque* tea salon that has been serving the best macaroons in Paris since 1862. *16 rue Royale, 75008 • Map D3*

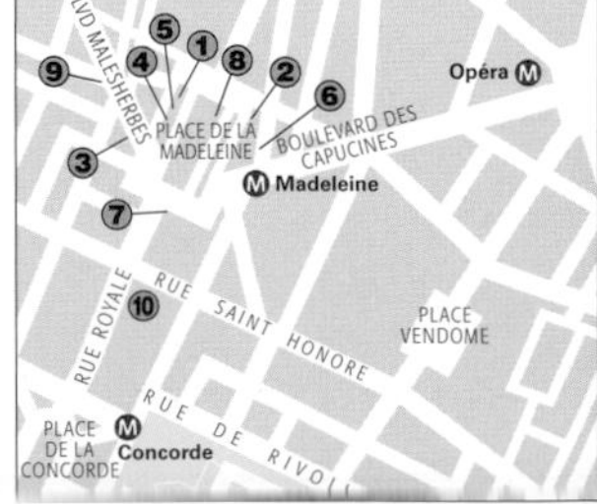

For more on shopping in Paris **See p169**

Price Categories

For a three-course meal for one with half a bottle of wine (or equivalent meal), taxes and extra charges		
	€	under €30
	€€	€30–€40
	€€€	€40–€50
	€€€€	€50–€60
	€€€€€	over €60

Left **Senderens** Right **Chartier**

Top 10 Places to Eat

1 Le Carré des Feuillants
Top chef Alain Dutournier prepares subtle dishes such as venison in an almond crust. *14 rue de Castiglione, 75001 • Map E3 • 01 42 86 82 82 • Closed Sat, Sun, Aug • No disabled access • €€€€€*

2 L'Espadon
Everything you would expect from a Michelin-starred restaurant: great service, decor and cooking. *Hôtel Ritz, 15 pl Vendôme, 75001 • Map E3 • 01 43 16 30 80 • €€€€€*

3 Le Grand Véfour
This beautiful 18th-century restaurant with three Michelin stars is hard to beat. *17 rue de Beaujolais, 75001 • Map E3 • 01 42 96 56 27 • Closed Fri D, Sat–Sun, Aug • No disabled access • €€€€€*

4 Senderens
The former Lucas Carton restaurant has renounced its Michelin stars but maintains its superb quality. *9 pl de la Madeleine, 75008 • Map D3 • 01 42 65 22 90 • Open daily • No disabled access • €€€€€*

5 Le Zinc d'Honoré
Join the lunchtime business crowds and the evening theatre-goers for well-priced bistro cuisine. *36 Place du Marché St-Honoré, 75001 • Map E3 • Open daily • €*

6 Higuma
This no-frills Japanese noodle house serves great value food. *32 bis rue Sainte-Anne, 75001 • Map E3 • 01 47 03 38 59 • €€€*

7 Il Cortile
Italian specialities such as veal with sage and strawberry soup, are served on a lovely patio in summer. *Hotel de Castille, 37 rue Cambon, 75001 • Map E3 • 01 44 58 45 67 • Closed Sat–Sun, Aug • €€€€€*

8 Willi's Wine Bar
This cosy bar and dining room is a popular haunt for lovers of modern French food and wines from small producers. *13 rue des Petits-Champs, 75001 • Map E3 • 01 42 61 05 09 • Closed Sun • €€€*

9 Restaurant du Paris Royal
Contemporary French cooking is served in the bucolic Palais Royal gardens *(see p64)*. *110 galerie de Valois, 75001 • Map E3 • 01 40 20 00 27 • Closed Sun • No disabled access • €€€€*

10 Chartier
Waiters race about serving simple soups, meat and fish dishes. No bookings are taken, but the inevitable queues move quickly. *7 rue du Faubourg-Montmartre, 75009 • Map E3 • 01 47 70 86 29 • €*

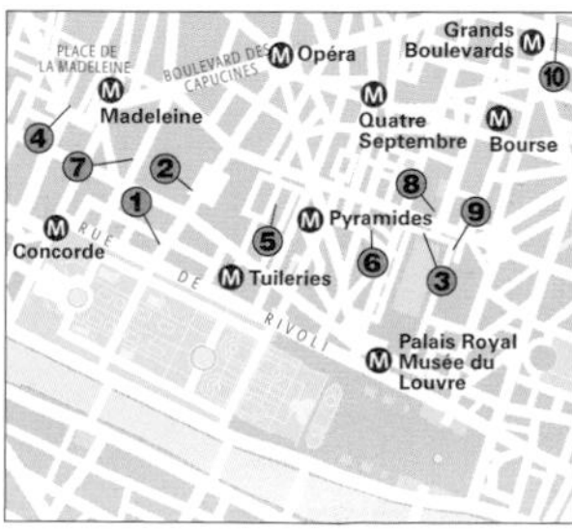

Note: *Unless otherwise stated, all restaurants accept credit cards and serve vegetarian meals*

BON
Bon
Bon
Bon

Left **Arc de Triomphe** Right **Palais de L'Elysée**

Champs-Elysées Quarter

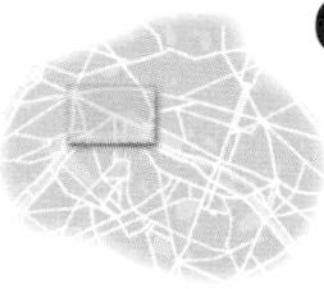

THE CHAMPS-ELYSEES IS UNDOUBTEDLY *the most famous street in Paris and the quarter which lies around it is brimming with wealth and power. It is home to the president of France, great* haute couture *fashion houses, embassies and consulates, and the five-star hotels and fine restaurants frequented by the French and foreign élite. The Champs-Elysées itself runs from the place de la Concorde to the place Charles de Gaulle, which is known as L'Etoile (the star) because of the 12 busy avenues that radiate out from it. It is the most stately stretch of the so-called Triumphal Way, built by Napoleon, where Parisians celebrate national events with parades or mourn at the funeral cortèges of the great and good.*

TOP 10 Sights

1. Arc de Triomphe
2. Avenue des Champs-Elysées
3. Grand Palais
4. Petit Palais
5. Pont Alexandre III
6. Palais de la Découverte
7. Rue du Faubourg-St-Honoré
8. Avenue Montaigne
9. Palais de l'Elysée
10. Musée Jacquemart-André

Home of La Marseillaise

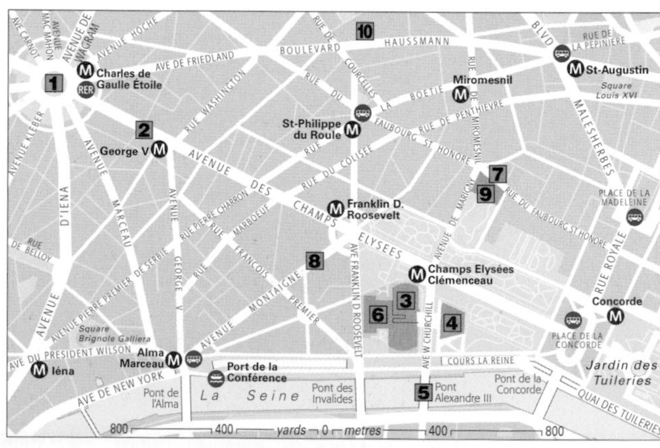

Preceding pages **French patisseries**

1 Arc de Triomphe

See pp24–5.

2 Avenue des Champs-Elysées

One of the most famous avenues in the world came into being when the royal gardener André Le Nôtre planted an arbour of trees beyond the border of the Jardin des Tuileries in 1667 *(see p95)*. First called the Grand Cours (Great Way), it was later renamed the Champs-Elysées (Elysian Fields). In the mid-19th century the avenue acquired pedestrian paths, fountains, gas lights and cafés, and became the fashionable place for socializing and entertainment. Since the funeral of Napoleon in 1840, this wide thoroughfare has also been the route for state processions, victory parades and other city events. The Rond Point des Champs-Elysées is the prettiest part, with chestnut trees and flower beds, but the upper end, near the Arc de Triomphe, has sadly lost its glamour with the influx of fast-food chains and tourist services. Yet a walk along the avenue is still an obligatory part of any visit to Paris. *Map C3*

3 Grand Palais

This immense *belle époque* exhibition hall was built for the Universal Exhibition in 1900. Its splendid glass roof is a landmark of the Champs-Elysées. The façade, the work of three architects, is a mix of Art Nouveau ironwork, Classical stone columns and a mosaic frieze, with bronze horses and chariots at the four corners of the roof. The Galleries du Grand Palais host temporary art exhibitions. *3 ave du Général-Eisenhower, 75008 • Map D3 • 01 44 13 17 17 • Open 10am–8pm Thu–Mon, 10am–10pm Wed (daily during exhibitions) • Closed 1 May, 25 Dec • Admission charge*

4 Petit Palais

The "little palace" echoes its neighbour in style. Set around a semi-circular courtyard, with Ionic columns and a dome, the building now houses the Musée des Beaux-Arts de la Ville de Paris. This includes medieval and Renaissance art, 18th-century furniture and a collection of 19th-century paintings. *Ave Winston-Churchill, 75008 • Map D3 • 01 53 43 40 00 • Open 10am–6pm Tue–Sun • Closed public hols*

Avenue des Champs-Elysées

La Marseillaise

The stirring French national anthem was written in 1792 by a French army engineer named Claude Joseph Rouget de Lisle. He lived for a time in this district, at 15 rue du Faubourg-St-Honoré. The rousing song got its name from the troops from Marseille who were prominent in the storming of the Tuileries during the Revolution *(see p45)*.

5 Pont Alexandre III

Built for the 1900 Universal Exhibition to carry visitors over the Seine to the Grand and Petit Palais, this bridge is a superb example of the steel architecture and ornate Art Nouveau style popular at the time. Named after Alexander III of Russia, who laid the foundation stone, its decoration displays both Russian and French heraldry. The bridge creates a splendid thoroughfare from the Champs-Elysées to the Invalides *(see p48)*. *Map D3*

6 Palais de la Découverte

Set in a wing of the Grand Palais, this museum showcasing scientific discovery was created by a physicist for the World's Fair of 1937. The exhibits focus on invention and innovation in various scientific areas, from biology to chemistry, to astronomy and physics, with interactive exhibits and demonstrations. The planetarium gives realistic views of space using fibre optics, while the Planète Terre (Planet Earth) rooms examine global warming. *Ave Franklin-D-Roosevelt, 75008 • Map D3 • Open 9:30am–6pm Tue–Sat, 10am–7pm Sun • Closed most public holidays • Admission charge*

Pont Alexandre III

7 Rue du Faubourg-St-Honoré

Running roughly parallel to the Champs-Elysées, the Paris equivalent of Fifth Avenue, Bond Street or Rodeo Drive is this high street of international glamour. From Christian La Croix and Versace to Gucci and Hermès, the shopfronts read like a *Who's Who* of fashion. Even if the prices may be out of reach, window-shopping is fun. There are also elegant antiques and art galleries. Look out for swallows that nest on many of the 19th-century façades. *Map D3*

8 Avenue Montaigne

In the 19th century the Avenue Montaigne was a night-life hotspot. Parisians danced the night away at the Mabille Dance Hall until it closed in 1870 and Adolphe Sax made music with his newly invented saxophone in the Winter Garden. Today this chic avenue is a rival to the rue Faubourg-St-Honoré as the home to more *haute couture* houses such as Christian Dior and Valentino. There are also luxury hotels, top restaurants, popular cafés, and the Comédie des Champs-Elysées and Théâtre des Champs-Elysées. *Map C3*

Rue du Faubourg-St-Honoré

9 Palais de l'Elysée

Built in 1718, after the Revolution this elegant palace was turned into a dance hall, then, in the 19th century, became the residence of Napoleon's sister Caroline Murat, followed by his wife Empress Josephine. His nephew, Napoleon III, also lived here while plotting his 1851 coup. Since 1873 it has been home to the president of France. For this reason, it is worth noting that the palace guards don't like people getting too close to the building *(see p42)*. *55 rue du Faubourg-St-Honoré, 75008 • Map D3 • Closed to the public*

10 Musée Jacquemart-André

This fine display of art and furniture, once belonging to avid art collectors Edouard André and his wife Nélie Jacquemart, is housed in a beautiful late 19th-century mansion. It is best known for its Italian Renaissance art, including frescoes by Tiepolo and Paolo Uccello's *St George and the Dragon* (c.1435). The reception rooms feature the art of the 18th-century "Ecole française", with paintings by François Boucher and Jean-Honoré Fragonard. Flemish masters are in the library. *158 blvd Haussmann, 75008 • Map C2 • 01 45 62 11 59 • Open 10am–6pm daily • Admission charge • www.musee-jacquemart-andre.com*

A Day of Shopping

Morning

The **Champs-Elysées** *(see p103)* is an area for leisurely strolls. Begin by window-shopping along one side of the **avenue Montaigne,** where Prada, Nina Ricci, Dior and many more have their flagship stores – the area oozes money. Have a break in the Bar des Théâtres, where fashion names and the theatre crowd from the Comédie des Champs-Élysées across the street sometimes hang out *(6 ave Montaigne • 01 47 23 34 63)*.

Return up the other side of avenue Montaigne to the Champs-Elysées, for the stroll to the Arc de Triomphe. This is where the "real world" shops, at more affordable prices. Break for lunch at **Spoon, Food and Wine**, but get there early to get a table *(see p109)*.

Afternoon

Continuing up the Champs-Elysées, look past the car showrooms and fast food outlets to note the many interesting buildings which house them.

Take the underpass to the **Arc de Triomphe** *(see pp24–5)* and climb to the top for the views. Notice how the Louvre and La Défense arch line-up perfectly. Walk or take the metro to the **rue du Faubourg-St-Honoré**, for more designer shops.

For tea and cakes, **Ladurée** *(see p109)* is a must on the Champs-Elysées, with its heart-warming macaroons and syrupy hot chocolate *(75 ave des Champs-Elysées • 01 40 75 08 75)*

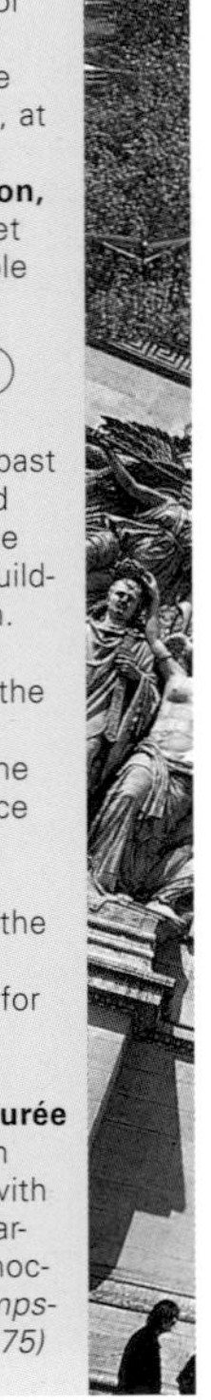

Left **Avenue de Marigny** Centre **Avenue Franklin-D.-Roosevelt** Right **25 Avenue Montaigne**

Top 10 International Connections

1 Avenue de Marigny
American author John Steinbeck lived here for five months in 1954 and described Parisians as "the luckiest people in the world". *Map C3*

2 8 Rue Artois
Here, in September 2001, the legendary Belgian mobster François Vanverbergh – godfather of the French Connection gang – fell victim to a drive-by assassin as he took his afternoon mineral water. *Map C2*

3 37 Avenue Montaigne
Having wowed Paris with her comeback performances, iconic German actress and singer Marlene Dietrich spent her reclusive final years in a luxury apartment here. *Map C3*

4 Pont de l'Alma
Diana, Princess of Wales, was killed in a tragic accident in the underpass here in 1997. Her unofficial monument nearby attracts thousands of visitors each year *(see p48)*. *Map C3*

5 31 Avenue George V, Hôtel George V
A roll-call of rockers – from the Rolling Stones and Jim Morrison to J-Lo and Ricky Martin – have made this their regular Paris home-from-home. *Map C3*

6 Hôtel d'Elysée-Palace
Mata Hari, the Dutch spy and exotic dancer, set up her lair in Room 113 before finally being arrested outside 25 Avenue Montaigne. *Map C3*

7 37 Avenue George V
Franklin D. Roosevelt and his new bride visited his aunt's apartment here in 1905. He was later commemorated in the name of a nearby avenue. *Map C3*

8 49 Avenue des Champs-Elysées
Author Charles Dickens may well have had "the best of times and the worst of times" when he resided here from 1855–6. Ten years earlier he had also lived at 38 Rue de Courcelles. *Map C3*

9 114 Avenue des Champs-Elysées
Brazilian aviation pioneer Alberto Santos-Dumont planned many of his amazing aeronautical feats – notably that of circling the Eiffel Tower in an airship in 1901 – from this address. *Map C2*

10 102 Boulevard Haussmann
Hypochondriac author Marcel Proust lived in a soundproofed room here, turning memories into a masterwork. *Map D2*

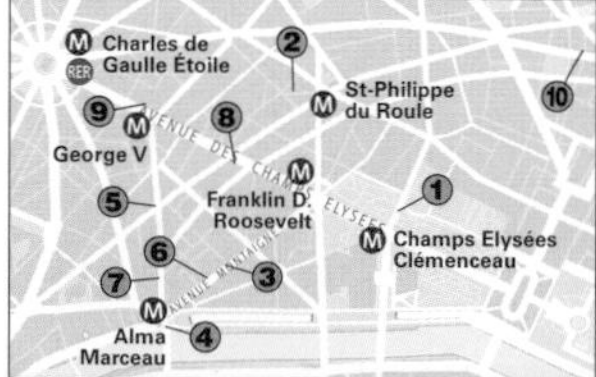

Left **Student riots, 1968** Right **Bastille Day celebrations**

TOP 10 Events on the Champs-Elysées

1 **1616**
Paris's grand avenue was first laid out when Marie de Médici, wife of Henri IV, had a carriage route, the Cours-la-Reine (Queen's Way), constructed through the marshland along the Seine.

2 **1667**
Landscape gardener Le Nôtre lengthened the Jardin des Tuileries to meet the Cours-la-Reine, and opened up the view with a double row of chestnut trees, creating the Grand Cours.

3 **1709**
The avenue was re-named the Champs-Elysées (Elysian Fields). In Greek mythology, the Elysian Fields were the "place of ideal happiness", the abode of the blessed after death.

4 **1724**
The Duke of Antin, overseer of the royal gardens, extended the avenue to the heights of Chaillot, the present site of the Arc de Triomphe *(see pp24–5)*.

5 **1772**
The Marquis of Marigny extended the avenue again, this time all the way to the Neuilly bridge over the Seine, the stretch of street now called avenue Charles-de-Gaulle.

6 **1774**
Architect Jacques-Germain Soufflot lowered the hill of the Champs-Elysées by 5 m (16 ft) to reduce the steep gradient, therefore making an easier and safer passage for residents' horses and carriages.

7 **1789**
On 14 July every year Parisians celebrate Bastille Day to commemorate the start of the French Revolution *(see p45)*. There are marching bands, military processions and Air Force jets fly overhead. In late July, "les Champs" is also the final stretch for the Tour de France bicycle race *(see pp56)*.

8 **26 August 1944**
Parisians celebrated the liberation of the city from the German Nazi Occupation of World War II with triumphant processions and festivities.

9 **30 May 1968**
The infamous student demonstrations of May 1968, when riotous students protested against state authority, spilled over to massive gatherings. The demonstration here, at one of the city's main focal points, captured world news.

10 **12 November 1970**
The death of President Charles de Gaulle was an immense event in France, as he had been the single most dominant French political figure for 30 years. He was honoured by a silent march along the Champs-Elysées.

Left **Christian Dior bag** Centre **Chanel** Right **Boutique Prada**

Top 10 Designer Shops

1 Christian Dior

The grey and white decor, with silk bows on chairs, makes a chic backdrop for fashions from lingerie to evening wear. *30 ave Montaigne, 75008 • Map C3*

2 Chanel

Chanel classics, from the braided tweed jackets to two-toned shoes as well as Lagerfeld's more daring designs, are displayed in this branch of the main rue Cambon store. *42 ave Montaigne, 75008 • Map C3*

3 Nina Ricci Mode

After treating yourself to the gorgeous lingerie or jewellery, go round the corner on rue François 1er to The Ricci Club for menswear or the discount shop where last year's fashions are sold. *39 ave Montaigne, 75008 • Map C3*

4 Emanuel Ungaro

This shop carries the less expensive U line as well as Ungaro's main collection. *2 ave Montaigne, 75008 • Map C3*

5 Boutique Prada

The signature bags, shoes and leather goods are displayed on the ground floor, while the fashions are upstairs. *10 ave Montaigne, 75008 • Map C3*

6 Joseph

The largest of the four Joseph stores in Paris, selling knitwear, evening wear and accessories. *14 ave Montaigne, 75008 • Map C3*

7 Jil Sander

Minimal and modern store, just like the clothes. Sander's trouser suits, cashmere dresses and overcoats in neutral colours are displayed on four floors. *56 ave Montaigne, 75008 • Map C3*

8 Chloé

Simple, classy, ready-to-wear designer womens' clothes and accessories are sold in this minimalist temple of feminine chic. *44 ave Montaigne, 75008 • Map C3*

9 Valentino

The Milanese designer's range of sophisticated clothes for the society set and casual fashions for the younger Miss Valentino label are displayed in this elegant marble boutique. *17–19 ave Montaigne, 75008 • Map C3*

10 MaxMara

The chic Italian womenswear label promotes a sleek, well-groomed look with beautiful fabrics. Suits, coats, evening wear and the trendier Sportmax line are sold here. *31 ave Montaigne, 75008 • Map C3*

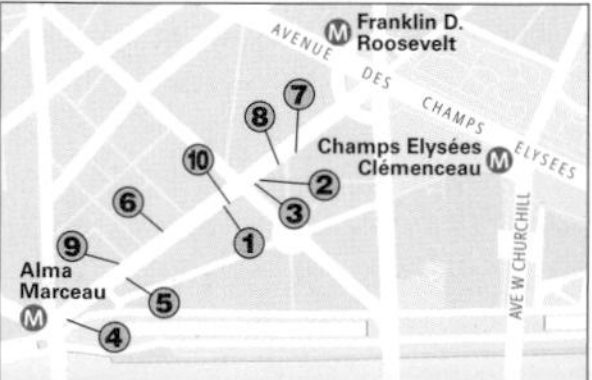

For more on shopping in Paris **See p169**

Price Categories

For a three-course meal for one with half a bottle of wine (or equivalent meal), taxes and extra charges		
	€	under €30
	€€	€30–€40
	€€€	€40–€50
	€€€€	€50–€60
	€€€€€	over €60

Above **Au Plaza Athénée**

Top 10 Places to Eat

1 Alain Ducasse au Plaza Athénée

Superchef Alain Ducasse's flagship restaurant. Langoustines with caviar is just one mouth-watering bite *(see p64)*. *Hôtel Plaza Athénée, 25 ave Montaigne, 75008 • Map C3 • 01 53 67 65 00 • Closed Mon–Wed L, Sat–Sun • €€€€€*

2 Guy Savoy

Another star chef, Guy Savoy is experimental with his food *(see p64)*. *18 rue Troyon, 75017 • Map C3 • 01 43 80 40 61 • Closed Sat L, Sun–Mon • €€€€€*

3 Les Ambassadeurs

Jacket and tie are required here. *Filet mignon* of suckling pig is one speciality. *Hôtel de Crillon, 10 pl de la Concorde, 75008 • Map D3 • 01 44 71 16 16 • €€€€€*

4 Spoon, Food and Wine

Alain Ducasse's affordable offshoot. *14 rue de Marignan, 75008 • Map C3 • 01 40 76 34 44 • Closed Sat–Sun, Aug • €€€€€*

5 Taillevent

One of the city's best dining experiences. Langoustine parcels with shellfish pastry is a signature dish *(see p64)*. *15 rue Lamennais, 75008 • Map C3 • 01 44 95 15 01 • Closed Sat–Sun, Aug • €€€€€*

6 Gagnaire

Chef Pierre Gagnaire is legendary for blending flavours, such as lamb cutlets with truffles. *6 rue Balzac, 75008 • Map C3 • 01 58 36 12 50 • Closed Sat–Sun, mid-Jul–mid-Aug • No disabled access • €€€€€*

7 Granterroirs

A rare and affordable place to eat around the Champs-Elysées, serving top quality salads and hot dishes. *30 rue de Miromesnil, 75008 • Map D2 • 01 47 42 18 18 • Closed Sat–Sun, Aug • €€*

8 Le Boeuf sur le Toit

Fabulous Art Deco setting, and *andouillettes* (tripe sausages) are a speciality. *34 rue du Colisée, 75008 • Map C3 • 01 53 93 65 55 • No disabled access • €€€*

9 L'Atelier des Chefs

This popular cooking school charges €15 per hour (30 minutes of cooking followed by a meal). Classes are in French, though English translations are available. *10 rue de Penthièvre, 75008 • Map D2 • 01 53 30 05 82 • €*

10 Ladurée

A tea room loved by locals and visitors alike. Regulars swoon over the hot chocolate and the delicious patisseries. *75 ave des Champs-Élysées, 75008 • Map C3 • 01 40 75 08 75 • €*

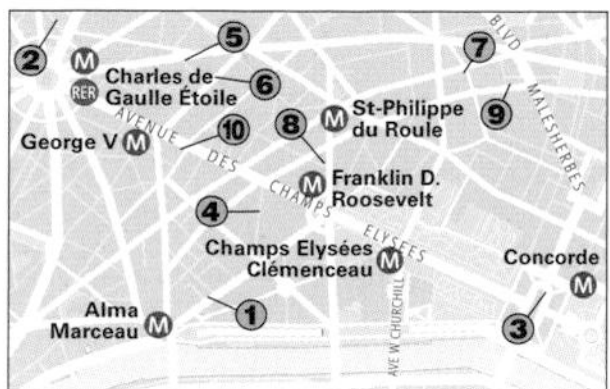

Note: *Unless otherwise stated, all restaurants accept credit cards and serve vegetarian meals*

Left **Dôme church** Centre **Eiffel Tower** Right **Champs-de-Mars**

Invalides and Eiffel Tower Quarters

TWO OF PARIS'S MOST BEAUTIFUL LANDMARKS, *the golden-domed Hôtel des Invalides and the world-famous Eiffel Tower, are found in these quarters. Large parts of the area were created in the 19th century, when there was still room to construct wide avenues and grassy esplanades leading to the monumental buildings. To the east of the Invalides are numerous stately mansions now converted into embassies, and the French parliament.*

Sights

1. Hôtel des Invalides
2. Eiffel Tower
3. Les Egouts
4. Musée de l'Armée
5. Musée Rodin
6. Musée du Quai Branly
7. Rue Cler
8. Ecole Militaire
9. UNESCO
10. Assemblée Nationale

The Thinker, Musée Rodin

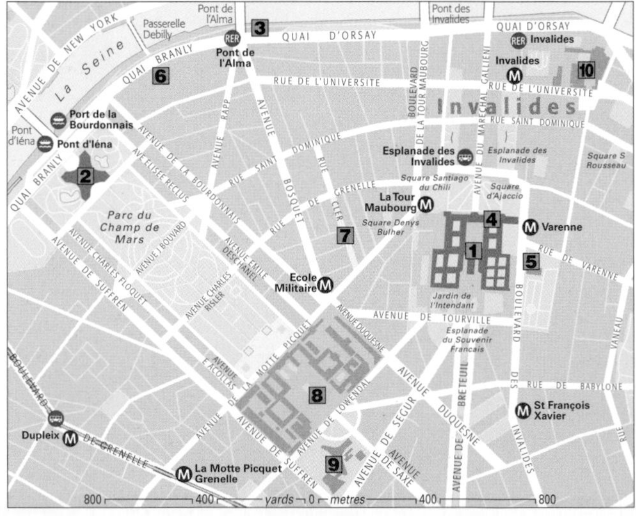

1 Hôtel des Invalides

see pp32–3.

2 Eiffel Tower

see pp16–17.

3 Les Egouts

In a city of glamour and grandeur, the sewers *(egouts)* of Paris are an incongruously popular attraction. They date from the Second Empire (1851–70), when Baron Haussmann was transforming the city *(see p45)*, and the sewers which helped to sanitize and ventilate Paris are considered one of his finest achievements. Most of the work was done by an engineer named Belgrand. The 2,100-km (1,300-mile) network covers the area from Les Halles to La Villette – if laid end-to-end the sewers would stretch from Paris to Istanbul. An hour-long tour includes a walk through some of the tunnels, where you'll see water pipes, telephone lines and various cables, while the museum tells the story of the city's water and sewers, from their beginnings to the present day. There is an audio-visual show and a room devoted to sanitation techniques of the future. *Face au 93, quai d'Orsay, 75007• Map C4 • Open May–Sep: 11am–5pm Sat–Wed; Oct–Apr: 11am–4pm Sat–Wed • Closed two weeks mid-Jan • Admission charge*

General Foch, Musée de l'Armée

4 Musée de l'Armée

The Army Museum contains one of the largest and most comprehensive collections of arms, armour and displays on military history in the world. There are weapons ranging from prehistoric times to the end of World War II, representing countries around the world. Housed in the Hôtel des Invalides, the galleries occupy the old refectories in two wings on either side of the courtyard. The museum ticket includes entry to the Musée des Plans-Reliefs, the Historial Charles de Gaulle, the Musée de L'Ordre de la Liberation and Napoleon's Tomb *(see p114)*. *Hôtel des Invalides, 75007 • Map C4 • Open 10am–6pm Wed–Mon, (until 9pm Tue & 5pm in winter) • Closed 1st Mon of month (except Jul–Sep), public hols • Admission charge*

5 Musée Rodin

An impressive collection of works by the sculptor and artist Auguste Rodin (1840–1917) is housed in a splendid 18th-century mansion, the Hôtel Biron *(see p116)*, where he spent the last nine years of his life. The rooms display his works roughly chronologically, including his sketches and watercolours. Masterpieces such as *The Kiss* and *Eve* are displayed in the airy rotundas. One room is devoted to works by his talented model and muse, Camille Claudel, and Rodin's personal collection of paintings by Van Gogh, Monet and other masters hang on the walls. The museum's other

Young Napoleon

The most famous alumnus of the Ecole Militaire was Napoleon Bonaparte, who was admitted as a cadet, aged 15, in 1784 and deemed "fit to be an excellent sailor". He graduated as a lieutenant in the artillery, and his passing-out report stated that "he could go far if the circumstances are right". The rest, as they say, is history.

highlight is the gardens, the third-largest private gardens in Paris, where famous works such as *The Thinker* and *The Gates of Hell* stand among the lime trees and rose bushes. *79 rue de Varenne, 75007 • Map C4 • Open 9:30am–5:45pm Tue–Sun (until 4:45pm in winter), gardens open one hour later • Admission charge • www.musee-rodin.fr*

6 Musée du Quai Branly

The aim of this museum is to showcase the arts of Africa, Asia, Oceania and the Americas. The collection boasts nearly 300,000 artifacts, including a fantastic array of African instruments, Gabonese masks, Aztec statues and 17th-century painted animal hides from North America (once the pride of the French royal family). Designed by Jean Nouvel, the building is an exhibit in itself: glass is ingeniously used to allow the surrounding greenery to act as a natural backdrop to the collection. *37 quai Branly, 75007 • Map B4 • Open 11am–7pm Tue–Sun (until 9pm Thu–Sat) • Admission charge*

7 Rue Cler

The cobblestone pedestrianized road that stretches south of rue de Grenelle to avenue de La Motte-Picquet is the most exclusive street market in Paris. Here greengrocers, fishmongers, butchers, and wine merchants sell top-quality produce to the well-heeled residents of the area. Tear yourself away from the mouth-watering cheeses and pastries, however, to feast your eyes on the Art Nouveau build ings at Nos. 33 and 151. *Map C4*

8 Ecole Militaire

At the urging of his mistress Madame Pompadour, Louis XV approved the building of the Royal Military Academy in 1751. Although its purpose was to educate the sons of impoverished officers, a grand edifice was designed by Jacques-Ange

Musée du Quai Branly

Gabriel, architect of the place de la Concorde *(see p95)* and the Petit Trianon at Versailles, and completed in 1773. The central pavilion with its quadrangular dome and Corinthian pillars is a splendid example of the French Classical style. *1 pl Joffre, 75007 • Map C5 • Open to the public by special permission only (apply in writing)*

9 UNESCO

The headquarters of the United Nations Educational, Scientific and Cultural Organization (UNESCO) were built in 1958 by an international team of architects from France (Zehrfuss), Italy (Nervi) and the United States (Breuer). Their Y-shaped building of concrete and glass may be unremarkable, but inside the showcase of 20th-century art by renowned international artists, is well worth a visit. There is a huge mural by Picasso, ceramics by Joan Miró, and a 2nd-century mosaic from El Djem in Tunisia. Outside is a giant mobile by Alexander Calder and a peaceful Japanese garden. *7 pl de Fontenoy, 75007 • Map C5 • 01 45 68 10 00 • By appointment only • Free*

10 Assemblée Nationale

Built for the daughter of Louis XIV in 1722, the Palais Bourbon has housed the lower house of the French parliament since 1827. The Council of the Five Hundred met here during the Revolution, and it was the headquarters of the German Occupation during World War II. Napoleon added the Classical riverfront façade in 1806 to complement La Madeleine *(see p97)* across the river. *33 Quai d'Orsay, 75007 • Map D4 • Open for tours only (identity papers compulsory) 10am, 2pm, 3pm Sat, except public hols and when parliament is in session • Free*

A Day Around the Invalides Quarter

Morning

Try to get to the **Eiffel Tower** *(see pp16–17)* early, to beat the worst of the queues, and take the lift to the top to admire the spectacular panorama. After descending, take tea at Le Dôme *(47 ave de la Bourdonnais, 01 45 51 45 41)*, whose terrace has a great view.

Walk towards the Seine and turn right before crossing the river. A stroll along the riverbank is always pleasant if the weather is kind *(see pp48–9)*, and before long you will reach the Place de la Résistance. Cross the road, staying on the south side of the river, where a ticket booth masks one of the city's great secrets, **Les Egouts** *(see p111)*. Don't worry about taking a torch or wearing special footwear – the area visited is well-lit and dry underfoot.

If the sewers don't put you off, you could lunch at the excellent fish restaurant, **Le Divellec** *(see p117)*.

Afternoon

After lunch, walk to the **Hôtel des Invalides** *(see pp32–3)* to see Napoleon's Tomb and the beautiful domed church, and then visit the almost adjacent **Musée Rodin** *(see p111)* and stroll in its gardens.

On leaving the museum turn right along rue de Varenne, until it meets rue du Bac. Here, at No. 109, is Le Bac à Glaces, a combined tearoom and ice cream parlour – perfect for a refreshing rest.

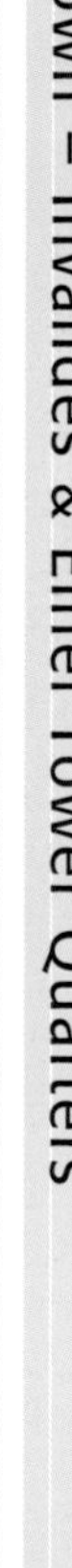

Left **The Abdication of Napoleon (1814), François Pigeot** Right **Suit of armour**

TOP 10 Musée de l'Armée Exhibits

1 Modern Department (1648–1792)

The modern King's army, from its birth under Louis XIV to the training of Revolutionary soldiers is related through objects, such as some fine early rifles.

2 Modern Department (1792–1871)

Displays here cover the beginnings of the Revolution to the Paris Commune, including the personal belongings of Napoleon I.

3 Ancient Armoury Department

The third-largest collection of armoury in the world is on show in the northeast refectory. Assembled over a 40-year period since the 1960s, these items had been lost since the Revolution.

4 17th-Century Murals

In the Ancient Armoury Department, restored 17th-century murals by Joseph Parrocel celebrate Louis XIV's military conquests.

5 The World Wars

Two rooms on the second floor are devoted to World War I and World War II. Documents, uniforms, maps, photographs and other memorabilia bring the conflicts of both wars to life, often to disturbing effect.

6 Banners and Trophies

A small collection of 17th–20th-century banners is displayed in the east wing.

7 Historial of Charles de Gaulle

This state-of-the-art display on the life of the former war-time president is in the Cour d'Honneur, Orient wing.

8 Musée des Plans Reliefs

On the fourth floor of the east wing is a collection of relief models of French towns showing the development of fortifications from the 17th century onwards.

9 Artillery

Over 800 canons are displayed inside and in front of the museum.

10 Salle Orientale

This collection of arms and armour reflects the military styles of different nations.

Verdun (1917), Felix Vallotton, Two World Wars

For the Musée de l'Armée **See p111**

Left **View from the Eiffel Tower** Right **Pont Alexandre III and Hôtel des Invalides**

TOP 10 Views

1 Top of the Eiffel Tower
There is nowhere in Paris to match the view from the top of the tower, so hope for good weather. With the Seine sparkling below and lush greenery, it is the highlight of any visit *(see pp16–17)*. *Map B4*

2 Pont d'Iéna
There is no bad approach to the Eiffel Tower, but the best is from the Trocadéro direction, walking straight to the tower across the Pont d'Iéna. *Map B4*

3 Base of the Eiffel Tower
Everybody wants to race to the top, but don't neglect the view from the ground. Looking directly up at the magnificent structure makes one appreciate the feat of engineering all the more *(see pp16–17)*. *Map B4*

4 Eiffel Tower at Night
Such was the success of Paris's breathtaking Millennium fireworks display, centred on the tower, that the city authorities continued the idea with an hourly lighting display that makes the whole edifice twinkle. *Map B4*

5 Saxe-Breteuil Market
This old street market in avenue de Saxe is a little off the usual tourist track, but the view of the Eiffel Tower above the fruit and vegetable stalls is totally Parisian and will especially appeal to photographers. *Map D5 • 7am–2:30pm Thu, 7am–3pm Sat*

6 Pont Alexandre III
The view of the Hôtel des Invalides, seen from the banks of the Seine, is stunning *(see p48)*. *Map D4*

7 Musée Rodin Gardens
The view of the golden Dôme church, through the branches of the trees that line these gardens, is awe-inspiring. *Map D5*

8 Napoleon's Tomb
You cannot help but be impressed as you enter the Dôme Church and stand gazing down at the massive tomb which holds the body of the diminutive emperor *(see pp32–3)*. *Map D4*

9 Pont de la Concorde
The Egyptian obelisk at the centre of place de la Concorde *(see p95)* is at its most impressive from the bridge. *Map D4*

10 Hôtel des Invalides
Walk into the centre of the courtyard to fully appreciate this magnificent set of buildings *(see pp32–3)*. *Map D4*

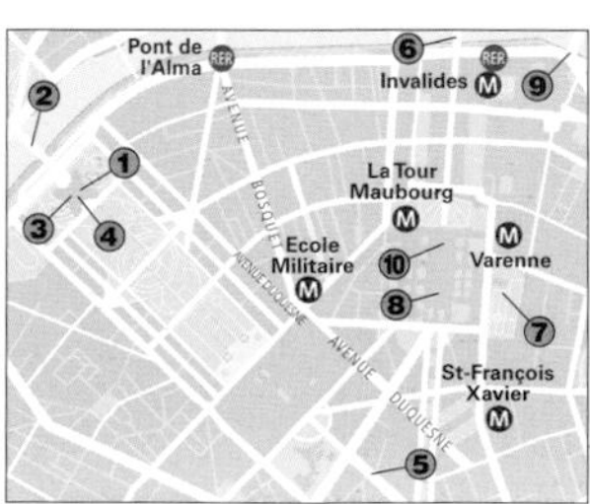

Left **Hôtel de Biron** Right **Hôtel de Villeroy**

Top 10 Mansions

1 Hôtel Biron
Built in 1730, this elegant mansion was home to the duc de Biron. From 1904 it was transformed into state-owned artists' studios and among its residents was Auguste Rodin (1840–1917), who agreed to donate his works to the nation in return for his flat and studio space. After the sculptor's death the house became the Musée Rodin *(see p111)*.

2 Hôtel de Villeroy
Built in 1724 for Charlotte Desmarnes, an actress at the Comédie-Française, it is now the Ministry of Agriculture. *78–80 rue de Varenne, 75007 • Map D4*

3 Hôtel Matignon
One of the most beautiful mansions in the area, built in 1721, is now the official residence of the French prime minister. *57 rue de Varenne, 75007 • Map D4*

4 Hôtel de Boisgelin
Built in 1732 by Jean Sylvain Cartaud, this mansion has housed the Italian Embassy since 1938. *47 rue de Varenne, 75007 • Map D4*

5 Hôtel de Gallifet
This attractive mansion was built in 1739 with Classical styling. It is now the Italian Institute. *50 rue de Varenne, 75007 • Map D4*

6 Hôtel d'Estrées
Three floors of pilasters feature on this 1713 mansion. Formerly the Russian embassy, Czar Nicolas II lived here in 1896. It is now a government building. *79 rue de Grenelle, 75007 • Map B5*

7 Hôtel d'Avaray
Dating from 1728, this mansion belonged to the Avaray family for nearly 200 years. It became the Dutch Embassy in 1920. *85 rue de Grenelle, 75007 • Map B5*

8 Hôtel de Brienne
This mansion houses the Ministry of Defence, so no photos are allowed. Napoleon's mother lived here from 1806–17. *14–16 rue St Dominique, 75007 • Map D4*

9 Hôtel de Noirmoutiers
Built in 1722, this was once the army staff headquarters and World War I commander Marshal Foch died here in 1929. It now houses ministerial offices. *138–140 rue de Grenelle, 75007 • Map B5*

10 Hôtel de Monaco de Sagan
Now the Polish Embassy, this 1784 mansion has fountains framing the entrance. It served as the British Embassy until 1825. *57 rue St-Dominique, 75007 • Map D4*

For more historic buildings in Paris **See pp42–3**

Price Categories

For a three-course meal for one with half a bottle of wine (or equivalent meal), taxes and extra charges	
€	under €30
€€	€30–€40
€€€	€40–€50
€€€€	€50–€60
€€€€€	over €60

Above **Vin Sur Vin**

Top 10 Places to Eat

1 Le Jules Verne

Book a window table for the view and a menu that roams the world. Reserve in advance. *2nd Level, Eiffel Tower, Champ-de-Mars, 75007 • Map B4 • 01 45 55 61 44 • No disabled access • €€€€€*

2 Le Divellec

One of the best fish restaurants in town, including oysters, salmon and sea bass at. *107 rue de l'Université, 75007 • Map C4 • 01 45 51 91 96 • Closed Sat–Sun, Aug, 1 wk Dec–Jan • €€€€€*

3 L'Arpège

Among the best restaurans in the city. Chef Alain Passard produces exquisite food. *84 rue de Varenne, 75007 • Map D4 • 01 47 05 09 06 • Closed Sun–Mon • No disabled access• €€€€€*

4 Le Violin d'Ingres

Chef Christian Constant is another shining star. Sea bass in almond pastry appeals. *135 rue St-Dominique, 75007 • Map C4 • 01 45 55 15 05 • Closed Sun–Mon • €€€€*

5 Vin Sur Vin

Owner Patrice Vidal knows his wine. Club-like atmosphere; booking essential. *20 rue de Montessuy, 75007 • Map C4 • 01 47 05 14 20 • Closed Sat L, Sun–Mon L • €€€€*

6 Le Soleil

This piece of the Riviera is just steps from the Eiffel Tower. Simple cooking with a southern French influence. *153 rue de Grenelle, 75007 • Map C4 • 01 45 51 54 12 • Closed Sun–Mon, 5 weeks Jul–Aug • €€€€*

7 L'Ami Jean

Inventive Basque dishes such as marinated scallops with ewe's milk cheese. *27 rue Malar, 75007 • Map C4 • 01 47 05 86 89 • Closed Sun, Mon • No disabled access • €€€€*

8 L'Agassin

Try classic skate wing with caper-butter sauce at this traditional French restaurant. *8 rue Malar, 75007 • Map C4 • 01 47 05 94 27 • Closed Sun–Mon, Aug • €€€*

9 L'Auberge du Champ de Mars

Inexpensive choice near the Eiffel Tower, with a cosy feel. *18 rue de l'Exposition, 75007• Map B4 • 01 45 51 78 08 • Closed Sat L, Sun–Mon L, Aug • No disabled access • €€*

10 Chez les Anges

Owner Jacques Lacipière ensures that the daily changing menu features the freshest ingredients. *54 boulevard La Tour Maubourg, 75007 • Map C4 • 01 47 05 89 86 • Closed Sat–Sun • €€€€*

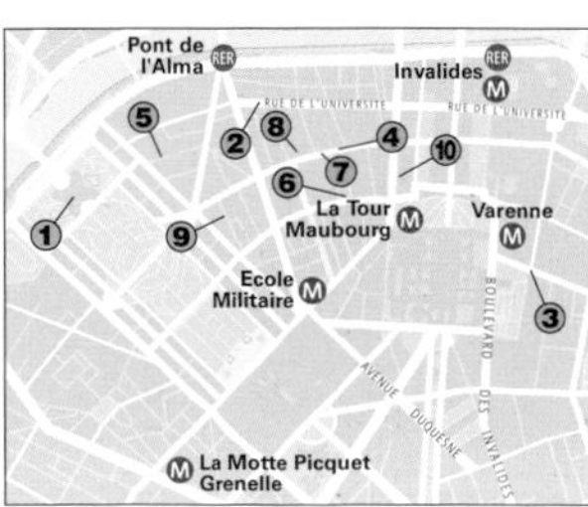

Note: *Unless otherwise stated, all restaurants accept credit cards and serve vegetarian meals*

Left **Musée d'Orsay** Centre **Panthéon** Right **St-Sulpice**

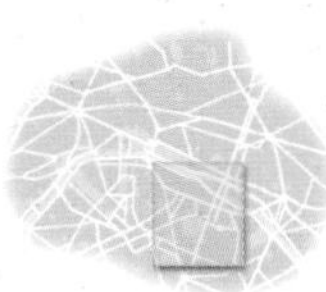

St-Germain, Latin and Luxembourg Quarters

THIS AREA OF THE LEFT BANK IS *possibly the most stimulating in Paris. St-Germain-des-Prés, centred around the city's oldest church, is a synonym for Paris's café society, made famous by the writers and intellectuals who held court here in the first half of the 20th century. Although it's more touristy today, a stroll around the back streets reveals lovely old houses plastered with plaques noting famous residents. The Latin Quarter takes its name from the Latin spoken by students of the Sorbonne until the Revolution. The scholastic centre of Paris for more than 700 years, it continues to buzz with student bookshops, cafés and jazz clubs. It was also the site of a Roman settlement and remains from that era can be seen in the Musée du Moyen-Age. The area's western boundary is the bustling boulevard Saint-Michel and to the south is the tranquil greenery of the Luxembourg Quarter.*

Jardin du Luxembourg

Top 10 Sights

1. Musée d'Orsay
2. Panthéon
3. Jardin du Luxembourg
4. St-Sulpice
5. La Sorbonne
6. Musée du Moyen-Age
7. Boulevard St-Germain
8. Boulevard St-Michel
9. Quai de la Tournelle
10. Musée Maillol

1 Musée d'Orsay

See pp12–15.

2 Panthéon

See pp28–9.

3 Jardin du Luxembourg

This 25-ha (60-acre) park is a swathe of green paradise on the very urban Left Bank. The formal gardens are set around the Palais du Luxembourg *(see p43)*, with broad terraces circling the central octagonal pool. A highlight of the garden is the beautiful Medici Fountain *(see p39)*. Many of the garden's statues were erected during the 19th century, among them the monument to the painter Eugène Delacroix and the statue of Ste Geneviève, patron saint of Paris. There is also a children's playground, open-air café, a bandstand, tennis courts, a puppet theatre and even a bee-keeping school *(see p38)*. *Map L6*

4 St-Sulpice

Begun in 1646, this enormous church unsurprisingly took 134 years to build. Its Classical façade by the Florentine architect Giovanni Servandoni features a two-tiered colonnade and two incongruously matched towers. Notice the two holy water fonts by the front door, made from huge shells given to François I by the Venetian Republic. *Jacob*

Medici Fountain, Jardin du Luxembourg

Clock, La Sorbonne

Wrestling with the Angel and other splendid murals by Delacroix (1798–1863) are in the chapel to the right of the main door. *Pl St-Sulpice, 75006 • Map L5 • Open 7:30am–7:30pm daily • Free*

5 La Sorbonne

Paris's world-famous university *(see p43)*, was founded in 1253 and was originally intended as a theology college for poor students but it soon became the country's main centre for theological studies. It was named after Robert de Sorbon, confessor to Louis IX. Philosophers Thomas Aquinas (c.1226–74) and Roger Bacon (1214–92) taught here; Italian poet Dante (1265–1321), St Ignatius Loyola (1491–1556), the founder of the Jesuits, and church reformer John Calvin (1509–64) are among its list of alumni. Its tradition for conservatism led to its closure during the Revolution (it was reopened by Napoleon in 1806) and to the student riots of 1968 *(see p45)*. *47 rue des Ecoles, 75005 • Map M5 • 01 40 46 21 11 • Group tours only, Mon–Fri and one Sat each month (advance booking) • Admission charge*

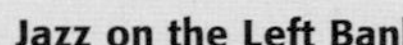

Jazz on the Left Bank

Jazz has been played in Paris, especially on the Left Bank, since the 1920s. Numbers of black musicians moved here from the US as they found France less racially prejudiced, and Paris became a second home for many jazz musicians such as Sidney Bechet *(see p63)*. The city has never lost its love of jazz, nor jazz its love for the city.

6 Musée National du Moyen-Age

This impressive mansion was built by the abbots of Cluny in 1330 and now houses a magnificent collection of medieval art, from Gallo-Roman antiquity to the 15th century. It adjoins the ruins of 2nd-century Roman baths *(thermes)* with their huge vaulted *frigidarium* (cold bath). Nearby are the 21 carved stone heads of the kings of Judea from Notre-Dame, decapitated during the Revolution. The museum's highlight is the exquisite *Lady and the Unicorn* tapestry series, representing the five senses *(see p34)*. *6 pl Paul-Painlevé, 75005 • Map N5 • Open 9:15am–5:45pm Wed–Mon • Closed 1 Jan, 1 May, 25 Dec • Admission charge • www.musee-moyenage.fr*

7 Boulevard St-Germain

This famous Left Bank boulevard runs for more than 3 km (2 miles) anchored by the bridges of the Seine at either end. At its heart is the church of St-Germain-des-Prés, established in 542, although the present church dates from the 11th century. Beyond the famous cafés, Flore and Les Deux Magots *(see p125)*, the boulevard runs west past art galleries, bookshops and designer boutiques to the Pont de la Concorde. To the east, it cuts across the Latin Quarter through the pleasant street market in the place Maubert, to join the Pont de Sully which connects to the Ile St-Louis *(see p69)*. *Map J3*

8 Boulevard St-Michel

The main drag of the Latin Quarter was created in the late 1860s as part of Baron Haussmann's city-wide makeover *(see p45)*, and named after a chapel that once stood near its northern end. It's now lined with a lively mix of cafés, clothes shops and cheap restaurants. Branching off to the east are rues de la Harpe and de la Huchette, which date back to medieval times. The

Boulevard St-Germain

Quai de la Tournelle

latter is an enclave of the city's Greek community, with many *souvlaki* stands and Greek restaurants. In the place St-Michel is a huge bronze fountain that depicts St Michael killing a dragon. *Map M4*

9 Quai de la Tournelle

From this riverbank, just before the Pont de l'Archevêché there are lovely views across to Notre-Dame. The main attraction of this and the adjacent Quai de Montebello, however, are the dark-green stalls of the *bouquinistes (see p122)*. The Pont de la Tournelle also offers splendid views up and down the Seine. *Map P5*

10 Musée Maillol

Dina Vierny, who modelled for the artist Aristide Maillol (1861–1944) from the ages of 15 to 25, went on to set up this foundation dedicated largely to his works. Set in an 18th-century mansion, it features his sculpture, paintings, drawings, engravings and terracotta works. A wonderful collection of works by other 20th-century artists, many of whom worked in Paris, including Picasso, Matisse, Dufy, Duchamp, Kandinsky and Poliakoff, is also on show. *59–61 rue de Grenelle, 75007 • Map J4 • Open 11am–6pm Wed–Mon • Admission charge • www.museemaillol.com*

A Day on the Left Bank

Morning

This area is as much about atmosphere as sightseeing, so take time to soak up some of that Left Bank feeling. Begin on the **Quai de la Tournelle**, strolling by the booksellers here and on the adjacent Quai de Montebello. As well as admiring the views of Notre-Dame, you might find an unusual souvenir.

From here head south down any street away from the river and you will meet the busy **boulevard St-Germain**. Turn right in the direction of two famous cafés, the **Flore** and the **Deux Magots**, and stop for a break in either of them *(see p125)* amid the locals talking the morning away.

Cut your way south to the rue de Grenelle and the **Musée Maillol**, a delightful lesser-known museum. Then enjoy lunch at L'Oeillade (*10 rue St-Simon • 01 42 22 01 60*), a bistro full of Gallic atmosphere.

Afternoon

The later you reach the **Musée d'Orsay** *(see p12–15)* the less crowded it will be. Spend an hour or two exploring the collection. The most popular displays are the Impressionists on the upper level.

After the museum visit, enjoy tea and a cake at **Christian Constant**, one of the best chocolate-makers in Paris (*37 rue d'Assas, 75006 • 01 53 63 15 15*). Or if it's dinner time, stay at the Musée d'Orsay and indulge in their set menu (Thu only).

Left **Bouquinistes** Right **The Village Voice**

Top 10 Booksellers

1 Shakespeare and Co
Bibliophiles spend hours in the rambling rooms of Paris's renowned English-language bookshop. There are books in other languages too and poetry readings most Mondays at 8pm. *37 rue de la Bûcherie, 75005 • Map N5*

2 Bouquinistes
The green stalls of the booksellers *(bouquinistes)* on the quays of the Left Bank are a Parisian landmark. Pore over the posters, old postcards, magazines, hardbacks, paperbacks, comics and sheet music. *Map N5*

3 Musée d'Orsay Bookshop
As well as its wonderful collections, the museum has a bewilderingly large and busy art bookshop *(see pp12–15).*

4 La Hune
Landmark literary hangout. Good collections on art, photography and literature. *170 blvd St-Germain, 75006 • Map K4*

5 Gibert Jeune
A cluster of bookshops that sell everything from travel guides and French literature to cookery books and children's stories. *3 and 5 place St-Michel, 27 quai St-Michel, 37 rue de la Huchette, 75005*

6 Album
Specialist in comic books, which are big business in France, from Tintin to erotica. *8 rue Dante, 75005 • Map L4*

7 Librairie Présence Africaine
Specialist on books on Africa, as the name suggests. Good information point, too, if you want to eat African food or hear African music. *25 bis rue des Écoles, 75005 • Map P6*

8 Tea & Tattered Pages
An excellent venue for a relaxed afternoon's browsing among thousands of English-language books; you can have a cuppa, too. *24 rue Mayet, 75006 • Map D5 / D6*

9 Librairie Maeght
Specialist in books on art adjoining the Maeght art gallery, with a good collection of posters, postcards and other items. *42 rue du Bac, 75007 • Map N5*

10 The Village Voice
North American bias, but works by writers from around the world as well. *6 rue Princesse, 75006 • Map L4*

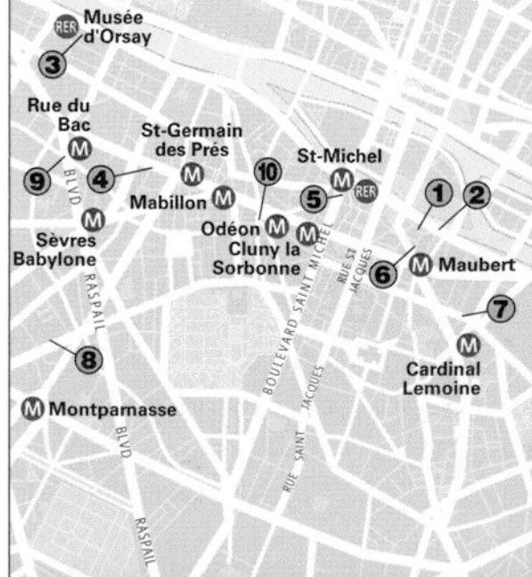

For more on shopping in Paris See p169

Left **Paris chocolatier** Right **Patisserie**

Top 10 Specialist Food Shops

1 Patrick Roger
One of a new generation of *chocolatiers*, Patrick Roger already has legions of fans thanks to his lifelike sculptures and ganache-filled chocolates. *108 boulevard St Germain, 75006 • Map F5 • Closed Sun*

2 Michel Chaudun
Michel Chaudun produces chocolates so divine that *le tout* Paris drops by in chauffeur-driven cars for a regular fix. *149 rue de l'Université, 75007 • Map C4 • Closed Sun*

3 Jean-Paul Hévin
Another of the distinguished *chocolatiers* of Paris, where it is regarded as an honoured profession. Also sells pastries and cakes. *3 rue Vavin, 75006 • Map E6*

4 Poilâne
Founded in the 1930s, this tiny bakery produces rustic, naturally leavened loaves in a Roman-style, wood-fired oven. *8 rue du Cherche-Midi, 75006 • Map E5*

5 La Dernière Goutte
The owners of this English-speaking wine shop, which has a good selection of bottles from small producers, also run the nearby wine bar Fish. *6 rue Bourbon Le Château, 75006 • Map E5*

6 Debauve & Gallais
This shop dates from 1800 when chocolate was sold for medicinal purposes. *30 rue des Sts-Pères, 75007 • Map K4*

7 Pierre Hermé Paris
Here are some of the city's very finest cakes and pastries, including what is said to be the best chocolate gâteau in Paris. *72 rue Bonaparte, 75006 • Map L5*

8 Ryst Dupeyron
A specialist wine shop, selling French wines, spirits and liqueurs and champagne. *79 rue du Bac, 75007 • Map N5*

9 Sadaharu Aoki
Aoki cleverly incorporates Japanese flavours such as yuzu, green tea, and black sesame into intoxicating classic French pastries that taste as good as they look. *35 rue de Vaugirard 75006 • Map E5 • Closed Mon*

10 Gérard Mulot
Here you'll find some of the finest pastries in Paris, along with some truly miraculous macaroons. *76 rue de Seine, 75006 • Map L4*

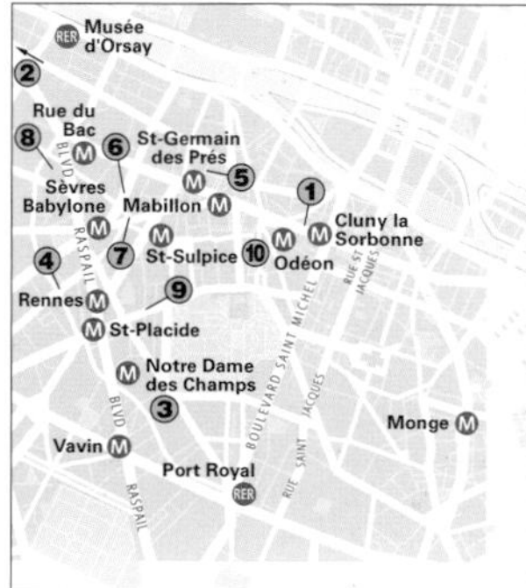

Left **Le Bar Dix** Right **Café Mabillon**

TOP 10 Late-Night Bars

1 Le Bar Dix

Incredibly lively bar, aimed at people who like to talk, smoke and drink. Happy hour 6–9pm. *10 rue de l'Odéon, 75006 • Map L5*

2 Le Crocodile

Potent cocktails are what this schoolroom-themed bar is all about. Choose from 350 combinations. Happy hour runs from 10pm until midnight. *6 rue Royer-Collard, 75005 • Map F6 • 01 43 54 32 37 • Closed Sun*

3 El Palenque

This lively Argentinian place brings Latin America to the Latin Quarter. Also serves great meat dishes. *5 rue de la Montagne-Ste-Geneviève, 75005 • Map N4*

4 Café Mabillon

The place that never closes. Hang out on the terrace with a few drinks and watch the world go by. Happy hour 7–9pm. *164 blvd St-Germain, 75006 • Map N4*

5 L'Assignat

Pleasant, bright family-run bar, full of regulars propping up the bar with a beer or a glass of wine. *7 rue Guénégaud, 75006 • Map L3*

6 Mezzanine

The place to see and be seen. The beer, wine and cocktails are not expensive given the buzz and the wonderful location. *Alcazar, 62 rue Mazarine, 75006 • Map L3*

7 Le Mondrian

Just the place to wind down after a night of *joie de vivre.* *148 blvd St-Germain, 75006 • Map N4*

8 Le Bob Cool

On a quiet backstreet, this shabby-chic bar plays host to thirsty local nighthawks as well as trendier partygoers on late-night cocktails. *15 rue des Grands Augustins, 75006 • Map M4*

9 Coolin

An Irish bar that doesn't try too hard. Appeals to drinkers, talkers and listeners of all ages, who like their draught Guinness with a blarney chaser. *15 rue Clément, 75006 • Map L4*

10 L'Urgence Bar

Hit this hospital-themed bar for cocktails with names like "Laxative" and "Liposuction", served in either a test-tube or baby's bottle. *45 rue Monsieur le Prince, 75006 • Map M5*

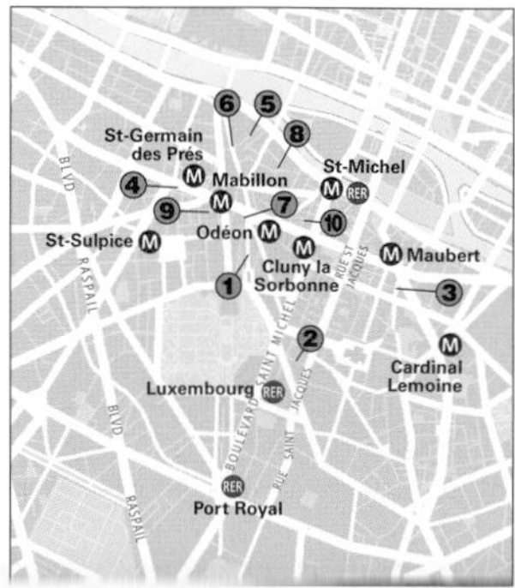

For more cafés and bars in Paris See pp52–3

Left **Café de Flore** Right **Shakespeare and Co**

TOP 10 Literary Haunts

1 La Palette
This café has been patronized by the likes of Henry Miller Apollinaire and Jacques Prévert. *43 rue de Seine, 75006 • Map L4 • Open 8am–2am Mon–Sat*

2 Les Deux Magots
This was home to the literary and artistic élite of Paris as well as a regular haunt of Surrealists such as François Mauriac *(see p52)*. *6 pl St-Germain-des-Prés, 75006 • Map K4 • Open 8am–2am daily*

3 Café de Flore
Guillaume Apollinaire founded his literary magazine, *Les Soirées de Paris,* here in 1912 *(see p52)*. *172 blvd St-Germain, 75006 • Map K4 • Open 7am–1:30am daily*

4 Le Procope
The oldest café in Paris, this was a meeting place for writers such as Voltaire, Hugo, Balzac and Zola. *13 rue de l' Ancienne-Comédie, 75006 • Map L4 • Open noon–1am daily*

5 Brasserie Lipp
Ernest Hemingway pays homage to this café in *A Moveable Feast*. It was also visited by Symbolist novelist André Gide. *151 blvd St-Germain, 75006 • Map L4 • Open 12:15pm–2am daily*

6 Hotel Pont Royal
Henry Miller drank here at the time of writing his *Tropic of Capricorn* and *Tropic of Cancer*. *5–7 rue de Montalembert, 75007 • Map J3 • Open 8am–midnight daily*

7 Shakespeare and Co
This bookshop has played host to many celebrated writers including Hemingway, Fitzgerald, Gide and Stein *(see p122)*.

8 Le Sélect
F Scott Fitzgerald and Truman Capote were among many American writers who drank in this café-restaurant. *99 blvd du Montparnasse, 75006 • Map E6 • Open 8am–2am daily*

9 La Coupole
Opened in 1927, this former coal depot was transformed by artists into a lavish, Art Deco brasserie. It attracted such luminaries as Louis Aragon and François Sagan *(see p157)*.

10 Le Petit St-Benoît
Camus, de Beauvoir and James Joyce are among the many writers who once took their daily coffee here. *4 rue St Benoît, 75006 • Map K3 • Open noon–midnight daily*

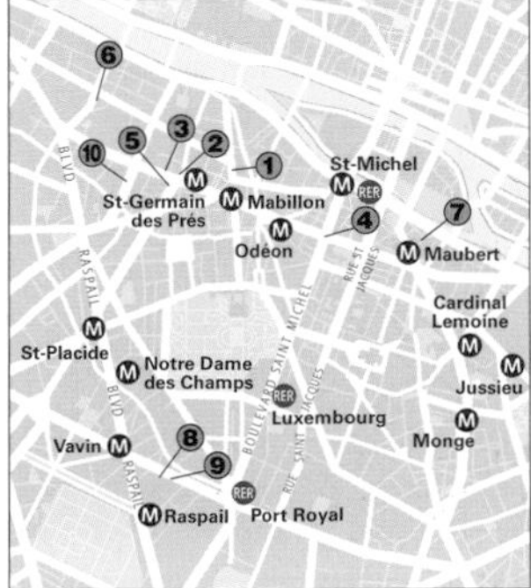

For more on writers in Paris **See p47**

Left **Rue de Buci market** Right **Parisian patisserie**

Top 10 Picnic Providers

1 Rue de Buci Market

Head for this chic daily market where you'll find the very best regional produce, wine and pastries *(see p54)*. *Map L4*

2 Poilâne

Get the best bread for your picnic, made from the recipe of the late king of bread-makers, Lionel Poilâne. *8 rue du Cherche-Midi, 75006 • Map J5*

3 Maubert Market

A small market specializing in organic produce every Tuesday, Thursday and Saturday morning. A good place to pick-up olives, cheese, tomatoes and fruit. *Pl Maubert, 75006 • Map N5*

4 Fromagerie Quatrehomme

The crème de la crème of cheese in Paris. Aged slowly and sold at peak ripeness. *62 rue de Sèvres, 75007 • Map D5*

5 Charcuterie Charles Nicole

This award-winning charcuterie shouldn't be missed. Flavoured sausages and *boudin blanc* are specialities. *10 rue Dauphine, 75006 • Map M4*

6 Marché Biologique

This organic Sunday morning market brings together some of the best farmers in the region. *Blvd Raspail, 75006 • Map J4*

7 Bon

Wonderful patisserie, with an especially good line in small fruit tarts, such as lemon and strawberry. Fat-free cheesecake for the health-conscious, too. *159 rue St-Jacques, 75005 • Map N5*

8 La Grande Epicerie de Paris

This gourmet supermarket offers takeaway meals on the spot. Hunt for treasures such as Breton seaweed butter and *coucou de Rennes*, a pedigreed chicken. *Le Bon Marché, 38 rue de Sèvres, 75007 • Map D5*

9 Charcuterie Coesnon

Produce from Normandy is sold at this charcuterie – pâtés, ham, cheese and cider too. *30 rue Dauphine, 75006 • Map M4*

10 Kayser

If you don't want to make up your own picnic then try a ready-made sandwich from the bakery. Mouthwatering combinations include goat's cheese with pear. *14 rue Monge, 75005 • Map P6*

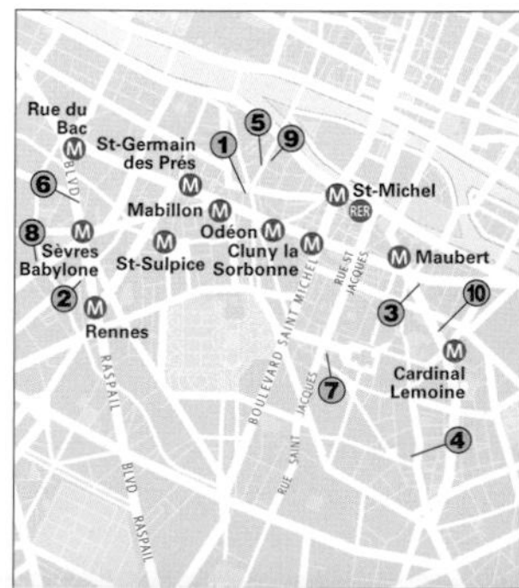

For more shops and markets in Paris See pp54–5

Price Categories		
For a three-course meal for one with half a bottle of wine (or equivalent meal), taxes and extra charges	€	under €30
	€€	€30–€40
	€€€	€40–€50
	€€€€	€50–€60
	€€€€€	over €60

Left **Alcazar** Right **L'Atelier Maitre Albert**

TOP 10 Places to Eat

1 L'Épi Dupin
The dishes are sublime, such as cod with saffron leeks *(see p64)*. *11 rue Dupin, 75006 • Map J5 • 01 42 22 64 56 • Closed Sat–Sun, Mon L, Aug • €€*

2 La Tour d'Argent
This two-star Michelin restaurant has views of Notre-Dame and duck *à l'orange* as the speciality. *15 quai de la Tournelle, 75005 • Map P5 • 01 43 54 23 31 • Closed Mon, Tue L • No disabled access • €€€€€*

3 Les Bouquinistes
This bistro, owned by Guy Savoy, offers creative cooking at affordable prices. *53 quai des Grands-Augustins, 75006 • Map M4 • 01 43 25 45 94 • Closed Sat L, Sun • No disabled access • €€€*

4 Alcazar
A stylish brasserie with a mix of French, Asian and British food. *62 rue Mazarine, 75006 • Map L3 • 01 53 10 19 99 • €€€*

5 Lapérouse
Classic French cuisine including fabulous desserts. *51 quai des Grands-Augustins, 75006 • Map M4 • 01 43 26 68 04 • Closed Sat L, Sun, Aug • €€€€€*

6 L'Atelier Maître Albert
Spit-roasted meats and signature dishes by top chef Guy Savoy. Aim for a table in front of the giant fireplace. *1 rue Maître Albert, 75001 • Map F5 • 01 56 81 30 01 • Closed Sat, Sun L • €€€€*

7 La Bastide Odéon
A taste of Provence, with rich and hearty dishes. Try the risotto with scallops. *7 rue Corneille, 75006 • Map L5 • 01 43 26 03 65 • Closed Sun– Mon, Aug • No disabled access • €€€*

8 Le Pré Verre
Dine on classic French cooking with Asian flourishes. *19 rue du Sommerard, 75005 • Map F5 • 01 43 54 59 47 • Closed Sun–Mon, Aug • €€*

9 Les Papilles
Pick your wine straight off the shelves to accompany the stunning menu *(see p65)*. *30 rue Gay Lussac, 75005 • Map F6 • 01 43 25 20 79 • Closed Sun • No disabled access • €€*

10 Au Moulin à Vent
One of the best bistros in Paris, with frogs' legs, *escargots* and Châteaubriand on the menu. *20 rue des Fossés-St-Bernard, 75005 • Map P6 • 01 43 54 99 37 • Closed Sat L, Sun–Mon, Aug • €€€*

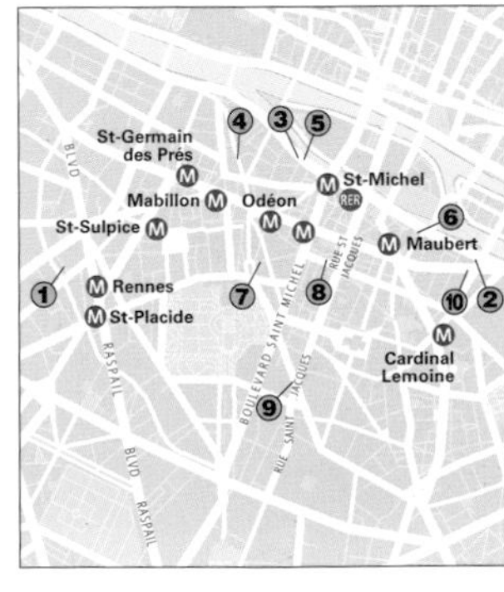

Note: *Unless otherwise stated, all restaurants accept credit cards and serve vegetarian meals*

Left **Jardin des Plantes** Centre **Natural History Museum** Right **Institut du Monde Arabe exhibit**

Jardin des Plantes Quarter

TRADITIONALLY ONE OF THE MOST PEACEFUL *areas of Paris, the medicinal herb gardens which give the quarter its name were established here in 1626. It retained a rural atmosphere until the 19th century, when the city's population expanded and the surrounding streets were built up. Near the gardens is the Arènes de Lutèce, a well-preserved Roman amphitheatre. The rue Mouffetard, winding down the hill from the bustling place de la Contrescarpe, dates from medieval times and has one of the best markets in the city. The area is also home to a sizeable Muslim community, focused on the Institut du Monde Arabe cultural centre and the Paris Mosque. In contrast to the striking Islamic architecture are the grey slab 1960s buildings of the Paris university Jussieu campus.*

Riding a stone hippopotamus at the Ménagerie

Top 10 Sights

1. Jardin des Plantes
2. Muséum National d'Histoire Naturelle
3. Ménagerie
4. Institut du Monde Arabe
5. Mosquée de Paris
6. Rue Mouffetard
7. Arènes de Lutèce
8. Place de la Contrescarpe
9. St-Médard
10. Manufacture des Gobelins

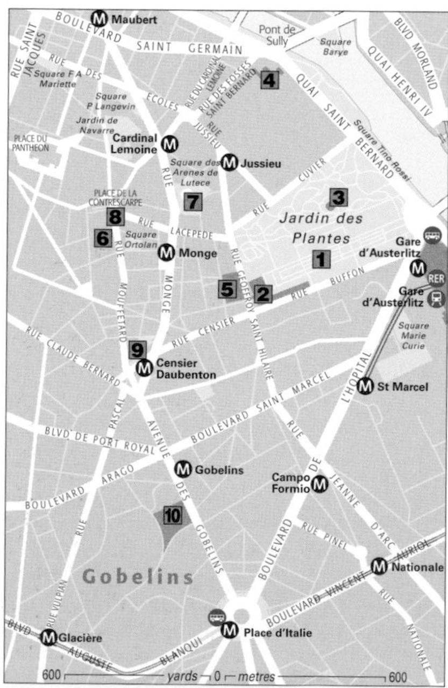

1 Jardin des Plantes

The 17th-century royal medicinal herb garden was planted by Jean Hérouard and Guy de la Brosse, physicians to Louis XIII. Opened to the public in 1640, it flourished under the curatorship of Comte de Buffon. It contains some 10,000 species, including the first Cedar of Lebanon planted in a French tropical greenhouse, and Alpine, rose and winter gardens *(see p132)*. *57 rue Cuvier, 75005 • Map G6 • 01 40 79 30 00 • Open 8am–5:30pm daily, to 6pm summer*

2 Muséum National d'Histoire Naturelle

Separate pavilions in the Jardin des Plantes house exhibits on anatomy, fossils, geology, mineralogy and insects. The Grande Galerie de l'Evolution *(see p60)* is a magnificent collection of stuffed African mammals, a giant whale skeleton and an endangered species exhibit *(see p34)*. *57 rue Cuvier, 75005 • Map G6 • Pavilions: open 10am–5pm Wed–Mon; Evolution Gallery: open 10am–6pm Wed–Mon • Closed 1 May • Admission charge • www.mnhn.fr*

3 Ménagerie

The country's oldest public zoo was founded during the Revolution to house the four surviving animals from the royal menagerie at Versailles. Other animals were donated from circuses and abroad, but during the Siege of Paris in 1870–71 *(see p45)* the unfortunate creatures were eaten by hungry citizens. A favourite with children *(see p60)*, the zoo has since been rehoused with monkeys, large cats, birds and reptiles. *Jardin des Plantes, 75005 • Map G6 • Open 9am–5pm daily • Admission charge*

4 Institut du Monde Arabe

This institute was founded in 1980 to promote cultural relations between France and the Arab world. The stunning building (1987) designed by architect Jean Nouvel *(see Musée du Quai Branly p112)* features a southern wall of 1,600 photo-sensitive metal screens that open and close like a camera aperture to regulate light entering the building. The design is based on the latticed wooden screens of Islamic architecture. Inside are seven floors of Islamic artworks, from 9th-century ceramics to contemporary art. *1 rue des Fossés-St-Bernard, 75005 • Map G5 • 01 40 51 38 11 • Open 10am– 6pm Tue–Sun • Admission charge • www.imarabe.org*

5 Mosquée de Paris

Built in 1922–6, the mosque complex is the spiritual centre for Parisian Muslims *(see p41)*. The beautiful Hispano-Moorish decoration, particularly the grand patio, was inspired by the Alhambra in Spain. The minaret soars nearly 33 m (100 ft). There is also an Islamic school, tea room and Turkish baths, open to men and women on separate days. *2 bis pl du Puits-de-l'Ermité, 75005 • Map G6 • Tours: 9am–noon, 2– 6pm Sat–Thu; closed Islamic hols • Admission charge*

Minaret, Mosquée de Paris

French North Africa

France has always had close connections with North Africa, though not always harmonious. Its annexation of Algeria in 1834 led to the long and bloody Algerian war of Liberation (1954–62). Relations with Tunisia, which it governed from 1883 to 1956, and Morocco, also granted independence in 1956, were better. Many North Africans now live in Paris.

6 Rue Mouffetard

Although the rue Mouffetard is famous today for its lively street market held every Tuesday to Sunday *(see p55)*, it has an equally colourful past. In Roman times this was the main road from Paris to Rome. Some say its name comes from the French word *mouffette* (skunk), as a reference to the odorous River Bièvre (now covered over) where waste was dumped by tanners and weavers from the nearby Gobelins tapestry factory. Though no longer poor or Bohemian, the neighbourhood still has lots of character, with its 17th-century mansard roofs, old-fashioned painted shop signs and affordable restaurants. In the market you can buy everything from Auvergne sausage to horse meat and ripe cheeses. *Map F6*

Arènes de Lutèce

7 Arènes de Lutèce

The remains of the 2nd-century Roman amphitheatre from the settlement of Lutetia *(see p44)* lay buried for centuries and were only discovered in 1869 during construction of the rue Monge. The novelist Victor Hugo, concerned with the preservation of his city's historic buildings, including Notre-Dame *(see p21)*, led the campaign for the restoration. The original arena would have had 35 tiers and could seat 15,000 spectators for theatrical performances and gladiator fights. *49 rue Monge, 75005 • Map G6 • Open 9am–9pm daily (summer); 8am–5pm daily (winter) • Free*

8 Place de la Contrescarpe

This bustling square has a village community feel, with busy cafés and restaurants and groups of students from the nearby university hanging out here after dark. In medieval times it lay outside the city walls, a remnant of which still stands. Notice the memorial plaque above the butcher's at No. 1, which marks the site of the old Pine Cone Club, a café where François Rabelais and other writers gathered in the 16th century. *Map F5*

9 St-Médard

The church at the bottom of rue Mouffetard dates back to the 9th century, when it was a parish church dedicated to St Médard, counsellor to the Merovingian kings. The present church, completed in 1655, is a mixture of Flamboyant Gothic and Renaissance styles. Among the fine paintings inside is the 17th-century *St Joseph Walking with the Christ Child* by Francisco de Zurbarán. The churchyard was the scene of hysterical fits in the 18th century, when a cult of "*convulsionnaires*" sought miracle cures at the grave of a Jansenist deacon. *141 rue Mouffetard, 75005 • Map G6 • Open 9am–noon, 2:30–7pm Tue–Sat, 9am–noon Sun • Free*

10 Manufacture des Gobelins

This internationally renowned tapestry factory was originally a dyeing workshop, founded by the Gobelin brothers in the mid-15th century. In 1662, Louis XIV's minister Colbert set up a royal factory here and gathered the greatest craftsmen of the day to make furnishings for the palace at Versailles *(see p151)*. You can see the traditional weaving process on a guided tour. *42 ave des Gobelins, 75013 • Metro Gobelins • Tours: 2pm and 3pm Tue–Thu (arrive 30 minutes prior), open for temporary exhibitions only noon–6pm Tue–Sun • Tickets must be bought prior to the visit at a branch of FNAC*

A Day in the Gardens

Morning

If it's a fine morning get an early start and enjoy a stroll in the **Jardin des Plantes** *(see p129)* before the city gets truly busy. The **Muséum National d'Histoire Naturelle** *(see p129)* doesn't open until 10am, but the garden is close enough to **rue Mouffetard** to enable you to enjoy the fabulous market, which gets going by about 8am. Don't forget to take your eyes off the stalls every now and then to see the splendid old buildings on this medieval street. Then return to the museum and its Evolution Gallery.

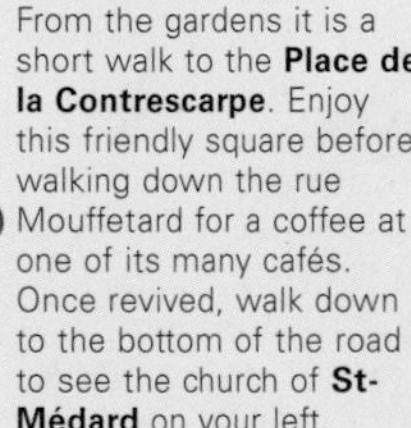

From the gardens it is a short walk to the **Place de la Contrescarpe**. Enjoy this friendly square before walking down the rue Mouffetard for a coffee at one of its many cafés. Once revived, walk down to the bottom of the road to see the church of **St-Médard** on your left.

Turn left along rue Monge to the **Arènes de Lutèce**. A couple of minutes away is a little bistro, Le Buisson Ardent (*25 rue Jussieu • 01 43 54 93 02*), which is ideal for lunch.

Afternoon

You can spend part of the afternoon at the **Institut du Monde Arabe** *(see p129)*,exploring its beautiful Islamic artworks, before walking down to admire the Moorish architecture of the **Mosquée de Paris** *(see p129)*. Finish the day with a mint tea at the Café de la Mosquée (*pl du Puits-de-l'Ermité • 01 43 31 18 14*).

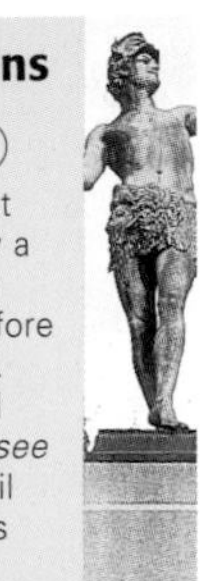

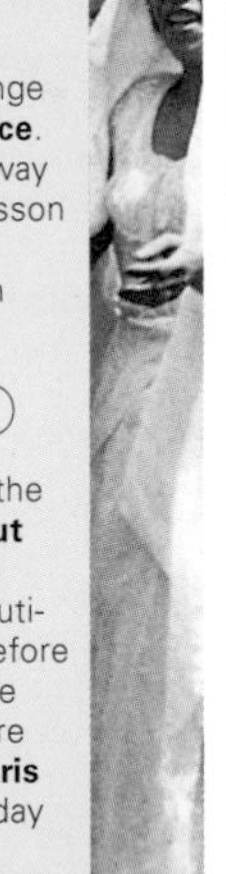

Left **Flowers in the Jardin des Plantes** Right **Dinosaur model**

TOP 10 Jardin des Plantes Sights

1 Dinosaur Tree

One of the trees in the Botanical Gardens is the *Ginkgo biloba*, which is 150 years old but the species is known to have existed in exactly the same form in the days of the dinosaurs, 125 million years ago.

2 Cedar of Lebanon

This magnificent tree was planted in 1734, and came from London's Botanic Gardens in Kew, although a story grew up that its seed was brought here all the way from Syria in the hat of a scientist.

3 Rose Garden

Although only a fairly recent addition, being planted in 1990, the beautiful *roseraie* has some 170 species of roses and 180 rose bushes on display. Spectacular when they are in full bloom in spring and summer.

4 Alpine Gardens

One of the stars of the Botanical Gardens, with more than 3,000 plants from the world's many diverse Alpine regions. There are samples from Corsica to the Caucasus, from Morocco to the Himalaya.

5 Sophora of Japan

Sent to Paris under the label "unknown seeds from China" by a Jesuit naturalist living in the Orient, this tree was planted in 1747, first flowered in 1777, and still flowers today.

6 Iris Garden

An unusual feature is this designated garden which brings together more than 400 different varieties of iris.

7 Dinosaur Model

Outside the Palaeontology Gallery, which is crammed with precious dinosaur skeletons, is a huge dinosaur model of a stegosaurus *(see p60)*.

8 Nile Crocodile

The crocodile in the Reptile House now has a better home than he once did. This creature was found in a Paris hotel room, left behind as an unwanted pet! It has yet to reach its full size of 5 m (16.5 ft).

9 Two Art Deco Greenhouses

Otherwise known as *Les Grandes Serres*, these 19th-century greenhouses used to be the largest in the world. Today, they house a prickly Mexican cacti garden and a tropical winter garden kept at a constant 22°C (74°F) and 80 per cent humidity.

10 Young Animal House

One of the zoo's most popular features for children is this house where young creatures, which for one reason or another cannot be looked after by their natural parents, are raised. Once they reach adulthood they are returned to thoir natural habitat.

For the Jardin des Plantes **See p129**

Price Categories

For a three-course meal for one with half a bottle of wine (or equivalent meal), taxes and extra charges	
€	under €30
€€	€30–€40
€€€	€40–€50
€€€€	€50–€60
€€€€€	over €60

Above **L'Avant-Goût**

Top 10 Places to Eat

1 Le Terroir
The kind of place locals like to keep secret, because it's good, inexpensive and has a great atmosphere. *11 blvd Arago, 75013 • Metro Gobelins • 01 47 07 36 99 • Closed Sat–Sun, Easter, Aug • €€€*

2 Léna et Mimile
Those in the know avoid the touristy restaurants around rue Mouffetard to savour a meal at this ambitious bistro with a peaceful terrace. *32 rue Tournefort, 75005 • 01 47 07 72 47 • Closed Sun–Mon Oct–Apr • €€€*

3 Au Petit Marguery
One for meat lovers, with plenty of steak, veal and game on the menu. Boisterous atmosphere. *9 blvd de Port-Royal, 75013 • Map F6 • 01 43 31 58 59 • Closed Sun–Mon, Aug • No vegetarian options • €€€€*

4 Le Buisson Ardent
This creative bistro is a romantic nightime destination. *25 rue Jussieu, 75005 • Map G6 • 01 43 54 93 02 • Closed Sun, Sat L • €€€*

5 La Truffière
A 17th-century building, a wood fire and welcoming staff all make for a great little bistro. The menu features truffles. *4 rue Blainville, 75005 • Map F6 • 01 46 33 29 82 • Closed Sun, Mon • €€€€€*

6 Restaurant Marty
An Art Deco brasserie serving delicious classics such as pan-fried *foie-gras* with apples, and Provençal-style scallops. *20 ave des Gobelins, 75005 • Metro Gobelins • 01 43 31 59 51 • €€€*

7 Chez Paul
Not the best place for vegetarians, with *pot au feu*, tongue and other meaty delights, but there is also fish. *22 rue de la Butte-aux-Cailles, 75013 • Metro Place d'Italie • 01 45 89 22 11 • €€€*

8 Au Coco de Mer
Spicy Seychelles cuisine, such as octopus curry or smoked swordfish. Vegetarians should book ahead. *34 blvd St-Marcel, 75005 • Map G6 • 01 47 07 06 64 • Closed Sun, Mon L, Aug • €€*

9 L'Avant-Goût
Small and noisy with tables crammed together. Try the pork *pot au feu* or apple flan, if available, though the menu changes daily. *26 rue Bobillot, 75013 • Metro Place d'Italie • 01 53 80 24 00 • Closed Sat–Mon • €€*

10 Chez Gladine
A lively atmosphere with waiters running around serving huge portions of Basque cuisine. Arrive early to get a table. *30 rue des Cinq Diamants, 75013 • 01 45 80 70 10 • Open daily • €*

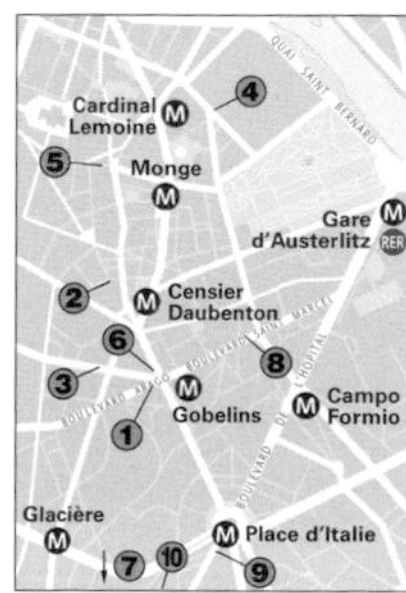

Note: *Unless otherwise stated, all restaurants accept credit cards and serve vegetarian meals*

Left **Jardins du Trocadéro** Center **Cinéaqua** Right **Café Carette**

Chaillot Quarter

CHAILLOT WAS A SEPARATE VILLAGE *until the 19th century, when it was swallowed up by the growing city and bestowed with wide avenues and lavish mansions during the Second Empire building spree* (see p45). *Its centrepiece is the glorious Palais de Chaillot which stands on top of the small Chaillot hill, its wide white-stone wings embracing the Trocadéro Gardens and its terrace gazing across the Seine to the Eiffel Tower. Behind the palace is the place du Trocadéro, laid out in 1858 and originally called the place du Roi-de-Rome (King of Rome), the title of Napoleon's son. The square is ringed with smart cafés, overlooking the central equestrian statue of World War I hero Marshal Ferdinand Foch. Many of the elegant mansions in this area now house embassies, and there are numerous fine dining spots. To the west are the exclusive residential neighbourhoods of the Parisian bourgeoisie (middle-classes).*

Top 10 Sights

1. Palais de Chaillot
2. Cinéaqua
3. Musée de la Marine
4. Cité de l'Architecture et du Patrimoine
5. Musée d'Art Moderne de la Ville de Paris
6. Cimetière de Passy
7. Jardins du Trocadéro
8. Musée du Vin
9. Maison de Balzac
10. Musée National des Arts Asiatiques-Guimet

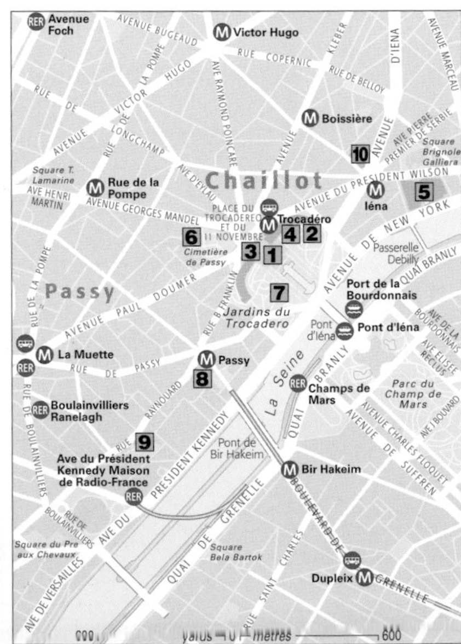

Exhibit at the Musée du Vin

1 Palais de Chaillot

The fall of his empire scuppered Napoleon's plans for an opulent palace for his son on Chaillot hill, but the site was later used for the original Trocadéro palace, built for the Universal Exhibition of 1878. It was replaced by the present Neo-Classical building with its huge colonnaded wings for another exhibition in 1937. The two pavilions house three museums *(see below)*. The broad terrace between the wings is the domain of souvenir sellers and skate-boarders by day, while at night it is crowded with busloads of tour groups stopping off for the splendid view of the Eiffel Tower across the Seine. Two bronzes, *Apollo* by Henri Bouchard and *Hercules* by Pommier, stand to the front of the terrace. Beneath the terrace is the 1,200-seat Théâtre National de Chaillot. *17 pl du Trocadéro, 75016 • Map B4*

2 Cinéaqua

Originally built in 1878 for the Universal Exhibition, Paris' aquarium reopened in 2006 after a 21-year closure. It is home to over 500 species, including seahorses, stonefish and some spectacular sharks and rays. Built into a former quarry, the site has been designed to blend in with the Chaillot hillside. There is also a futuristic cinema complex, Cinéaqua, hence its name. *Ave Albert de Mun, 75016 • Map B4 • Open 10am–10pm daily • Admission charge • Cinéaqua 2 ave des Nations Unies, 75016 • www.cineaqua.com*

3 Musée de la Marine

French naval history is the focus of this museum, whether in war, trade and commerce, or industries such as fishing. The displays range from naval art to

Palais de Chaillot

science to maritime adventure and popular legends and traditions. Among the highlights is an outstanding collection of model ships, from the feluccas of ancient Egypt, to medieval galleys to nuclear submarines. You can also watch craftsmen at work on the models. Napoleon's royal barge is also on show *(see p35)*. *Palais de Chaillot, 75016 • Map B4 • Open 10am–6pm Wed–Mon • Closed 1 Jan, 1 May, 25 Dec • Admission charge • www.musee-marine.fr*

4 Cité de l'Architecture et du Patrimoine

Occupying the east wing of the Palais Chaillot (built for the Universal Exhibition of 1937), this museum is a veritable ode to French architectural heritage, showcasing its development through the ages as well as contemporary architecture. The Galerie des Moulages (Medieval to Renaissance) contains moulded portions of churches and great French cathedrals such as Chartres. The Galerie Moderne et Contemporain includes a reconstruction of an apartment designed by Corbusier, and

General Foch

General Ferdinand Foch (1851–1929), whose statue stands in the centre of place du Trocadéro, was the commander-in-chief of the Allied armies by the end of World War I. His masterful command ultimately led to victory over the Germans in 1918, whereupon he was made a Marshal of France and elected to the French Academy.

architectural designs from 1990 onwards. The wall-painting gallery in the Pavillon de Tête has a stunning collection of frescoes copied from medieval murals. *Palais de Chaillot, 75116 • Map B4 • Open 11am–7pm Wed–Mon (until 9pm Thu) • 01 58 51 52 00 • Admission charge • www.citechaillot.fr*

5 Musée d'Art Moderne de la Ville de Paris

This modern art museum is housed in the east wing of the Palais de Tokyo, built for the 1937 World Fair. Its permanent collection includes such masters as Chagall, Picasso, Modigliani and Léger; further highlights include Raoul Dufy's enormous mural *The Spirit of Electricity* (1937), and Picabia's *Lovers (After the Rain)* (1925). The museum is also keen to promote up-and-coming artists by showcasing their work in frequent temporary exhibitions on the same site. *11 ave du Président-Wilson, 75016 • Map B4 • Open 10am–6pm Tue–Sun (until 10pm Thu during temporary exhibitions) • 01 53 67 40 00 • Admission charge*

6 Cimetière de Passy

This small cemetery covers only 1 ha (2.5 acres), yet many famous people have been laid to rest here with the Eiffel Tower as their eternal view *(see p138)*. It is worth a visit just to admire the striking sculptures on the tombs. *Pl du Trocadéro (entrance rue du Commandant Schloessing) 75016, • Map A4*

7 Jardins du Trocadéro

Designed in 1937, the tiered Trocadéro Gardens descend gently down Chaillot Hill from the palace to the Seine and the Pont d'Iéna. The centrepiece of this 10-ha (25-acre) park is the long rectangular pool lined with stone and bronze statues, including *Woman* by Georges Braque (1882–1963). Its illuminated fountains are spectacular at night. With flowering trees, walkways and bridges over small streams, the gardens are a romantic place for a stroll *(see p39)*. *Map B4*

Cimetière de Passy

8 **Musée du Vin**

The vaulted 14th-century cellars where the monks of Passy once made wine are an atmospheric setting for this wine museum. Waxwork figures depict the history of the wine-making process, and there are displays of wine paraphernalia. There are tasting sessions, wine for sale and a restaurant. *5 square Charles-Dickens, 75016 • Map A4 • Open 10am–6pm Tue–Sun • Admission charge • www.museeduvinparis.com*

9 **Maison de Balzac**

The writer Honoré de Balzac *(see p46)* rented an apartment here from 1840–44, and assumed a false name to avoid his many creditors. He worked on several of his famous novels here, including *La cousine Bette* and *La comédie humaine*. The house is now a museum displaying first editions and manuscripts, personal mementoes and letters, and paintings and drawings of his friends and family. *47 rue Raynouard, 75016 • Map A4 • Open 10am–6pm Tue–Sun • Closed public hols • Admission charge • www.balzac.paris.fr*

10 **Musée National des Arts Asiatiques-Guimet**

One of the world's foremost museums of Asiatic and Oriental art, founded by industrialist Emile Guimet in Lyon in 1879. The Khmer Buddhist temple sculptures from Angkor Wat are the highlight of the finest collection of Cambodian art in the west. Guimet's original collection tracing Chinese and Japanese religion from the 4th to 19th centuries is also on display, as are artifacts from India, Indonesia and Vietnam. *6 pl d'Iéna, 75016 • Map B3 • Open 10am–6pm Wed–Mon • Admission charge • www.guimet.fr*

A Day in Chaillot

Morning

It would be hard to imagine a better start to a day in Paris than going to the **Palais de Chaillot** *(see p135)* and seeing the perfect view it has across the Seine to the **Eiffel Tower** *(see pp16–17)*. Then tour the fascinating collections of the **Cité de l'Architecture** *(see pp135–6)* and, if marine history is your thing, the **Musée de la Marine** *(see p135)*, both in the palace. Outside the palace, take a break in the Café du Trocadéro *(8 pl du Trocadéro • 01 44 05 37 00)* and watch the comings and goings in the square.

Afterwards, head along rue Benjamin Franklin and rue Raynouard, where you will find first the **Musée du Vin** and the **Maison de Balzac**. Walk to the far side of the Maison de Radio France building for a brunch or lunch at **Zebra Square** *(see p139)*.

Afternoon

Revived, walk back along the Seine towards the Palais de Chaillot, and head up to the place d'Iéna to the recently refurbished and much improved **Musée National des Arts Asiatiques-Guimet** for its spectacular Eastern artworks.

By now you will definitely be in need of a rest, so return to the place du Trocadéro for a coffee at the Café Kléber No. 4 *(01 47 27 86 65)*. End the day in the peaceful **Cimetière de Passy** and admire its ornate tombs, before heading back to your hotel.

Left **Manet bust** Centre **Debussy's grave** Right **Fernandel's grave**

Top 10 Graves in Cimetière de Passy

1 Edouard Manet
Born in Paris in 1832, Manet became the most notorious artist in the city when works such as *Olympia* and *Le Déjeuner sur l'Herbe (see p12)* were first exhibited. He died in Paris in 1883.

2 Claude Debussy
The French composer (1862–1918) achieved fame through works such as *Prélude à l'Après-midi d'un Faune* and *La Mer*, and was regarded as the musical equivalent of the Impressionist painters.

3 Berthe Morisot
The French Impressionist artist was born in Paris in 1841, posed for Edouard Manet and later married his lawyer brother Eugène. She never achieved the fame of the male Impressionists, and died in Paris in 1895.

4 Fernandel
The lugubrious French film actor known as Fernandel was born in Marseille in 1903 and made more than 100 films in a career that lasted from 1930 until his death in Paris in 1971.

5 Marie Bashkirtseff
This Russian artist was more renowned as a diarist after her death from tuberculosis in 1884. Despite living for only 24 years she produced 84 volumes of diaries and their posthumous publication created a sensation due to their intimacy.

6 Henri Farman
The French aviator was born in Paris in 1874 and died here in 1958. He was the first man to make a circular 1-km (0.5-mile) flight, and the first to fly across the Atlantic to New York. His gravestone shows him at the controls of a primitive plane.

7 Antoine Cierplikowski
The grave of this fairly obscure artist of the 1920s attracts attention because of its immensely powerful sculpture of a man and woman joined together and seeming to soar from the grave to the heavens.

8 Comte Emanuel de las Cases
Born in 1766, this historian and friend of Napoleon shared the emperor's exile on the island of St Helena and recorded his final thoughts. The Comte himself died in Paris in 1842.

9 Gabriel Fauré
The French composer, probably best known today for his *Requiem*, was a great influence on the music of his time. He died in Paris in 1924, at the age of 79.

10 Octave Mirbeau
The satirical French novelist and playwright was also an outspoken journalist. Born in 1848, he died in Cheverchemont in 1917 and his body was brought to Passy for burial.

For Cimetière de Passy **See p136**

Price Categories

For a three-course meal for one with half a bottle of wine (or equivalent meal), taxes and extra charges		
	€	under €30
	€€	€30–€40
	€€€	€40–€50
	€€€€	€50–€60
	€€€€€	over €60

Left **La Butte Chaillot** Right **Le Bistrot de Vignes**

Top 10 Places to Eat

1 Le Relais du Parc

The fixed-price lunch menu is a bargain, offering the cuisine of superchefs Alain Ducasse and Joel Robuchon. *59 ave Raymond Poincaré, 75016 • Map B3 • 01 44 05 66 66 • Closed Sat L, Sun–Mon • €€€€€*

2 La Table de Babette

This high-class West Indian restaurant is run by star chef Babette de Rozières. Expect exotic dishes such as stuffed crab with chilies and bananas flambéed in rum. *32 rue de Longchamp, 75016 • Map A3 • 01 45 53 00 07 • Closed Sat L, Sun, Aug • €€€€€*

3 La Butte Chaillot

This arty bistro from super-chef Guy Savoy is a winner, with dishes that belie the price. *110 bis ave Kléber, 75016 • Map B3 • 01 47 27 88 88 • Closed Sat L • No disabled access • €€€€*

4 L'Astrance

Pascal Barbot's exciting restaurant, serving fusion food at its best. Book at least one month in advance. *4 rue Beethoven 75116 • Map B4 • 01 40 50 84 40 • Closed Sat & Sun • No disabled access • €€€€€*

5 Maison Prunier

Fish dishes reign at this restaurant with 1930s decor. *16 ave Victor-Hugo, 75016 • Map B3 • 01 44 17 35 85 • Closed Sun, Aug • No disabled access • €€€€€*

6 Le Scheffer

Superb food, friendly, and reasonable prices, so book ahead. Try the red mullet Provençale. *22 rue Scheffer, 75016 • Map B3 • 01 47 27 81 11 • Closed Sat, Sun, Jul–Aug • €€*

7 Le Petit Rétro

Cosy atmosphere in this 1900s bistro and affordable prices. *Blanquette de Veau* is delicious. *5 rue Mesnil, 75016 • Map B3 • 01 44 05 06 05 • Closed Sat L, Sun, Aug • No disabled access • €€*

8 Le Bistrot des Vignes

Unpretentious little bistro of the type everyone hopes to find in Paris. *1 rue Jean-Bologne, 75016 • Map B4 • 01 45 27 76 64 • Closed Sun • No disabled access • €€*

9 La Table Lauriston

Serge Barbey believes in the best ingredients prepared simply. La Table Lauriston is a hit with local gourmets who tuck into his gargantuan steak and rum-doused *baba* in the jewel-toned dining room. *129 rue Lauriston, 75116 • Map A3 • 01 47 27 00 07 • Closed Sun, Sat L • €€€€*

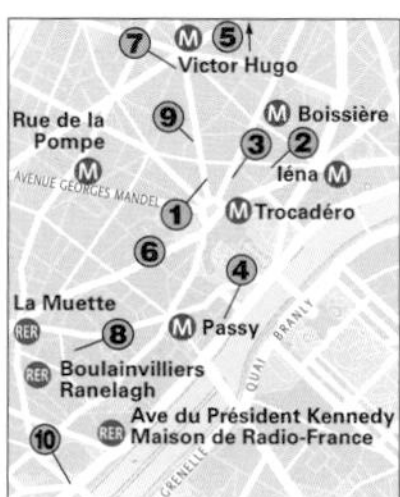

10 Zebra Square

Media hang-out as it's close to a Paris radio station. Noted for its steak tartare. Weekend brunches are popular. *3 pl Clément-Ader, 75016 • Map A4 • 01 44 14 91 91 • €€€*

***Note:** Unless otherwise stated, all restaurants accept credit cards and serve vegetarian meals*

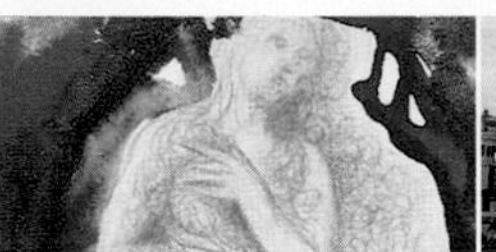

Left **Sacré-Coeur** Centre **Espace Montmartre Salvador Dalí** Right **Place Pigalle**

Montmartre and Pigalle

PAINTERS AND POETS, from Picasso to Apollinaire, put the "art" in Montmartre, and it will forever be associated with their Bohemian lifestyles of the late 19th and early 20th centuries. There are plenty of artists around today too, painting quick-fire portraits of tourists in the place du Tertre. Some say the name comes from "Mount of Martyrs", commemorating the first bishop of Paris, St Denis, who was decapitated here by the Romans in AD 250. Parisians, however, call it the "Butte" (knoll) as it is the highest point in the city. Throngs of tourists climb the hill for the stupendous view from Sacré-Coeur, crowding the main square, but you can still discover Montmartre's charms along the winding back streets, small squares and terraces. Below the hill, Pigalle, once home to dance halls and cabarets, has largely been taken over by sleazy sex shows along the boulevard de Clichy.

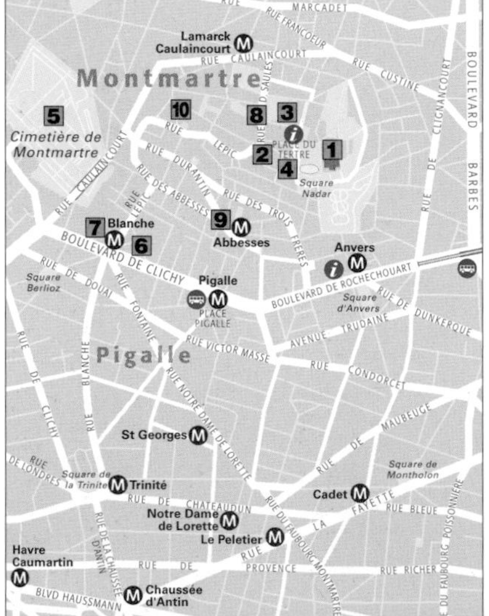

Streetside painter, Montmartre

Top 10 Sights

1. Sacré-Coeur
2. Espace Montmartre Salvador Dalí
3. Musée de Montmartre
4. Place du Tertre
5. Cimetière de Montmartre
6. Musée d'Erotisme
7. Moulin Rouge
8. Au Lapin Agile
9. Place des Abbesses
10. Moulin de la Galette

1 Sacré-Coeur
see pp22–3.

2 Espace Montmartre Salvador Dalí
The Dalí works here may not be the artist's most famous or best, but this museum is still a must for any fan of the Spanish Surrealist *(see p144)*. More than 300 of his drawings and sculptures are on display amid high-tech light and sound effects, including Dalí's voice, meant to create a "surreal" atmosphere. There are also bronzes of his memorable "fluid" clocks *(see p37)*. *11 rue Poulbot, 75018 • Map F1 • Open 10am–6pm daily • Admission charge • www.daliparis.com*

3 Musée de Montmartre
The museum is set in Montmartre's finest townhouse, known as Le Manoir de Rose de Rosimond after the 17th-century actor who once owned it. From 1875 it provided living quarters and studios for many artists. Using drawings, photographs and memorabilia, the museum presents the history of the Montmartre area, from its 12th-century convent days to the present, with an emphasis on the Bohemian lifestyle of the *belle époque*. There is even a re-created 19th-century bistro. *12 rue Cortot, 75018 • Open 11am–6pm Tue–Sun • Closed 1 Jan, 1 May, 25 Dec • Admission charge • www.museedemontmartre.fr*

4 Place du Tertre
At 130 m (430 ft), Montmartre's old village square, whose name means "hillock", is the highest point in the city. Any picturesque charm it might once have had is now sadly hidden under the tourist-trap veneer of over-priced restaurants and portrait artists hawking their services, although the fairy lights at night are still atmospheric. No. 21 houses the Old Montmartre information office, with details about the area. Nearby is the church of St-Pierre de Montmartre, all that remains of the Benedictine abbey which stood here from 1133 until the Revolution. *Map F1*

5 Cimetière de Montmartre
The main graveyard for the district lies beneath a busy road in an old gypsum quarry, though it's more restful than first appears when you actually get below street level. The illustrious tombs, many with ornately sculpted monuments, packed tightly into this intimate space reflect the artistic bent of the former residents, who include composers Hector Berlioz and Jacques Offenbach, writers Stendhal and Alexandre Dumas, Russian dancer Nijinsky and the film director François Truffaut. *20 ave Rachel, 75018 • Map E1*

Street art, Montmartre

The Montmartre Vineyards

It's hard to imagine it today, but Montmartre was once a French wine region said to match the quality of Bordeaux and Burgundy. There were 20,000 ha (50,000 acres) of Parisian vineyards in the mid-18th century, but today just 1,000 bottles of wine are made annually from the remaining 2,000 vines in Montmartre, and sold for charity.

6 Musée de l'Erotisme

With more than 2,000 items from around the world, this museum presents all forms of erotic art from painting, sculpture, photos and drawings to objects whose sole purpose seems to be titillation. It's all tastefully presented, however, reflecting the sincere interest of the three collectors who founded the museum in 1997 to explore the cultural aspects of eroticism. The displays range from spiritual objects of primitive cultures to whimsical artworks. *72 blvd de Clichy, 75018 • Map E1 • Open 10am–2am daily • Admission charge • www.musee-erotisme.com*

7 Moulin Rouge

The Moulin Rouge ("red windmill") is the most famous of the *belle époque* dance halls which scandalized respectable citizens and attracted Montmartre's artists and Bohemians. Henri de Toulouse-Lautrec immortalized the era with his sketches and posters of dancers such as Jane Avril, some of which now grace the Musée d'Orsay *(see p13)*. Cabaret is still performed here *(see p58)*. *82 blvd de Clichy, 75018 • Map E1 • Shows daily at 9pm & 11pm (dinner at 7pm) • www.moulinrouge.fr*

8 Au Lapin Agile

This *belle époque* restaurant and cabaret was a popular hang-out for Picasso, Renoir, and poets Apollinaire and Paul Verlaine. It took its name from a humorous painting by André Gill of a rabbit *(lapin)* leaping over a cooking pot, called the "Lapin à Gill". In time it became known by its current name ("nimble rabbit") *(see p58)*. *22 rue des Saules, 75018 • Map F1 • Open 9pm–2am Tue–Sun • www.au-lapin-agile.com*

Au Lapin Agile

Moulin de la Galette

9 Place des Abbesses

This pretty square lies at the base of the Butte, between Pigalle and the place du Tertre. Reach it via the metro station of the same name to appreciate one of the few original Art Nouveau stations left in the city. Designed by the architect Hector Guimard, it features ornate green wrought-iron arches, amber lanterns and a ship shield, the symbol of Paris, on the roof. Along with Porte Dauphine, it is the only station to retain its original glass roof. A mural painted by local artists winds around the spiral staircase at the entrance. But don't walk to the platform, take the elevator – it's the deepest station in Paris, with 285 steps. *Map E1*

10 Moulin de la Galette

Montmartre once had more than 30 windmills, used for pressing grapes and grinding wheat; this is one of only two still standing. During the siege of Paris in 1814 its owner, Pierre-Charles Debray, was crucified on its sails by Russian soldiers. It became a dance hall in the 19th century and inspired paintings by Renoir and Van Gogh *(see p144)*. It is now a restaurant, but it can be admired from outside, and rue Lepic is worth a visit for its shops and restaurants. *79 rue Lepic, 75018 • Map E1*

A Day in Montmartre

Morning

As with all the city's busy attractions, the sooner you get to **Sacré-Coeur** *(see pp22–3)* the more you will have it to yourself – it opens at 8am. Later in the morning, enjoy the bustle of Montmartre with tourists having their portraits painted by the area's street artists in the place du Tertre. There are plenty of places to choose for a coffee, but the one most of the artists frequent is the Clairon des Chasseurs *(3 pl du Tertre • 01 42 62 40 08)*.

For art of a more surreal kind, pay a visit to the **Espace Montmartre Salvador Dalí** *(see p141)*. Head down rue des Saules to continue the artistic theme with lunch at La Maison Rose *(2 rue de l'Abreuvoir • 01 42 57 66 75)*. Utrillo once painted this pretty pink restaurant.

Afternoon

After lunch, the **Musée de Montmartre** *(see p141)* is nearby, as are the Montmartre Vineyards, and the little Cimetière St-Vincent where you will find Maurice Utrillo's grave.

Head back up to rue Lepic to see the **Moulin de la Galette** before heading towards the boulevard de Clichy. Here you will see the sleazy side of Pigalle life, although the **Musée de l'Erotisme** is a more tasteful interpretation.

To the east is a great bar for an apéritif, La Fourmi *(74 rue des Martyrs • 01 42 64 70 35)*. Then end the day with a show at the world-famous **Moulin Rouge** cabaret.

Left **Dalì sculpture** Centre **Pablo Picasso** Right **Moulin de la Galette, Renoir**

Top 10 Artists who Lived in Montmartre

1 Pablo Picasso
Picasso (1881–1973) painted *Les Demoiselles d'Avignon* in 1907 while living at the Bateau-Lavoir. It is regarded as the painting which inspired the Cubism movement, which he launched with fellow residents Georges Braque and Juan Gris.

2 Salvador Dalí
The Catalan painter (1904–89) came to Paris in 1929 and held his first Surrealist exhibition that year. He kept a studio in Montmartre, and his work is now celebrated in the Espace Montmartre Salvador Dalì *(see p141)*.

3 Vincent Van Gogh
The Dutch genius (1853–90) lived on the third floor of 54 rue Lepic. Many of his paintings were inspired by the Moulin de la Galette windmill *(see p143)*.

4 Pierre-Auguste Renoir
Renoir (1841–1919) is another artist who found inspiration in the Moulin de la Galette, when he lived at 12 rue Cortot. For a time he laid tables at Au Lapin Agile *(see p142)*.

5 Edouard Manet
Manet (1832–83) spent a lot of time in Montmartre and scandalized the art world with his paintings of nudes, including the famous *Olympia* *(see p13)*.

6 Maurice Utrillo
Utrillo (1883–1955) often painted the Auberge de la Bonne-Franquette, an atmospheric depiction of old Montmartre. His mother was the artist Suzanne Valadon and they both lived at 12 rue Cortot, now the Musée de Montmartre *(see p141)*.

7 Henri de Toulouse-Lautrec
More than any other artist, Toulouse-Lautrec (1864–1901) is associated with Montmartre for his sketches and posters of dancers at the Moulin Rouge and other dance halls. They epitomize the era to this day *(see p13)*.

Toulouse-Lautrec

8 Raoul Dufy
The painter Dufy (1877–1953) lived at Villa Guelma on the boulevard de Clichy from 1911 to 1953, when he was at the height of his career.

9 Amedeo Modigliani
The Italian painter (1884–1920) and sculptor arrived in Paris in 1906, when he was 22, and was greatly influenced by Toulouse-Lautrec and the other artists on the Montmartre scene.

10 Edgar Degas
Edgar Degas was born in Paris in 1834 and lived in the city for the whole of his life, most of the time in Montmartre. He died here in 1917 and is buried in the Montmartre cemetery *(see p141)*.

Left **Art brut, Halle Saint Pierre** Right **Rue de Poteau market**

TOP 10 Places to Escape the Crowds

1 St-Jean l'Evangéliste de Montmartre
This 1904 church is a clash of styles, from Moorish to Art Nouveau. *21 rue des Abbesses, 75018 • Map E1 • Open daily • Free*

2 Montmartre City Hall
On display in this fine building are two Utrillo paintings. *1 pl Jules-Joffrin, 75018 • Metro Jules Joffrin*

3 Hameau des Artistes
This little hamlet of artists' studios is private, but no one will mind if you take a quiet look round. *11 ave Junot, 75018 • Map E1*

4 Musée de la Vie Romantique
Writer George Sand frequently visited the owner of this house, artist Ary Scheffer. The building is now devoted to her works. *16 rue Chaptal, 75009 • Map E1 • Open 10am–6pm Tue–Sun • Admission charge*

5 Musée Gustave Moreau
The former home of symbolist artist Moreau now displays a large collection of his works. *14 rue de La Rochefoucauld, 75009 • Map E2 • Open 10am–12:45pm, 2–5:15pm Wed–Mon • Admission charge • www.musee-moreau.fr*

6 Halle Saint Pierre
A fascinating cultural centre that exhibits naive, folk and "raw" art *(art brut)*. *2 rue Ronsard, 75018 • Map F1 • 01 42 58 72 89 • Open 10am–6pm daily • Admission charge*

7 Cité Véron
This cul-de-sac is home to the intriguing Ophir, a warehouse of theatre costumes and stage props. *92 blvd de Clichy, 75018 • Map E1*

8 Square Suzanne-Buisson
Named after a World War II Resistance fighter, this square is a romantic spot. *Map E1*

9 Rue de Poteau Market
This great food market is a long way from the tourist crowds. *Metro Jules Joffrin*

10 Chapelle des Martyrs
Also known as the Martyrium, this 19th-century chapel is said to be on the spot where St Denis was beheaded by the Romans in AD 250. *11 rue Yvonne-Le-Tac, 75018 • Map E1 • Chapel: open 10am–6pm Tue–Sun; crypt: open 3–6pm Fri • Admission charge*

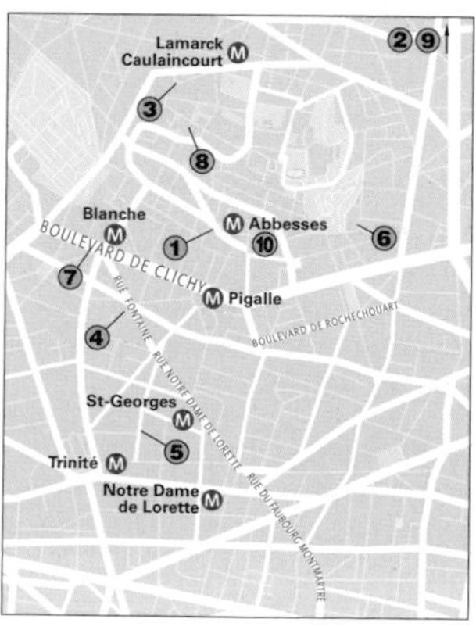

Left **Au Lapin Agile** Right **Moulin Rouge**

TOP 10 Cabarets and Clubs

1 Au Lapin Agile
Poets and artists not only drank in this cabaret club, some such as Renoir and Verlaine also laid tables. Picasso even paid his bill with one of his Harlequin paintings *(see p142)*.

2 Moulin Rouge
As old as the Eiffel Tower (1889) and as much a part of the Parisian image, today's troupe of 60 Doriss Girls are the modern versions of Jane Avril and La Goulue *(see p142)*. *82 blvd de Clichy, 75018 • Map E1*

3 Autour de Midi et Minuit
Tuck into delicious bistro food before heading into the small vaulted cellar for a jazz concert. *11 rue Lepic, 75018 • Map E1 • Closed Sun, Mon, Aug*

4 Chez Madame Arthur
The entertainment at this club is provided by drag artists and transsexuals – you won't need much French to understand. *75 bis rue des Martyrs, 75018 • Map E1*

5 La Nouvelle Eve
One of the lesser-known cabaret venues. Its intimate nature does not undermine the professionalism of the shows. *25 rue Fontaine, 75009 • Map E1*

6 Hammam Club
This North African-style restaurant turns into a late-night club with DJ and a dance floor. *94 rue d'Amsterdam, 75009 • Map E1*

7 Cabaret Michou
Outrageous show of drag artists and a compère whose behaviour can never be predicted, this is close to the original spirit of Montmartre cabaret. *80 rue des Martyrs, 75018 • Map E1*

8 Folies Pigalle
This former strip club is now a leading dance venue and popular among the gay community. *11 pl Pigalle, 75018 • Map E1*

9 La Loco
Next to the Moulin Rouge, this vast club couldn't be more different, attracting young dancers who want to dance all night. *90 blvd de Clichy, 75018 • Map E1*

10 Le Divan du Monde
World music is played here, live and DJ, with regular dance events and concerts too. *75 rue des Martyrs, 75018 • Map E1*

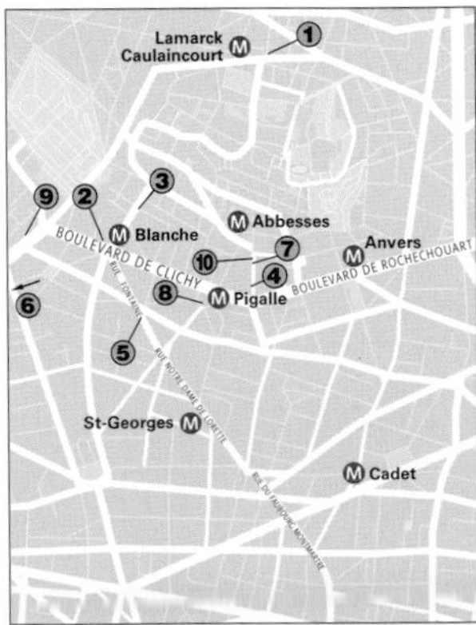

For more jazz clubs in Paris **See pp62–3**

Left **Café Burq**

Price Categories

For a three-course meal for one with half a bottle of wine (or equivalent meal), taxes and extra charges	
€	under €30
€€	€30–€40
€€€	€40–€50
€€€€	€50–€60
€€€€€	over €60

TOP 10 Places to Eat

1 Café Burq
A genuine Montmartre bistro with a trendy clientele. Roasted Camembert with honey is a favourite. *6 rue Burq, 75018 • Map E1 • 01 42 52 81 27 • Closed Sun, Aug • No disabled access • €€*

2 Le Barramundi
The emphasis here is on unpretentious international cuisine. *3 rue Taitbout, 75009 • Map E3 • 01 47 70 21 21 • Closed Sat L, Sun • €€*

3 L'Alsaco
This Alsatian bar-restaurant is a boisterous place noted for its *charcuterie* and wines. *10 rue Condorcet, 75009 • Map E1 • 01 45 26 44 31 • €*

4 Chez Jean
This 1950s wood-panelled brasserie boasts one of the city's most whimsical chefs. *8 rue St-Lazare, 75009 • Map E1 • 01 48 78 62 73 • Closed Sat L, Sun, Aug • €€€*

5 Spring
American Daniel Rose offers a no-choice four-course menu based on the day's market produce. Book months ahead for a table. *28 rue de la Tour d'Auvergne, 75009 • Map F2 • 01 45 96 05 72 • Closed Sun, Mon • €€€€*

6 Rose Bakery
The square quiches, carrot cakes and sticky puddings have made this eatery legendary. *46 rue des Martyrs, 75009 • Map F2 • 01 42 82 12 80 • Closed Mon • €*

7 Charlot "Roi des Coquillages"
Art Deco brasserie, specializing in seafood. *81 blvd de Clichy, 75009 • Map E1 • 01 53 20 48 00 • No disabled access • €€€*

8 L'Entracte
Off-the-beaten-track bistro. Simple dishes like pepper steak. *44 rue d'Orsel, 75018 • Map E1 • 01 46 06 93 41 • Closed Aug • €€*

9 Le Ch'ti Catalan
The cooking at this friendly bistro hops from northern France to southern Spain with happy results. *4 rue de Navarin, 75009 • Map F2 • 01 44 63 04 33 • Closed Sun • €€€*

10 Au Négociant
A cross between bar, pub and restaurant. Simple dishes such as pâté or potato pie. *27 rue Lambert, 75018 • Map E1 • 01 46 06 15 11 • Closed Sat–Sun, Aug • €*

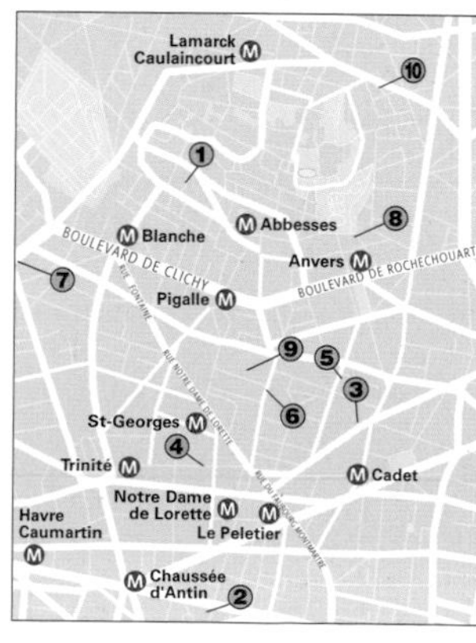

Note: *Unless otherwise stated, all restaurants accept credit cards and serve vegetarian meals.*

Left **Bois de Boulogne** Centre **Cimetière Père-Lachaise** Right **Parc Monceau**

Greater Paris

CENTRAL PARIS HAS MORE THAN ENOUGH on offer to keep any visitor occupied, but if time permits you should make at least one foray out of the centre, whether your interest is in the sumptuous Palace of Versailles, former home of the "Sun King" Louis XIV, or in the Magic Kingdom of Disneyland Paris. The excellent metro system makes for easy day trips to the area's two main parks, the Bois de Boulogne and the Bois de Vincennes, for a wide range of outdoor activities, from boating to riding or in-line skating, or just strolling amid pleasant greenery. In contrast to these bucolic pleasures is the cutting-edge modern architecture of La Défense. Visually stunning, it comprises Paris's stylish new business district to the west of the city, with added attractions in its exhibition centres. Two large cemeteries outside the centre are worth a visit for their ornate tombs.

Sights

1. **Versailles**
2. **Disneyland Resort Paris**
3. **La Défense**
4. **Bois de Vincennes**
5. **Bois de Boulogne**
6. **Parc de la Villette**
7. **Montparnasse**
8. **Cimetière du Père Lachaise**
9. **Parc Monceau**
10. **Musée Marmottan-Claude Monet**

Sculptures, Versailles

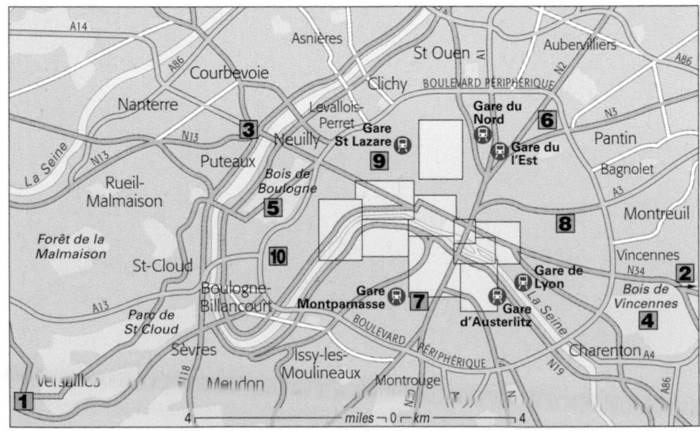

Preceding pages **Versailles gardens**

1 Versailles

The top day-trip from Paris has to be Versailles. This stunning chateau, begun by Louis XIV in 1664, is overwhelming in its opulence and scale. Plan carefully what you want to see as even a full day may not be long enough. Much of the palace is only accessible on a guided tour, so arrive early as on sunny days the queues can be long *(see p42)*. *Versailles 78000 • RER line C to Versailles-Rive Gauche • Open Apr–Oct: 9am–6:30pm Tue–Sun; Nov–Mar: 9am–5:30pm Tue–Sun (gardens open daily) • Admission charge • www.chateauversailles.fr*

2 Disneyland Resort Paris

Visitors with children will probably have no choice about whether they visit the Paris branch of Disneyland or not. However, even parents will enjoy the hi-tech workings and imagination behind such attractions as "Pirates of the Caribbean" and "The Haunted House" *(see p60)*. The new Walt Disney Studios Park involves visitors interactively through film, with a professional stunt show at the end and special effects rides. *Marne-la-Vallée • RER line A to Marne-la-Vallée Chessy/Disneyland • Open Sep–Jun: 9am–8pm daily; Jul–Aug: 9am–11pm daily (Studios Sep–Jun: 9am–6pm daily; Jul–Aug 9am–8pm daily); times vary for Walt Disney Studios Park • Admission charge • www.disneylandparis.com*

3 La Défense

The flair of French artistic vision and Parisian style are both clearly shown by this modern urban development. This new business and government centre was purposely built to the west of the city to allow the centre to remain unmarred by skyscrapers. More than just offices, however, the area is also an attraction in its own right, with stunning sights such as the Grande Arche, a cube-like structure with a centre large enough to contain Notre-Dame, and surrounded by artworks, a fountain, cafés and restaurants. *Metro Esplanade de la Défense or RER line A to Grande-Arche-de-la-Défense*

4 Bois de Vincennes

To the southeast of the city centre lies the parkland of the Bois de Vincennes. The park has three lakes, including a boating lake, along with the "Parc Floral" and its Four-Seasons Garden, a zoo, Buddhist Centre, and a summer amusement park. The beautiful Château de Vincennes, surrounded by a dry moat, was the French royal residence before Versailles. It has the tallest dungeon in Europe. *Vincennes, 94300 • Metro Château de Vincennes/RER Vincennes • Park: open dawn–dusk daily; château: Sep–Apr 10am–5pm; May–Aug 10am–6pm • Closed public hols • www.chateau-vincennes.fr*

Grande Arche, La Défense

The Treaty of Versailles

France, Great Britain, the USA, Italy and the German Republic negotiated this agreement after World War I at Versailles, which required Germany to demilitarize parts of its territory, reduce the size of its army, abolish conscription, cease trading in military equipment and to pay compensation. The Treaty was signed on 28 June 1919.

5 Bois de Boulogne

This enormous park is the Parisians' favourite green retreat, especially on summer weekends when its 865 ha (2,135 acres) can become crowded. There is plenty to do, apart from simply walking and picnicking, such as cycling, riding, boating or visiting the various attractions. These include parks within the park, two race courses *(see p51)* and an art and folk museum. The park is open 24 hours a day, but avoid after dark. *Map A2*

6 Parc de la Villette

More than just a park, this landscape was created in 1993 to a futuristic design. It provides the usual park features of paths and gardens, but modern sculptures, zany park benches and several major hi-tech attractions offer a different edge. These include the interactive science museum, the Cité des Sciences et de l'Industrie, a 60-seater mobile hydraulic cinema, an Omnimax cinema, play areas for younger children and a music museum *(see p60)*. *30 ave Corentin-Cariou, 75019 • Metro Porte de Pantin • 01 40 03 75 75 • Opening times vary depending on the attraction • Admission charge • www.villette.com*

7 Montparnasse

Montparnasse's location is highly visable due to the 209-m (685-ft) Tour du Montparnasse which offers spectacular views. Five minutes' walk away is the area's main draw, the Cimetière du Montparnasse, where the great writers Maupassant, Sartre, de Beauvoir, Baudelaire and Samuel Beckett are buried *(see p156)*. For breathtaking views of Paris by night visit the rooftop restaurant "Le Ciel de Paris." *Metro Gare Montparnasse • Tour du Montparnasse: open 9:30am–11:30pm daily (winter until 10:30pm Sun–Thu); admission charge • Cemetery: open 8:30am–5:30pm daily; free • www.tourmontparnasse.com*

Parc de la Villette

8 Cimetière du Père Lachaise

This is the most visited cemetery in the world, largely due to rock fans who come from around the world to see the grave of the legendary singer Jim Morrison of The Doors. There are about one million other graves here, in some 70,000 different tombs, including those of Chopin, Oscar Wilde, Balzac, Edith Piaf, Colette, Molière and Delacroix *(see p156)*. There are maps posted around the cemetery to enable you to find these notable resting places, or a more detailed plan can be bought at the kiosks around the grounds. *16 rue du Repos • Metro Père-Lachaise • Open 8am–5:30pm Mon–Sat, 9am–5:30pm Sun, but phone to check (01 55 25 82 10) • Free*

9 Parc Monceau

This civilized little park is no further from the city centre than Montmartre, yet it goes unnoticed by many visitors. It was created in 1778 by the Duc de Chartres and is still frequented by well-heeled residents. The grounds are full of statues and an air of well-being *(see p38)*. *Blvd de Courcelles, 75008 • Metro Monceau*

10 Musée Marmottan-Claude Monet

Paul Marmottan was an art historian and his 19th-century mansion now houses the world's largest collection of works by Claude Monet *(see p13)*, including his *Impression Soleil Levant* which gave the Impressionist movement its name. The collection was donated by the artist's son in 1971, and includes the artist's collection of works by Renoir and Gauguin. *2 rue Louis-Boilly, 75016 • Metro Muette • Open 10am–6pm Tue–Sun • Admission charge • www.marmottan.com*

A Taste of Greater Paris

Morning

You won't cover Greater Paris in a day, and **Disneyland Resort Paris** and **Versailles** *(see p151)* both need at least a day.

If you want variety, go to **Montparnasse** by métro and, in front of the busy mainline station, is the Tour Montparnasse – take a trip to the top to admire the view and take a coffee break in the Panoramic Bar.

When you leave, walk down boulevard Edgar Quinet. On your right is the entrance to the **Cimetière du Montparnasse**. An hour should be plenty of time here.

Walk towards the Vavin metro station to the historic café/brasserie **La Coupole** *(see p157)*, to have lunch.

Afternoon

Take the metro at Vavin, changing at Réaumur-Sébastopol, to **Cimetière du Père Lachaise** and explore the city's other great cemetery. Spend one or two hours searching out the famous names buried here and admiring the architecture of the monuments. Have a coffee afterwards at a neighbourhood café, Le Saint Amour *(2 ave Gambetta • 01 47 97 20 15 • Metro Père-Lachaise)*. From Père-Lachaise it is again just one change on the metro, at Nation, to the **Bois de Vincennes**, where you can spend the late afternoon in the park and admire the château.

Left **Marble courtyard** Right **Palace gardens**

TOP 10 Versailles Sights

1 The Hall of Mirrors
The spectacular 70-m (233-ft) long Galerie des Glaces (Hall of Mirrors) is one of the few rooms at Versailles that can be visited without a guide. It was in this room that the Treaty of Versailles was signed in 1919, to formally end World War I.

2 Chapelle Royale
The Royal Chapel is regarded as one of the finest Baroque buildings in the country. Finished in 1710, the elegant, white marble Corinthian columns and numerous murals make for an awe-inspiring place of prayer.

3 Salon de Venus
In this elaborate room decorated mainly in marble, a statue of Louis XIV, the creator of Versailles, stands centre stage, exuding regal splendour beneath the fine painted ceiling.

4 Queen's Bedroom
In this ornate room filled with white-and-gold woodwork, the queens of France gave birth to their children in public view: 19 royal infants were born here.

5 Marble Courtyard
Approaching the front of the palace across the vast open courtyard, visitors finally come to the splendour of the black-and-white marble courtyard. This is the original area of the palace, before the north and south wings were added.

6 L'Opéra
The stunningly opulent opera house was built in 1770, to be ready in time for the marriage of the *dauphin*, the future Louis XVI, to Marie-Antoinette. The floors were designed so that they could be raised to stage level during special festivals.

7 Grand Trianon
In the southeast corner of the gardens stands the Grand Trianon, a miniature palace built by Louis XIV to enable him to retreat from royal duties and enjoy a little private female company.

8 Palace Gardens
The palace gardens are scattered with walkways, landscaped topiary, fountains, pools, statues and the Orangery, where exotic plants were kept in the winter. The magnificent Fountain of Neptune is to the north of the North Wing.

9 Salon d'Apollon
Louis XIV's throne room is, naturally, one of the palace's centrepieces, and features a suitably regal portrait of the 18th-century king. Dedicated to the god Apollo, it reflects the divine way in which the French monarchy saw themselves.

10 Stables of the King
The magnificent stables have been restored and they now house the famous Zingaro equine training academy.

Not all sights are open at once, so check upon arrival

Left **Boating on lake** Right **Cycling in the Bois de Boulogne**

TOP 10 Bois de Boulogne Features

1 Parc de Bagatelle
Differing garden styles feature in this park, including English and Japanese, though the major attraction is the huge rose garden, best seen in June.

2 Pré Catelan Park
This park-within-a-park is at the very centre of the Bois. Its lawns and wooded areas include a 200-year-old beech tree said to have the largest spread of branches in Paris.

3 Jardin d'Acclimatation
The main children's area of the Bois incorporates a small amusement park, a zoo with a farm and a pets' corner, and a Herb Museum aimed especially at children *(see p60)*.

4 Lakes
Two long, thin lakes adjoin each other. The larger of the two, confusingly called Lac Inférieur (the other is Lac Supérieur) has boats for hire and a motor boat to take you to the islands.

5 Musée en Herbe
This small museum aims to introduce children to art via regular, changing exhibitions. There is an admission charge.

6 Parc des Princes
This stadium has been host to many football cup finals and rugby internationals and is home to the National Sports Museum.

7 Château de Longchamp
At the same time as he re-designed central Paris *(see p45)*, Baron Haussmann created the Bois de Boulogne. This chateau was given to Haussmann as a thank-you from Napoleon III.

8 Shakespeare Garden
Inside Pré Catelan park is a little garden planted with all the trees, flowers and herbs mentioned in the plays of Shakespeare. There's an open-air theatre nearby.

Shakespeare Garden

9 Jardin des Serres d'Auteuil
This 19th-century garden has a series of greenhouses where ornamental hothouse plants are grown. In the centre is a palm house with tropical plants.

10 Horse-Racing
The Bois is home to two race courses. To the west is the Hippodrome de Longchamp, where flat racing takes place including the Prix de l'Arc de Triomphe *(see p57)*; in the east, the Hippodrome d'Auteuil holds steeplechases.

For more on the Bois de Boulogne **See p152**

Left **Père Lachaise cemetery** Centre **Jim Morrison's grave** Right **Edith Piaf's tomb**

TOP 10 Graves

1 Jim Morrison, Père Lachaise Cemetery
The American lead singer of The Doors rock band spent the last few months of his life in Paris and died here in 1971. Fans still hold vigils at his grave, which is covered with scrawled messages from all over the world.

2 Oscar Wilde, Père Lachaise Cemetery
The Dublin-born author and wit died in 1900, after speaking his alleged last words in his Paris hotel room: "Either that wallpaper goes, or I do." His tomb is unmissable, with a huge monument by Jacob Epstein.

3 Fredéric Chopin, Père Lachaise Cemetery
The Polish composer was born in 1810 but died in Paris at the age of 39. The statue on his tomb represents "the genius of music sunk in grief".

4 Edith Piaf, Père Lachaise Cemetery
The "little sparrow" was born in poverty in the Belleville district of Paris in 1915, less than 1,500 m (5,000 ft) from where she was buried in 1963 in a simple black tomb *(see p63)*.

5 Marcel Proust, Père Lachaise Cemetery
The ultimate chronicler of Paris, the writer was born in the city in 1871. He is buried in the family tomb *(see p47)*.

6 Samuel Beckett, Montparnasse Cemetery
The Irish-born Nobel prize-winning writer settled in Paris in 1937, having previously studied here. He died in 1989 and his gravestone is a simple slab, reflecting the writer's enigmatic nature *(see p47)*.

7 Jean-Paul Sartre and Simone de Beauvoir, Montparnasse Cemetery
Joined together in death as in life, even though they never lived together, their joint grave is a remarkably simple affair. Both of these philosophers were born, lived and died in Paris.

8 Guy de Maupassant, Montparnasse Cemetery
The great French novelist and short-story writer died in Paris in 1893, and his grave with its luxuriant growth of shrubs stands out because of the open book carving *(see p46)*.

9 Charles Baudelaire, Montparnasse Cemetery
The poet who shocked the world with his frank collection of poems *Les Fleurs du Mal* was born in Paris in 1821 and died here in 1867.

10 Charles Pigeon Family, Montparnasse Cemetery
This charming and touching grave shows Charles Pigeon and his wife in bed, reading by the light of the gas lamp he invented.

For Greater Paris cemeteries **See pp152–3**

Price Categories

For a three course meal for one with half a bottle of wine (or equivalent meal), taxes and extra charges		
	€	under €30
	€€	€30–€40
	€€€	€40–€50
	€€€€	€50–€60
	€€€€€	over €60

Left **Le Dôme**

TOP 10 Places to Eat

1 Le Pré Catelan

Tucked away in the Bois de Boulogne *(see p152)* is this high-class dining pavilion. Romantic setting and elegant service. *Route de Suresnes, Bois de Boulogne, 75016 • Metro Porte Maillot • 01 44 14 41 14 • €€€€€*

2 Les Trois Marches

Eating in this Michelin-starred restaurant is a sublime experience. Leek and mushroom tart is just one speciality. *Hôtel Palais Trianon, 1 blvd de la Reine, Versailles • RER line C to Versailles • 01 39 50 25 08 • Closed Sun–Mon & Aug • €€€€€*

3 Marée de Versailles

Versailles may be a long way from the sea, but this restaurant serves whatever fish is fresh that day. Its terrace is the perfect place for oysters and white wine. *22 rue au Pain, Versailles • RER line C to Versailles • 01 30 21 73 73 • Closed Sun–Mon • €€€€*

4 La Coupole

Near the Cimetière du Montparnasse *(see p152)* is this Parisian landmark. Eclectic menu features dishes such as Welsh rarebit. *102 blvd du Montparnasse, 75014 • Map E6 • 01 43 20 14 20 • €€*

5 La Closerie des Lilas

With its piano bar and terrace, this is a Montparnasse institution. The brasserie is cheaper and steaks are good. *171 blvd du Montparnasse, 75006 • Map E6 • 01 40 51 34 50 • €€€€€*

6 Le Dôme

The prime fish restaurant in the area, once frequented by Sartre. Great food and grand decor. *108 blvd du Montparnasse, 75014 • Map E6 • 01 43 35 25 81 • Closed Sun–Mon & Aug • €€€€*

7 La Gare

If visiting the Bois de Boulogne, include La Gare on the itinerary. This stylish brasserie in a former railway station has a summer terrace and rotisserie-style food. *19 chaussée de la Muette, 75016 • Metro La Muette • 01 42 15 15 31 • €€*

8 Colimaçon (Ma Pomme)

Handy after a visit to Père Lachaise *(see p153)*. The food is first class, from ostrich and fish dishes to pastas and salads. *107 rue de Ménilmontant, 75020 • Metro Gambetta • 01 40 33 10 40 • Closed Sat L, Sun, Mon L • €*

9 L'Echappée

Not far from Père Lachaise is this family-run bistro. The food is value for money and the atmosphere perfect. *38 rue Boyer, 75020 • Metro Gambetta • 01 47 97 44 58 • Closed Sun, Aug • €*

10 Relais d'Auteuil

At the southern end of the Bois de Boulogne is this gourmet restaurant. Sea bass in a pepper crust is just one delicious speciality. *31 blvd Murat, 75016 • Metro Boulogne Jean Jaurés • 01 46 51 09 54 • Closed Sun • €€€€€*

***Note:** Unless otherwise stated, all restaurants accept credit cards and serve vegetarian meals*

STELLA ARTOIS
BAR
RAITEUR
AP
ASIE
PRESTIGE
SANDWICH
TURC

STREETSMART

Left **Parisian hotel** Centre **Parisian restaurant** Right **French perfume**

Top 10 Planning Your Trip

1 When to Go

April in Paris may be a cliché but it is still a good time to visit. Spring and autumn are both pleasant and there are plenty of parks and tree-lined boulevards to enjoy. Although certain places shut down in August, when most Parisians take their holidays, there is still plenty to see and do.

2 Choosing an Area

The Left Bank is a good choice if you like a Bohemian atmosphere of cafés and clubs. The Marais has many good museums and restaurants and the Opéra and Louvre quarters are central to everything. To save money, stay just outside the centre and use the excellent yet cheap metro.

3 Choosing a Hotel

If space is important, ask about the size of the rooms: some can be very cramped. It is also worth checking whether the rooms face busy, noisy roads and what is the hotel's nearest metro station. Ask if there is an elevator to all floors, as in some older buildings this may not be the case.

4 Choosing a Restaurant

If you like to eat well, or want to try a particular restaurant, phone and book a few weeks ahead of your visit. If you decide to take pot luck, however, the city is full of good places to eat and you should always be able to find a table.

5 What to See

Don't expect to see the whole of Paris on a weekend visit – you would not even see the whole of the Louvre in this time *(see pp8–11)*. Even on a longer visit, don't be over-ambitious: leave time for wandering the streets or relaxing in a bar or café, the way the Parisians do. It's all part of the experience.

6 What to Pack

The weather can be unpredictable, so allow for unexpected cold or wet spells at almost any time of year by bringing a pullover and an umbrella. Parisians are casual but chic, so take a few smart outfits for dining out. Only the most expensive restaurants require men to wear a tie.

7 How much Money to Take

You can use the major credit cards (Visa, MasterCard, American Express) almost everywhere, and there are cash dispensers (ATMs) all over Paris which display symbols of cards they accept. Make sure you have a few euros in cash when you arrive, however, to pay for metro tickets or a taxi. *Bureaux de change* offices also abound throughout the city.

8 Passports and Visas

No visa is required for citizens of EU countries, the USA, Canada, Australia or New Zealand if you are staying for less than three months, although your passport will need to be valid for at least three months beyond the end of your stay. Citizens of other countries should consult their French embassy or consulate for information before travelling.

9 Customs

For EU citizens there are no limits on goods that can be taken into or out of France, provided they are for your personal use. Outside the EU, you may import the following allowances duty-free: 200 cigarettes or equivalent in tobacco; 4 litres of wine, or 2 litres of wine plus 1 litre of spirits; 60ml of perfume and 250ml of eau de toilette; €350 worth of other items.

10 Travelling with Children

Now that public places are non-smoking, Paris is more child friendly than ever. Some hotels allow children under a certain age to share their parents' room for free *(see p179)*. Most Parisians don't take children to restaurants, seeing them as places to drink, but there are plenty of child-friendly options *(see pp60–61)*.

For hotels in Paris **See pp172–9**

Left **Metro exit sign** Right **Restaurant prices**

Top 10 Things to Avoid

1 Crime
As long as you avoid the quieter areas after dark, you will find Paris a reasonably safe city. Crime in busy areas is rare, except for pick-pockets. Muggings are not common but theft is, so make sure your hotel room and car are locked and secure.

2 Health Costs
In case you fall ill, avoid expensive health care by taking out insurance. For any minor health problems, pharmacies are plentiful and marked by a green cross; if one is closed, the address of the nearest open pharmacy will be shown in the window.

3 Beggars
Avoid displaying large amounts of bank-notes in front of the many beggars and buskers who frequent the metro and some of the city streets. The choice of whether to offer them money is up to you, but do so with small change.

4 Pickpockets
Pickpockets do frequent busy tourist places and public transport so keep a watchful eye on your belongings. Men should never keep their wallet in a back pocket and women should make sure their handbags are closed and held firmly in front of them if possible.

5 Taking the Wrong Metro
To avoid taking the wrong route, check the number of the line you want on a map and the name of the end station for the direction in which you wish to travel. All signs in metro stations work in this way and the system is simple. There is always a panel on the wall just before you reach the platform; this panel will have a list of the train's destinations, so you can double check *(see p164)*.

6 Transport Fines
When using the metro, put your ticket through the machine as you enter, but remember to retrieve it as you should keep it with you until your journey is completed. You will be fined if you are not found to be carrying a validated ticket by an inspector. This also applies to travelling by bus.

7 Tourist Traps
It is more difficult to eat badly in Paris than in many cities, but there are places which look for a fast profit at the expense of the tourist who will never return. Avoid signs that say *"Menu Touristique"* – they may be fine, but places that attract local people are far better.

8 Hidden Charges in Cafés or Bars
When paying a bill, check if service is included – it usually is. If you want to save money, take your drink or snack at the counter. Prices are lower and no tip is expected.

9 Over-Tipping
Restaurants and cafés normally include a 10–15 per cent service charge, so only leave a further small gratuity for very good service. Taxi drivers should get 10–15 per cent but this is not obligatory. Porters can be tipped €1.5–3 per bag and chambermaids a similar amount per day, usually left at the end of your stay.

10 Queues
Get to popular tourist attractions a little before they open – this could save you time later. Late afternoon is also a good time to avoid the queues. Some museums also allow you to pre-purchase tickets on their website.

Queues to enter Notre-Dame

Left **Eurostar train** Centre **Ice cream parlour in Gare du Nord** Right **Orlyval high-speed train**

Top 10 Arriving in Paris

1 Eurostar

Eurostar trains arrive at Gare du Nord, slightly north of the city centre. The station is served by three metro lines and three RER lines, and has a taxi rank outside, usually manned by assistants to help newly arrived visitors.

2 Gare du Nord Facilities

Gare du Nord is a large station with several places to eat and drink and shops selling books, newspapers and snacks. The metro station is reached from the concourse and is clearly signposted. There is also a tourist office by the Grandes Lignes exit.

3 CDG Airport

Roissy-Charles-de-Gaulle Airport is the arrival point for most international flights, 23 km (14 miles) northeast of the city centre. Its main terminals are some distance apart, so check which one you require when returning. A 24-hour English-language information service is available. ✆ *CDG information: 39 50.*

4 Connections from CDG Airport

CDG is connected to central Paris by Air France and Roissy bus services, and (the easiest option) the RER train line B. This links with Gare du Nord, Les Halles and St Michel, among other central stations. Taxis take at least 30 minutes to the city centre, sometimes more, and cost about €50.

5 Orly Airport

Orly is 14 km (8.5 miles) south of the city centre and is used by French domestic services and some international airlines. It also has two terminals: Orly-Sud is mainly for international flights; Orly-Ouest is for domestic flights. English-language information is available 6am–11:30pm. ✆ *Orly information: 39 50.*

6 Connections from Orly Airport

Air France and other bus services link Orly with the city centre and metro stations, while the high-speed and frequent Orlyval train runs to the Orlyval RER station, for onward RER links to central Paris. Taxis take about 30 minutes and cost about 40 euros.

7 Beauvais Tillé Airport

Beauvais Tillé Airport is some 70 km (43 miles) north of Paris and is used by low-cost airlines Ryanair (Ireland and Scotland), and Wizzair (Eastern Europe). There is a connecting bus link with Porte Maillot metro station; allow at least an hour for the journey.

8 Arriving by Road

All motorways from whichever direction eventually link with Paris' Boulevard Périphérique (Outer Ring Road). Access to central Paris is via different exits *(portes)*, so drivers should always check their destination before setting off and know which exit they will need.

9 Parking

To park on the street you will need the nerves and ability of a local: they often park illegally, seemingly with impunity. Visitors are advised to use one of the official car parks, which are plentiful.

10 Arriving by Bus

The main operator, Eurolines, has services from the UK, Ireland, Germany and several other European countries. Coaches arrive at Gare Routière Internationale, east of the city centre but are linked to the metro from the Galliéni station on Line 3.

Eurolines long-distance bus

For information on getting around Paris **See p164**

Left **Paris tourist office sign** Right **Parisian listings magazines**

TOP 10 Sources of Information

1 French Tourist Offices
The French Tourist Office has branches in many major international cities.

2 Office de Tourisme de Paris
The main office is near the Pyramides metro station. It is well stocked with brochures, and has hotel and tour reservation services. *25 rue des Pyramides, 75001 • Map E3 • 08 92 68 30 00* (€0.34/ min) *• Open 10am–7pm Mon–Sat, 11am–7pm Sun (9am–7pm Jun–Oct) • Closed 1 May • www.parisinfo.com*

PARIS
Convention and Visitors Bureau
Tourist Office

3 Espace du Tourisme d'Ile de France
This tourist facility serves Paris and the wider Ile de France region. It has a good range of brochures, especially for outside Paris, and can book tours and accommodation. *99 rue de Rivoli, 75001 • Map M2 • 01 44 50 19 98 • www.cestsoparis.com*

4 Websites
Two official sites are the state tourist office (www.paris.fr) and the city tourist office (www.parisinfo.com), with lots of information and links in French and English. Most major attractions such as the Musée du Louvre (www.louvre.fr) also have their own sites.

5 A Nous Paris
If you are able to read French, this free, weekly magazine, found in certain central Paris metro stations, is a good source of information about current events in the city.

6 Officiel des Spectacles & Pariscope
These two events guides can be bought at newspaper stands and are ideal if you want more general information about current exhibitions.

7 Paris Free Voice
This monthly magazine is published by the American Church and aimed at US residents in Paris. Available from English-language bookshops, it is a good source of information on what is happening in the city. It also has a website www.parisvoice.com

8 Francofile electronic newsletter
This monthly mailing available via the linked website (www.paris-anglo.com) is sent out in English to visitors, residents and anyone interested in what's going on in Paris. It covers exhibitions, politics, restaurant openings and closings and offers a question-and-answer service.

9 Libraries
Public libraries are found all over Paris and all of them are free to enter. Most have selections of newspapers and magazines, as well as notices that may be useful to visitors. Only Paris residents, however, can borrow material.

10 Newspapers
Foreign newspapers are available on the day of publication in many newsagents. The *International Herald Tribune* is published from Paris. French-speakers can also keep in touch with world events via France's national publications such as *Le Monde* or *Le Figaro*, or the city's own paper, *Le Parisien*.

French Tourist Offices Overseas

www.franceguide.com

UK
Lincoln House, 300 High Holborn, London WC1V 7JH • 0906 8244 123 (UK only).

USA
825 Third Ave, 29th floor, New York, NY 10022 • 514 288 1904.

Australia
25 Bligh St, Level 13, Sydney, NSW 2000 • 02 9231 5244.

Canada
1800 McGill College, Suite 1010, Montréal, QUE H3A 3J6 • 514 288 20 26.

Left **Metro sign** Centre **Locator map outside a metro station** Right **Walking in Paris**

TOP 10 Getting Around Paris

1 Metro

The Paris metro system is cheap and efficient. The network is comprehensive and the service is very frequent. The service operates from roughly 5:30am–12:30am (until 1:30–2am Fri, Sat and the evening before bank holidays) and exact times for each line are given at stations. *www.ratp.fr*

2 RER

The RER train system (5am–12:30am; to 1.30am Fri, Sat and the eve before public holidays) has only five lines, but the network goes further into the suburbs. Metro tickets are only valid on RER trains in the central zones (1 and 2). If travelling further, you must buy a separate RER ticket.

3 Buses

Buses run from approximately 6:30am–8:30pm, although some services operate through the night (Noctilien Buses). A *Grand Plan de Paris* available from metro stations shows all bus routes. Metro tickets are valid in Zones 1 and 2, but you cannot switch between bus and metro on the same ticket. Bus stops show the line route.

Parisian bus

4 Taxis

There are 470 taxi ranks in Paris and you can also call taxis from a hotel or restaurant. Fares are not expensive, but make sure the meter is switched on when you get on board. The final fare will be more than the metered fare if you have luggage with you or were picked up at a mainline station. Some drivers will not take more than three people in their taxi, to avoid passengers in the front seat.

5 Arrondissements

Paris is divided into 20 *arrondissements* (districts), which radiate out in a clockwise spiral from the centre. The first is abbreviated to 1er (Premier) and follow on as 2e, 3e (Deuxième, Troisième) etc. The postal address for the first district is 75001, and again these follow on – the second district is 75002.

6 Asking Directions

The Parisians' reputation for rudeness is unjustified. Most are polite and will try to help even if you do not speak French (many Parisians speak English). Politeness, is all-important, however, so begin any enquiry with "*Excusez moi*" ("Excuse me").

7 Cycling

In this city of heavy traffic, cycling might seem like madness, but there is an ever-expanding network of cycle lanes. Get the free map *Paris à Vélo (Paris by Bike)* from tourist offices and bike shops. RATP rents bikes from €14 per day. Try the Vélib', Paris's self-service bikes available from €1–4 for 30 minutes. *www.rouelibre.fr*

8 Rollerblading

Parisians are mad about rollerblading and on Friday nights and Sunday afternoons organized *balades* (outings) often take place, beginning at Montparnasse. *www.pari-roller.com*

9 Boat

The Batobus runs for roughly 11 months a year and its eight stops link major attractions such as the Eiffel Tower, Louvre Museum and Notre-Dame. Boats run every 15–30 minutes, from 10am–7pm (until 9pm Jun–Sep; 10:30am–4:30pm winter). A day pass is advisable if you plan to make more than one journey. *08 25 05 01 01, www.batobus.com*

10 Walking

Central Paris is fairly compact, and even a walk from the Arc de Triomphe to the Bastille should only take an hour. Be sure to look up to see the beautiful old buildings – and down to avoid the evidence of Parisian dogs.

Left **Canal tour boat** Centre **Pedestrian walk sign** Right **Bus tour**

Top 10 Guided Tours

1 Boat Tours

The long-established Bateaux-Mouches operate daily with regular day and evening dinner cruises. *Bateaux-Mouches: 01 42 25 96 10, www.bateaux-mouches.fr • Bateaux Parisiens: 01 46 99 43 13, www.bateauxparisiens.com • Vedettes de Paris: 01 44 18 19 50, www.vedettesdeparis.com • Les Vedettes du Pont Neuf: 01 46 33 98 38, www.vedettesdupontneuf.fr*

2 Walking Tours

Tours are available on a wide range of themes and in several languages. Paris Walkabout, Secrets of Paris and Paris Walks are three of the leading English-language companies. Also check out the website www.paris-expat.com *Paris Walkabout: www.pariswalkabout.com • Paris Walks: 01 48 09 21 40, www.paris-walks.com • Secrets of Paris: www.secretsofparis.com*

3 Cycle Tours

Several companies offer guided cycling tours, with multilingual guides, including night-time tours and medieval Paris tours. For the less energetic, Segway Tours hire out electric scooters. *Paris à Vélo: 01 48 87 60 01, www.parisvelosympa.com • Fat Tire Bike Tours: 01 56 58 10 54, www.fattirebiketoursparis.com • City Segway Tours: 01 56 58 10 54, www.citysegwaytours.com*

4 Canal Tours

Less well-known than river trips, these tours take you into the fascinating backwaters of the Paris canal system. Commentaries will often only be in French, but they may include English if many English speakers are on board.

Sign for Paris canal tour

Canauxrama and Navettes de la Villette: 01 42 39 15 00, www.canauxrama.com • Paris Canal: 01 42 40 96 97, www.pariscanal.com

5 Bus Tours

Numerous bus tours are available – the main tourist office on rue des Pyramides *(see p163)* is the best place to begin. Tours usually last up to two hours but many of the companies allow you to hop on and off at any of their stops.

6 Gourmet Tours

Promenades Gourmandes offers tailor-made French- or English-language tours of the city's markets, food shops, kitchenware shops or anything else in Paris that is of food-related interest. *Promenades Gourmandes: 01 48 04 56 84 • www.promenadesgourmandes.com*

7 Parks and Gardens Tours

Paris City Hall organizes tours of parks, gardens and cemeteries, for groups or individuals with a specialist interest. Ask at any tourist office for details or call City Hall. *City Hall: 01 43 28 47 63*

8 Shopping and Fashion Tours

Pay a guide to direct you to the best shops. You can then choose from a range of themes. *Shopping Plus: 01 47 53 91 17, www.frenchforaday.com*

9 Themed Tours

American company Paris Through Expatriate Eyes runs several tours, revealing many secrets even Parisians don't know. Visit www.parisinfo.com for other tour operators. *Paris Through Expatriate Eyes: 06 70 98 13 68, www.paris-expat.com*

10 Sports Tour

Sports fans can take a guided one-and-a-half hour tour of the huge and world-famous arena the Stade de France. *Stade de France: 08 92 70 09 00 • Tours 10am-5pm on the hour daily except on event days (English-language tour 10:30am & 2:30pm) • www.stadefrance.fr*

Left **Paris bus** Centre **Budget hotel** Right **Eating at the bar**

TOP 10 Paris on a Budget

1 Public Transport

There is a bewildering array of discount travel passes available *(see p164 & 168)*, so be sure to study them to find the best one for you. You can buy one-, two-, three- and five-day passes (called a Paris Visite ticket), with options for different zones. Savings can be considerable, provided the pass gives you what you want. ✆ www.ratp.fr

2 Hostels and Camping

It is perfectly feasible to find acceptable accommodation in central Paris for €40–50 per night. Even cheaper options include the following hostel groups. ✆ *www.cheaphostel.com • FUAJ 01 44 89 87 27 • Camping du Bois de Boulogne: 01 45 24 30 00, www.campingparis.fr • St Christopher's Inn: www.st-christophers.co.uk*

3 Bed-and-Breakfast

Several companies offer rooms with Parisian families on a bed-and-breakfast basis. Most are located either centrally or close to a metro station, and can cost as little as €30 per person per night, if sharing. ✆ *Alcove & Agapes: 01 44 85 06 05, www.bed-and-breakfast-in-paris.com • Good Morning Paris: 01 47 07 28 29, www.goodmorningparis.fr*

Paris metro sign

4 Cheap Eats

For a coffee or snack, standing at the bar is cheaper than sitting down. In restaurants, the *prix-fixe* (fixed-price) menus offer good deals and the *plat du jour* (dish of the day) is usually inexpensive. If you want to sample fine dining, do it at lunchtime when it's often cheaper.

5 Cheap Seats

Half-price theatre and concert tickets are available for same-day performances only from kiosks at Place de la Madeleine *(see p97)*. Cinemas usually offer discounts in the mornings, and on Wednesdays.

6 Cheap Treats

Several attractions including the Louvre, Musée Picasso and Arc de Triomphe are free on the first Sunday of each month. The Louvre also reduces its admission price after 6pm on Wednesday and Friday *(see p8)*. The Paris City Passport, available from tourist offices, gives 10–50 per cent off entry to 47 museums.

7 Paris Museum Pass

This gives unlimited visits to over 60 museums and monuments throughout Paris. There are two-, four- and six-day options but it is only a cheap deal if you visit many attractions on consecutive days. They are on sale at participating museums, tourist offices *(see p163)* and the Espace du Tourisme Ile de France in the Carousel du Louvre (99 rue de Rivoli, 75001). ✆ *www.parismuseumpass.fr*

8 Breakfast

Most hotels charge separately for breakfast and what is on offer varies widely. You can save money by opting out and choosing a small snack in a café or boulangerie instead.

9 Churches

As well as being free to visit, many churches also put on free or very inexpensive concerts, both at lunchtime and in the evening. If passing a church, take a look to see if any such concerts are being advertised.

10 Concessions

Many places offer free or discounted admission to various groups of people, particularly students, under-25s or over-60s. You will need proof of your age, such as a student pass or some other means of identification.

For budget hotels in Paris **See p175**

Left **Paris taxi** Right **Musée d'Orsay**

Top 10 Paris for the Disabled

1 Tourist Office Leaflets

The main tourist office in Paris *(see p163)* has information leaflets on facilities for the disabled. Their website also has useful addresses. *www.parisinfo.com*

2 Useful Organizations

Both the Association des Paralysés de France (APF) and the Groupement pour l'Insertion des Personnes Handicappées Physiques (GIHP) provide information on disabled facilities in Paris. *APF: 17 blvd Auguste Blanqui, 75013, 01 40 78 69 00 (www.apf.asso.fr) • GIHP: 32 rue du Paradis, 75010, 01 45 23 83 50 www.gihpidf.asso.fr*

3 Guided Tours

The Paris City Hall organizes numerous specialized tours of the city's parks, gardens and cemeteries for people with disabilities, including special visits for the blind. *City Hall: 01 43 28 47 63*

4 Itineraries

For those with wheelpower who want to go it alone in central Paris, APF have detailed information on negotiating various quarters of the city *(see above for address). Paris comme sur des roulettes* is also a useful guide with maps colour coding the quality of the pavements on given routes, access to public conveniences etc. *Editions Dakota, 45 rue St-Sébastien, 75011* (€8.99), *or from FNAC and large newsagents.*

5 Travel Agents

Holiday Care, in the UK, has a useful list of specialist tour operators. APF Evasion, in Paris, can also organize your entire stay. *Holiday Care: 0845 1249 971, outside UK +44 (0) 208 760 0072 (www.holidaycare.org.uk) • APF Evasion: 17 blvd Auguste Blanqui, 75013, 01 40 78 69 00*

6 Metro/RER

Few stations are easily accessible for wheelchairs and most require a station member of staff to operate lifts to avoid either stairs or escalators. The new Météor line, however, is wheelchair accessible. Main metro and RER stations have a leaflet on transport facilities, called *Handicaps et Déplacements en Région Ile-de-France.*

7 Buses

Paris buses are slowly being equipped with access for wheelchairs, and all buses already have seats reserved for disabled and elderly persons, war veterans and pregnant women.

8 Taxis

It is a legal requirement for taxi drivers to help people with disabilities to get in and out of their vehicle, and to carry guide dogs as passengers. This does not mean that all taxis are able to carry wheelchairs, so do check when booking. *Taxi G7 has a large fleet of cars: 01 47 39 47 39*

9 Hotels

Many older hotels are unsuitable for people with mobility problems as they are without elevators, so it is essential that you check before booking. Newer hotels and the modern hotel chains are usually wheelchair accessible, but always ask when making a reservation.

10 Attractions

While some of the older museums and monuments are not accessible for people in wheelchairs, most museums and galleries are, and they also increasingly cater for those with special needs. To be sure about the facilities on offer, get the relevant tourist office leaflet before you visit. APF publishes a guide to disabled access in Paris' museums, theatres and cinemas, *Guide 98 (see Useful Organizations).*

Wheelchair access sign

Left **Metro carnet tickets** Centre **Carte Orange** Right **Paris Visite**

Top 10 Tickets

1 Metro Tickets

Metro tickets can be bought in batches of 10 *(un carnet)*, which offer considerable savings on the price of a single ticket. Each ticket is valid for one journey, no matter how many changes of route are made. They must be stamped when you enter the metro and retained until you leave *(see p161)*. If staying for a few days, consider buying a *Carte Orange* (photo ID needed) or a *Paris Visite* card, which offer savings on all city transport.

2 Bus Tickets

One type of ticket serves all bus and metro routes and Zones 1 and 2 of the RER network. As with the metro, time-stamp your ticket when boarding the bus and keep it until the end of the journey. You will be fined if you are not in possession of a valid ticket.

3 RER Tickets

Using the purple metro and bus tickets on the central Zones 1 and 2 of the RER service makes for a convenient way of getting around. See the station maps for the extent of these zones.

4 SNCF Train Tickets

Tickets issued by the RATP (Régie Autonome des Transports Parisiens) are not valid on the mainline SNCF (Société Nationale des Chemins de Fer) services, France's national rail network. To find out about services to suburban stations, including Versailles *(see p151)*, ring the General Information and reservations line. *SNCF information: 3635 (special number) • www.sncf.com*

5 Theatre Tickets

These can be bought at the box office of the theatre, by telephone or at ticket agencies (including FNAC stores). Some theatres offer reduced-price tickets for students or stand-by seats 15 minutes before the performance. There is also a half-price ticket kiosk *(see p166)*.

6 Cinema Tickets

Prices are average for a European city, but ask about discounts that may be available for students, over-60s and families. Admission prices on Wednesdays are sometimes reduced. Larger cinemas take credit card reservations over the phone and online.

7 Clubs

Admission prices are high at all Paris clubs and are often increased at weekends or after midnight, but women can sometimes get in at a reduced rate or for free. Although the admission charge may include a first drink, subsequent drinks will usually be very pricey.

8 Tickets for Attractions

Some concessionary and discount tickets are available *(see p166)*. The Museum Pass saves queueing if you are planning to visit many of the major museums *(see pp34–5)*. Some museums have online booking, and the Louvre has automatic ticket machines *(see p8)*. Turning up early is another option.

9 Ticket Touts

Like elsewhere, Paris has its ticket touts, and the usual rules apply. It may get you tickets for an in-demand event, but be wary of forgeries and exorbitantly increased prices. Some Parisians carry a sign saying *"cherche une place"* ("I'm looking for a seat"), which sometimes finds a ticket at face-value from someone with one to spare.

10 Ticket Agencies

Tickets for concerts and theatre shows are sold at the main tourist information centre at 25 rue des Pyramides and at ticket agencies around the city, including at several branches of the FNAC chain of CD/book/video stores, and at the Virgin Megastore. There is abooking fee for using agencies. *FNAC, 74 ave des Champs-Elysées • Map C3 • Open 10am–midnight Mon–Sat, noon–midnight Sun*

Left **Paris chocolate shop** Centre **Street market stall** Right **Souvenir biscuit tins**

TOP 10 Shopping

1 What to Buy
Food and fashion are two of the things that Paris does supremely well and at all kinds of price ranges. Good wines can be found reasonably inexpensively. Galleries offer artworks from the traditional to the avant-garde and stationery shops tempt buyers with beautiful displays.

2 Shopping Hours
These vary enormously, though typically they will be from about 9:30am–7pm Monday to Saturday. Thursday is late-night shopping until 9pm in many shops. Sunday is very quiet but many small shops do open, particularly in the Marais, especially food shops in the morning. Shops may well close during August.

3 Taxes
Different rates of sales tax (TVA) apply to most goods, varying between 5–25 per cent and are generally included in the stated price. No refunds are available on purchases of food, wine or tobacco. On other goods, tax can be refunded to non-EU citizens who spend more than €175 in one shop. Ask the store for the appropriate form.

4 Clothes
Paris is still a fashion capital, for men and women, and a range of shopping options is available. There are the genuine *haute couture* stores, mostly on and near avenue Montaigne *(see p108)*, but many shops sell cut-price designer labels and there is a great choice of inexpensive fashion too.

5 Food and Drink
No visit to Paris is complete without going to one of the street markets. Don't let the stalls blind you to the shops, however, which are full of gastronomic delights. Place de la Madeleine has a high concentration of food stores *(see p98)*.

6 Lingerie
French fashion isn't all on the surface. Designers also produce stylish underwear, from subtly erotic to rather blatantly provocative.

7 Perfume and Cosmetics
Two more items to check out in Paris. There are many shops devoted to both, including the Sephora and Marionnaud chains where you can sample hundreds of scents. Prices are usually favourable, too.

Designer shoes

8 Department Stores
Paris's huge department stores come on a grand scale. You almost need a map to find your way round Galeries Lafayette and Au Printemps, which have separate buildings for their various sections *(see p54)*. BHV at Hôtel de Ville sells household goods and a vast array of DIY tools, plus clothes.

9 Music
Parisians are into music in a big way, and the large music stores reflect this. Try any of the FNAC chain of shops, which stock a huge range of CDs alongside books, videos and computer software. The Virgin Megastore on the Champs-Elysées has several floors, and has shop-floor headphones to let you listen to the stock.

10 Stationery
French stationery can be exquisite and there are plenty of specialist shops with tempting window displays. Handmade papers sit alongside beautifully designed pens and cards that anyone would be pleased to receive. Diaries and address books make tasteful presents.

For more shops in Paris **See pp54–5**

Left **Bureau de change** Centre **Paris postbox** Right **Newspapers on sale**

Top 10 Banking & Communications

1 Currency

The euro (€), the single European currency, is now operational in 16 of the 27 member states of the EU, including France. Euro banknotes have seven denominations: 5, 10, 20, 50, 100, 200 and 500. There are also eight coin denominations: €1 and €2, and 50, 20, 10, 5, 2 and 1 cents (also referred to as centimes!). Both notes and coins are valid and interchangeable within each of the 16 countries. Check on exchange rates against your own currency at the time of travel.

2 Credit Cards

These are widely accepted throughout Paris and you should have no difficulty paying for most things with plastic. The only possible exception is American Express because of the heavy commission it incurs. The Visa card is the most widely used.

Parisian public telephone

3 Cash Dispensers (ATMs)

There are cash dispensers all over Paris, and each one indicates the cards it accepts. Many of them also operate in several languages. If you know your PIN number, obtaining cash in this way is very easy.

4 Changing Money

Bureaux de Change exist throughout Paris, especially near tourist hotspots. Many banks also have either a *bureau de change* or foreign desk. "No commission" signs can be misleading, as they probably mean an unfavourable rate. If changing a large amount, a bank is usually best.

5 Post Offices

The main post offices in the heart of Paris are at 52 rue de Louvre (open 24 hours) and 71 ave des Champs-Elysées. They do not exchange currency or travellers' cheques but will exchange international postal cheques, giros and money orders.

6 Postcards

For simple letters and postcards home, you can buy stamps at a *tabac* (tobacconist) rather than try to find a post office. Not all of them advertise the service, but if they sell postcards it is worth asking. Some hotels and newsagents also sell postage stamps.

7 Telephones

Paris phone numbers begin with 01 and have eight subsequent digits, usually written in four sets of two digits. If calling Paris from overseas, drop the zero from "01". Most public telephones require a *télécarte* (phonecard), which can be bought from post offices, metro stations, tobacconists and a few other outlets.

8 Internet Cafés

These aren't as common as in some cities but are rapidly on the increase and it should not be hard to track one down. Many cafés also provide WIFI access. Try the internet café Paris-cy at 8 rue de Jouy, 75004: 01 42 71 37 37. Or search for one at www.cafes-wifi.com.

9 Newspapers and Magazines

A wide choice of the major foreign newspapers is available on the day of publication throughout Paris. The closer you are to the Champs-Elysées, the more you will see. The popular *International Herald Tribune* is published in Paris.

10 Television and Radio

Most hotels subscribe to multilingual cable and satellite channels, which vary the diet of French-language entertainment.

Left **Pedestrian stop sign** Centre **Paris police car** Right **Pharmacy sign**

Top 10 Security & Health

1 Crossing the Road

Take care when crossing Paris's roads. French drivers are not known for respecting pedestrians, though a red light will usually – although not always – make them stop. Pedestrians do not have automatic priority on a crossing, unless lights are also in their favour. On pedestrian crossings, motorists often have the right to turn right, so always look before you start to cross.

2 Pickpockets

Gangs of pickpockets do frequent tourist spots such as the Eiffel Tower and the Arc de Triomphe, as well as wandering the metro system. Some are amateur gangs and easy to spot, but others are more subtle so guard your belongings at all times.

3 Mugging

Mugging is less of a problem in Paris than in other big cities, but it can happen. Try not to travel alone late at night and avoid unlit streets. Try to avoid long interchanges between metro stations too: better a longer journey than an unfortunate experience. The main stations you should avoid at night are Les Halles and St Lazare.

4 Police

There are a number of police stations in central Paris. These are listed in the phone book, or call the Préfecture Centrale for details. All crimes should be reported, if only for insurance purposes. *Préfecture Centrale: 01 53 71 53 71 • Open 24 hours*

5 Women Travellers

Parisian men are generally courteous. A firm rebuttal usually halts unwanted attention. If not, try to seek the help of another man: they do not like to see a woman being pestered.

6 Insurance

Paris medical treatment is very good but it can be expensive, so be sure to have good health insurance. Visitors from EU countries should be equipped with a European Health Insurance card to avoid emergency fees. All other nationalities should take out private insurance. Report all crimes or lost property, and keep a copy of the statement you make to the police.

7 Hospitals

English-speaking visitors might want to contact the British or the American Hospitals, both open 24 hours a day. Paris hospitals are listed in the phone book, or call Hôpital Assistance Publique. *British Hospital: 01 46 39 22 22 • American Hospital: 01 46 41 25 25 • Hôpital Assistance Publique: www.aphp.fr*

8 Ambulances

If you need an ambulance, dial the emergency number. Fire stations also have ambulances and are qualified to carry out first aid.

9 Pharmacies

A green cross indicates a pharmacy (chemist). They are usually open between 9am–7pm Monday to Saturday. At other times, each pharmacy will have the address of the nearest one open on the door or window. Pharmacies can tell you where the nearest doctor is.

10 Dentists

These are listed in the Paris *Pages Jaunes (Yellow Pages)* under *Médecins Qualifiés*. In a dire emergency, a service called SOS Dentistes will provide a house call, but be prepared to pay. A large dental practice is at the Centre Médical Europe. *SOS Dentistes: 87 blvd Port Royal, 01 43 37 51 00 • Centre Médical Europe: 44 rue d'Amsterdam, 01 42 81 93 33*

Emergency Numbers

Police
17

Ambulance (SAMU)
15

Fire Department
18

Left **The Westin Paris** Centre **Hôtel le Parc** Right **Ritz Hotel**

Top 10 Luxury Hotels

1 Hôtel de Crillon

With one of the best locations in Paris, one of the best restaurants and one of the best reputations, the Crillon is for those who enjoy their comforts. From the marble lounge to the light and spacious rooms, the Crillon oozes class. *10 pl de la Concorde, 75008 • Map D3 • 01 44 71 15 00 • www.crillon.com • No disabled access • €€€€€*

2 Four Seasons George V

Recently modernized to great effect, all the rooms have been upgraded, while retaining certain features like the panelled Bar Anglais. The revamped restaurant, Le Cinq, has become one of "the" places to eat. *31 ave George V, 75008 • Map C3 • 01 49 52 70 00 • www.fourseasons.com/paris • €€€€€*

3 The Westin Paris

A world away from the usual anonymity of chain hotels, being set in a 19th-century building designed by Charles Garnier, also responsible for the Paris Opéra *(see p97)*. The original atmosphere has been retained, but the rooms offer everything you would expect from the name. *3 rue de Castiglione, 75001 • Map E3 • 01 44 77 11 11 • www.westin.com • €€€€€*

4 Lotti

An intimate version of a grand hotel, with the atmosphere of a private club. Most rooms are spacious and well equipped, but it has resisted the thorough modernization that many of its rivals have undergone. *7 rue Castiglione, 75001 • Map E3 • 01 42 60 60 62 • www.hotel-lotti-paris.com • €€€€€*

5 Meurice

The sumptuous antique decor of the Meurice may not be original, but you would never know it. The fading hotel has been completely restored rather than just refurbished, creating spacious guest rooms and state-of-the-art facilities, while retaining a traditional feel. And the location could not be better. *228 rue de Rivoli, 75001 • Map E3 • 01 44 58 10 15 • www.lemeurice.com • €€€€€*

6 Le Parc Sofitel Demeure

The façade of this 1912 mansion conceals a beautiful flower-filled courtyard, while the interior decor combines the feel of the old with the design of the new. Superchef Alain Ducasse has his top restaurant, 59 Poincaré, right next door *(see p139)*. *55–7 ave Raymond Poincaré, 75016 • Map B3 • 01 44 05 66 66 • www.sofitel.com • €€€€€*

7 Plaza Athénée

Surrounded by designer shops *(see p108)* is this venerable but thoroughly modernized hotel. Alain Ducasse has a restaurant in the hotel *(see p109)*. *25 ave Montaigne, 75008 • Map C3 • 01 53 67 66 65 • www.plaza-athenee-paris.com • €€€€€*

8 Hôtel Raphaël

One of the city's finest hotels. The antique decor is reflected in the rooms but they have been fully modernized in terms of facilities. Higher floors have stunning Parisian views. *17 ave Kleber, 75016 • Map B3 • 01 53 64 32 00 • www.raphael-hotel.com • €€€€€*

9 Ritz Hotel

The Ritz has never lost its glamour and still attracts visiting film stars, royalty and politicians. Antique furniture is backed up by every modern requirement. *15 pl Vendôme, 75001 • Map E3 • 01 43 16 30 30 • www.ritz.com • €€€€€*

10 Westminster

This hotel was built in the 18th century and has only been a hotel for 20 years, combining modern facilities with elegant English-style furnishings. *13 rue de la Paix, 75002 • Map E3 • 01 42 61 57 46 • www.warwickhotels.com • €€€€€*

***Note:** Unless otherwise stated, all hotels accept credit cards, have en-suite bathrooms and air conditioning*

Price Categories

For a standard, double room per night (with breakfast if included), taxes and extra charges.		
	€	under €100
	€€	€100–€150
	€€€	€150–€250
	€€€€	€250–€350
	€€€€€	over €350

Left **Brighton** Right **Hôtel du Panthéon**

TOP 10 Hotels in Great Locations

1 Hôtel Edouard VII

An elegant boutique hotel with eclectic design features and oodles of charm. Most rooms have the bonus of breath-taking balcony views over the spectacular Opéra National de Paris Garnier *(see p97)*. *39 avenue de l'Opéra, 75002 • Map E3 • 01 42 61 56 90 • www.edouard7hotel.com • info@edouard7hotel.com • No disabled access • €€€€€*

2 Brighton

Enjoy the rue de Rivoli location without paying the usual prices associated with this location. This old hotel is slowly being renovated, so try to get one of the newer rooms with a view over the Tuileries opposite *(see p95)*. *218 rue de Rivoli, 75001 • Map K1 • 01 47 03 61 61 • www.paris-hotel-brighton.com • No disabled access • €€€*

3 Bristol

Prices reflect the luxury standards and location, close to the fashionable shops of St-Honoré, and near the Elysée palaces *(see pp103–104)*. Rooms are large and fitted out with antique furniture and marble bathrooms. *112 rue du Faubourg-St-Honoré, 75008 • Map D3 • 01 53 43 43 00 • www.lebristolparis.com • resa@lebristolparis.com • €€€€€*

4 Hôtel du Jeu de Paume

Tucked away on the Ile St-Louis is this beautiful old building with beams. Rooms are small but the friendly atmosphere makes up for everything. *54 rue St-Louis-en-l'Ile, 75004 • Map Q5 • 01 43 26 14 18 • www.jeudepaumehotel.com • info@jeudepaumehotel.com • No air conditioning • No disabled access • €€€€*

5 Hôtel des Deux-Iles

To stay on one of the Seine islands is a treat, and to do it in this hotel is a double treat. The bedrooms may be small, due to the building's 17th-century origins, but the cheerful decor, the intimacy (only 17 rooms) and the hidden patio with its flowers and fountain more than compensate. *59 rue St-Louis-en-l'Ile, 75004 • Map Q5 • 01 43 26 13 35 • www.deuxiles-paris-hotel.com • No disabled access • €€€*

6 Hôtel d'Orsay

Art-lovers will enjoy this hotel, right by the magnificent Musée d'Orsay *(see pp12–15)*. The hotel's modern bright colours are strikingly offset with antique furniture here and there. Several more expensive suites are also available. *93 rue de Lille, 75007 • Map J2 • 01 47 05 85 54 • www.paris-hotel-orsay.com • €€€*

7 Hôtel du Panthéon

A small, family-run hotel set in an 18th-century building right by the Panthéon *(see pp28–9)*. *19 place du Panthéon, 75005 • Map N6 • 01 43 54 32 95 • www.hoteldupantheon.com • reservation@hoteldupantheon.com • €€€*

8 Pavillon de la Reine

The best hotel in the Marais, convenient for all the attractions of the area *(see pp84–7)*. Lovely rooms and a quiet court-yard. *28 pl des Vosges, 75003 • Map R3 • 01 40 29 19 19 • www.pavillon-de-la-reine.com • contact@pavillon-de-la-reine.com • €€€€€*

9 Hôtel de la Place du Louvre

A hotel that provides its guests with a superb view of the Louvre *(see pp10– 13)*. The rooms cleverly mix the historical with the modern. *21 rue des Prêtres-St-Germain-l'Auxerrois, 75001 • Map M2 • 01 42 33 78 68 • www.paris-hotel-place-du-louvre.com • No disabled access • €€*

10 Hôtel Castille

This sumptuous hotel is located close to many attractions. It also boasts a renowned restaurant. *33 rue Cambon, 75001 • Map E3 • 01 44 58 44 58 • www.castille.com • hotel@castille.com • €€€€€*

Recommend your favourite hotel on traveldk.com

Left **Hôtel Favart** Centre **Aviatic Hôtel** Right **Hôtel de l'Elysée Faubourg St-Honoré**

TOP 10 Romantic Hotels

1 Hôtel d'Aubusson

The rooms in this 17th-century building are spacious and many of them have beams. In winter there is a log fire in the guests' lounge. *33 rue Dauphine, 75006 • Map M4 • 01 43 29 43 43 • www.hoteldaubusson.com • €€€€*

2 Hôtel Favart

A venerable hotel with modern bedrooms. Mirrored bathrooms and beams in the first-floor rooms make for a romantic setting. *5 rue Marivaux, 75002 • Map E3 • 01 42 97 59 83 • www.hotel-paris-favart.com • €€*

3 Aviatic Hôtel

A homely hotel that bubbles with the delightful atmosphere of the Left Bank. Ask them to pack a picnic for you for a romantic stroll around the nearby Jardin du Luxembourg *(see p119)*. *105 rue de Vaugirad, 75006 • Map D6 • 01 53 63 25 50 • www. aviatic.fr • welcome@aviatic. fr • No disabled access • €€€*

4 L'Hôtel

This hotel has come up in the world since Oscar Wilde expired here, having uttered the famous words, "My wallpaper and I are fighting a duel to the death. One or the other of us has to go." Fashionable as it has become, with decor by Jacques Garcia, the hotel still has a quirky charm. *13 rue des Beaux-Arts, 75006 • Map E4 • 01 44 41 99 00 • www.l-hotel.com • €€€€€*

5 Hôtel de l'Elysée Faubourg St-Honoré

Some of the rooms have four-poster beds, so if planning a romantic getaway be sure to specify one of these. The public rooms are plush and the hotel is around the corner from the Presidential Palace. *12 rue des Saussaies, 75008 • Map D3 • 01 42 65 29 25 • www.france-hotel-guide.com • No disabled access • €€*

6 Five Hotel

Fibre-optic lighting creates a glittering atmosphere in many of this boutique hotel's 24 rooms. Guests can choose from nine colours, ranging from tranquil black to cheerful plum-and-pink, and five "olfactory ambiances" by Diptyque. The Five has already established a reputation as the perfect lovers' getaway. *3 rue Flatters, 75005 • 01 43 31 74 21 • www.thefivehotel.com • €€€*

7 Hôtel Costes

Book a first-floor room overlooking the courtyard for a romantic place to stay. Low lighting and dark furniture add to the mood, as does the Oriental-style swimming pool and trendy restaurant. *239 rue St-Honoré, 75001 • Map E3 • 01 42 44 50 00 • hotel.costes@wanadoo.fr • €€€€€*

8 Le Relais Christine

This 17th-century mansion offers a back-street haven from the St-Germain bustle. Opt for a terraced room overlooking the secluded garden and take breakfast in the vaulted room which was once an abbey's refectory. *3 rue Christine, 75006 • Map M4 • 01 40 51 60 80 • www.relais-christine.com • No disabled access • €€€€€*

9 Hôtel Lancaster

Pampering is paid for here, but the investment pays off with huge rooms in a 19th-century mansion just a stroll from the Champs-Elysées. *7 rue de Berri, 75008 • Map C3 • 01 40 76 40 76 • www.hotel-lancaster.fr • reservations@hotel-lancaster.fr • No disabled access • €€€€€*

10 Hôtel Caron de Beaumarchais

If you find your romance in the days of the 18th-century, then this hotel will be perfect. Period furniture and classical music attempt to capture that era. Rooms are beautiful and guests are truly pampered. *12 rue Vieille-du-Temple, 75004 • Map R2 • 01 42 72 34 12 • www.carondebeaumarchais.com • hotel@carondebeaumarchais.com • No disabled access • €€*

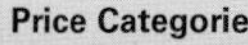

Price Categories

For a standard,	€	under €100
double room per	€€	€100–€150
night (with breakfast	€€€	€150–€250
if included), taxes	€€€€	€250–€350
and extra charges.	€€€€€	over €350

Left **Hôtel des Grandes Écoles** Right **Hôtel Lenox Montparnasse**

Top 10 Budget Hotels

1 Hôtel des Grandes Écoles

A secret hideaway in a lovely part of Paris, the two buildings that make up this 51-room hotel are set around a garden. The rooms are attractively decorated and the location is perfect as a base for exploring the Latin Quarter. *75 rue du Cardinal-Lemoine, 75005 • Map P6 • 01 43 26 79 23 • www. hotel-grandes-ecoles. com • No air conditioning • €€*

2 Hôtel Lenox Montparnasse

The flower-filled Lenox is close to Montparnasse cemetery *(see p151)*. The rooms are clean, with modern facilities. Some are on the small side so ask for a larger room if you don't like being too cramped: there is also a top-floor suite. *15 rue Delambre, 75014 • Map D6 • 01 43 35 34 50 • www. paris-hotel-lenox.com • No disabled access • €€€*

3 Hôtel Saint-André-des-Arts

This charmingly modest hotel offers unique character and a Left Bank location at bargain prices. The rooms are tiny, but for a cheap bolt-hole and truly Parisian Bohemian feel, it can't be beaten. *66 rue St-André-des-Arts, 75006 • Map M4 • 01 43 26 96 16 • hsaintand@ wanadoo.fr • No air conditioning • No disabled access • €*

4 Hôtel Amour

Situated just below Montmartre, this extremely trendy, vintage hotel and bistro has medium-sized rooms decorated with cutting edge photography and pop art (bare bottoms are much in evidence). As it is on a quiet residential street, guests can experience Parisian Bohemia without the usual crowds. *8 rue Navarin, 75009 • Map F1 • 01 48 78 31 80 • www.hotelamour.com • €€*

5 Grand Hôtel Lévêque

The only thing grand about this hotel is its name, but it remains a favourite for budget accommodation in Paris. Almost all rooms have fans, phone, TV, hairdryer and even a modem socket. *29 rue Cler, 75007 • Map C4 • 01 47 05 49 15 • www.hotel-leveque.com •info@hotel-leveque.com • No disabled access • €*

6 Hôtel de Lille

If you want a cheap central hotel, they come no cheaper nor more central than the Lille, just a minute's walk from the Louvre Museum. Rooms are clean but basic, and there is no breakfast and no elevator serving the five floors. *8 rue du Pélican, 75001 • Map M2 • 01 42 33 33 42 • No credit cards • No air conditioning • No disabled access • €*

7 Le Caulaincourt Square Hôtel

You may not get luxury but you do get a friendly atmosphere and access to the sights of Montmartre. *2 square Caulaincourt, 75018 • Map E1 • 01 46 06 46 06 • www.caulaincourt.com • No air conditioning • No disabled access • €*

8 Hôtel Plessis

Delightful hotel in an untouristed area of Paris. Rooms are compact, old fashioned but clean. Fifth-floor rooms have balconies; all have TV and phone. *25 rue du Grand Prieuré, 75011 • 01 47 00 13 38 • hotel.plessis@club-internet.fr • No air conditioning • No disabled access • €*

9 Hôtel du Globe

Set in a 17th-century building near the Jardin du Luxembourg, flowers fill the rooms and some have four-poster beds. *15 rue des Quatre Vents, 75006 • Map E6 • 01 43 26 35 50 • www.hotel-du-globe.fr • No air conditioning • No disabled access • €€*

10 Ermitage Hôtel

A wonderful family-run hotel in Montmartre. Some rooms have views over the city, others overlook a garden, and the furniture is antique or repro. *24 rue Lamarck, 75018 • Map E1 • 01 42 64 79 22 • www.ermitage sacrecoeur.fr • No credit cards • No air conditioning • No disabled access • €*

***Note:** Unless otherwise stated, all hotels accept credit cards, have en-suite bathrooms and air conditioning*

Left **Hôtel de Seine** Right **Hôtel de Banville**

Top 10 Medium-Priced Hotels

1 La Régence Étoile Hôtel

Very reasonably priced for its standard and location (a short walk from the Arc de Triomphe), the Régence has plush public areas and modern bedrooms with TVs, direct-dial phones, mini-bars and safe. *24 ave Carnot, 75017 • Map B2 • 01 58 05 42 42 • www. laregenceetoile.com • No disabled access • €€€*

2 Hôtel d'Angleterre

Hemingway once stayed in this long-established hotel. Most rooms are a good size with high ceilings, and some are decorated with antiques. The standard rooms are small so book a superior one at extra cost. *44 rue Jacob, 75006 • Map N5 • 01 42 60 34 72 • www.hotel-dangleterre. com • No air conditioning • No disabled access • €€€*

3 L'Abbaye Saint-Germain

This 16th-century former convent has a cobbled courtyard in a quiet location near St-Sulpice *(see p41)*. It is perfect for exploring much of the Left Bank, and is a haven to return to afterwards. The 46 rooms are all different, the best being the top-floor suites with their rooftop views. *10 rue Cassette, 75006 • Map K5 • 01 45 44 38 11 • www.hotel-abbaye.com • hotel.abbaye@wanadoo.fr • No disabled access • €€€*

4 Hôtel de Seine

Timbered rooms indicate the old-world nature of this mansion, close to the Jardin du Luxembourg. Some rooms have balconies. *52 rue de Seine, 75006 • Map L5 • 01 46 34 22 80 • www.hotel-de-seine.com • No air conditioning • No disabled access • €€€*

5 Hôtel Ferrandi

This bargain hotel combines old-fashioned comfort with modern convenience. *92 rue du Cherche-Midi, 75006 • Map J6 • 01 42 22 97 40 • www.france-hotel-guide. com • hotel.ferrandi@ wanadoo.fr • No disabled access • €€*

6 Hôtel Le Clos Médicis

Built in 1773 for the Médici family, ancient beams and artworks now combine with modern design. Rooms are small, but compensations are the garden, adjacent bar, and the location in a quiet street off boulevard St-Michel. *56 rue Monsieur-le-Prince, 75006 • Map M5 • 01 43 29 10 80 • www.closmedicis.com • message@closmedicis. com • 1 room suitable for disabled guests • €€€*

7 Hotel des Trois Poussins

In the Pigalle area but well away from the sleazy side. Some rooms are small, but the higher they go, the better the view. *15 rue Clauzel, 75009 • Map E1 • 01 53 32 81 81 • www. les3poussins. com • h3p@les3poussins. com • No disabled access • €€€*

8 Hôtel Saint-Merry

This hotel is unlike any other – one room even sports its own flying buttress. Carved bedboards and other features ensure an historical experience. *78 rue de la Verrerie, 75004 • Map P2 • 01 42 78 14 15 • www. hotelmarais.com • hotelstmerry@wanadoo.fr • No air conditioning • No disabled access • €€€*

9 Hôtel Saint-Paul

This 17th-century building has antique furniture and some rooms have four-poster beds and others overlook the Jardin du Luxembourg. *43 rue Monsieur-le-Prince, 75006 • Map M5 • 01 43 26 98 64 • www.hotelsaintpaul.fr • contact@hotelsaintpaul paris.com • €€€*

10 Hôtel de Banville

This wonderful 1928 mansion may be away from the centre but it oozes class and is filled with antiques. Several bedrooms have four-poster beds. *166 blvd Berthier, 75017 • Metro Porte de Clichy • 01 42 67 70 16 • www.hotelbanville. fr • €€€€*

Note: *Unless other-wise stated, all hotels accept credit cards, have en-suite bathrooms and air conditioning*

Price Categories

For a standard, double room per night (with breakfast if included), taxes and extra charges.

€	under €100
€€	€100–€150
€€€	€150–€250
€€€€	€250–€350
€€€€€	over €350

Left **Hotel Résidence Lord Byron** Right **Hôtel Chopin**

Top 10 Famous-Name Hotels

1 Hôtel Esmeralda

The proximity to Notre-Dame gives the hotel its name. Ask for a room with a cathedral view, and be prepared for a Bohemian atmosphere. The area is noisy and the rooms are not modernized, though most have en suite bathrooms. *4 rue St-Julien-le-Pauvre, 75005 • Map P4 • 01 43 54 19 20 • No air conditioning • No disabled access • €*

2 Résidence Lord Byron

An inexpensive hotel in an expensive area, with a pleasant courtyard garden for summer breakfasts. Top floor rooms are cheaper because the elevator doesn't go that far, but they do have good views. *5 rue Chateaubriand, 75008 • Map C2 • 01 43 59 89 98 • www.hotel-lordbyron.fr • lordbyron@hotel-lordbyron.fr • No disabled access • €€€*

3 Balzac

Fashionably chic, this luxurious hotel has a restaurant and a basement bar, both popular with locals. The 57 rooms and 13 apartments are simply but tastefully decorated, with terraced suites offering great views of the Eiffel Tower. *6 rue Balzac, 75008 • Map C2 • 01 44 35 18 00 • www.hotelbalzac.com • reservation-balzac@jjwhotels.com • No disabled access • €€€€€*

4 Hôtel Chopin

Hidden away in one of the city's *passages* *(see p50)*, the Chopin opened in 1846. At this price don't expect the best facilities, but it is a pleasant place to stay and the rooms are comfortable. Ask for an upper room for more light. *46 passage Jouffroy, 10 blvd Montmartre, 75009 • Map F2 • 01 47 70 58 10 • www.hotelbretonnerie.com • No air conditioning • No disabled access • €*

5 Hôtel Daguerre

Surprisingly smart hotel at the budget end of the market. Rooms are brightly decorated, if a little small, but some of the upper ones have views of Sacré-Coeur and others overlook the patio garden. *94 rue Daguerre, 75014 • Metro Gaîté • 01 43 22 43 54 • http://hoteldaguerre.monsite.wanadoo.fr • €*

6 Hôtel Flaubert

Terrific value, slightly out of the centre but not far from the metro. New owners have smartened it up; bamboo furniture complements lush gardens. Room sizes vary. *19 rue Rennequin, 75017 • Map C1 • 01 46 22 44 35 • www.hotelflaubert. com • paris@hotelflaubert.com • €€*

7 Hôtel Baudelaire Opéra

The French writer Baudelaire lived here in 1854, and today it makes a good bargain find in this central area. Rooms are brightly decorated, although most of them are small. *61 rue St-Anne, 75002 • Map H4 • 01 42 97 50 62 • www.paris-hotel.net • resa@paris-hotel.net • No air conditioning • No disabled access • €€€*

8 Hôtel Victor Hugo

This long-established hotel has some delightful features, including a vegetable cart that's used for the buffet in the garden breakfast room. *19 rue Copernic, 75016 • Map B3 • 01 45 53 76 01 • www.victorhugohotel.com • paris@victorhugohotel.com • No disabled access • €€€*

9 Hôtel Galileo

Tasteful decor and a walled garden, all just a short walk away from the Arc de Triomphe. *54 rue Galilée, 75008 • Map B2 • 01 47 20 66 06 • www.galileo-paris-hotel.com • No disabled access • €€€*

10 Grand Hôtel Jeanne d'Arc

You could pass a whole weekend in Paris without wandering far from this well-equipped hotel, surrounded as it is by Marais attractions. *3 rue de Jarente, 75004 • Metro St-Paul • 01 48 87 62 11 • www.hoteljeannedarc.com • information@hoteljeannedarc.com • No air conditioning • No disabled access • €*

Recommend your favourite hotel on traveldk.com

Left **Hotel Square** Centre **Hôtel du Quai Voltaire** Right **Le Notre-Dame**

Top 10 Rooms with a View

1 Hôtel Bourgogne et Montana

Stylish hotel, with the Musée d'Orsay *(see pp12–15)* and the Invalides close by. Top floor rooms have great views across the Seine. Paintings line the walls, antique furniture and gilt-lined mirrors abound. *3 rue de Bourgogne, 75007 • Map D4 • 01 45 51 20 22 • www.bourgogne-montana.com • No disabled access • €€€*

2 Artus Hôtel

Indulge yourself in the food shops of the Rue de Buci *(see p123)*, then indulge yourself even more back in this hotel – especially if you have booked the suite with a Jacuzzi from which there are great views of the Latin Quarter. *34 rue de Buci, 75006 • Map L4 •01 43 29 07 20 • www.artushotel.com • info@artushotel.com • No disabled access • €€€€*

3 Hotel Square

Boutique-style hotel with 22 rooms and views down the Seine to the Eiffel Tower. Slightly out of the centre, but makes up for it with style. *3 rue de Boulainvilliers, 75016 • Map A5 • 01 44 14 91 90 • www.hotelsquare.com • reservation@hotelsquare.com • €€€€*

4 Hôtel du Quai Voltaire

Impressionist artist Camille Pissarro (1831–1903) painted the view of the Seine and Notre-Dame visible from most of the guest rooms here. Rooms are small, but the warm welcome and the location more than make up for that. *19 quai Voltaire, 75007 • Map K2 • 01 42 61 50 91 • www.quai voltaire.fr • No air conditioning • No disabled access • €€*

5 Hôtel des Grands Hommes

Great views of the Panthéon *(see pp28–9)* from this intimate 32-room family hotel in an 18th-century house. The rooms are reasonably sized. *17 pl du Panthéon, 75005 • Map N6 • 01 46 34 19 60 • www.hoteldesgrandshommes.com • No disabled access • €€€*

6 Terrass Hôtel

The Terrass has fabulous views over Paris which can be enjoyed from its rooftop terrace. Most rooms in this early 19th-century building are now air-conditioned; all are comfortable. There is a bar, restaurant and other facilities. *12–14 rue Joseph-de-Maistre, 75018 • Map E1 • 01 44 92 34 14 • www.terrass-hotel.com • reservation@terrass-hotel.com • No disabled access • €€€€*

7 Le Notre-Dame

A great location right by the Seine with magnificent views of Notre-Dame, the bright decor here makes up for the size of the rooms. There are three suites. *1 quai St Michel, 75005 • Map N4 • 01 43 54 20 43 • www.paris-hotel-notredame.com • hotel.lenotredame@libertysurf.fr • No disabled access • €€€*

8 Les Rives de Notre-Dame

The view of Notre-Dame from this 10-room hotel is arguably the best in Paris. The decor is modern and the rooms are fairly spacious. *15 quai St-Michel, 75005 • Map N4 • 01 43 54 81 16 • www.rivesdenotredame.com • hotel@rivesdenotredame.com • No disabled access • €€€*

9 Hôtel Régina

Across the rue de Rivoli from the Louvre *(see pp8–11)* with views of the Tuileries, this is a splendid old hotel. *2 pl des Pyramides, 75001 • Map K1 • 01 42 60 31 10 • www.regina-hotel.com • €€€€€*

10 Metropolitan Hotel

There is a view of the Eiffel Tower from the top floors of this charming hotel. Rooms are equipped for business travellers, but there are family rooms. *86 rue de Longchamp, 75016 • Map A3 • 01 45 05 13 63 • www.metropolitan-paris.com • No disabled access*

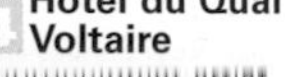

Note: *Unless otherwise stated, all hotels accept credit cards, have en-suite bathrooms and air conditioning*

Price Categories

For a standard, double room per night (with breakfast if included), taxes and extra charges.		
	€	under €100
	€€	€100–€150
	€€€	€150–€250
	€€€€	€250–€350
	€€€€€	over €350

Left **Relais St-Germain** Right **Fleurie**

TOP 10 Family-Friendly Hotels

1 Hôtel Baltimore

Part of the Sofitel hotel chain and situated between the Trocadéro and the Arc de Triomphe, the Baltimore caters well for families with good facilities and a friendly attitude. Rooms and suites are elegant. *88 bis avenue Kléber, 75016 • Map B3 • 01 44 34 54 54 • www.accorhotels.com • No disabled access • €€€€€*

2 Relais St-Germain

There are four apartments for rent in this hotel, close to the Jardin du Luxembourg for when the children simply want to play in the park. All have their own cooking facilities, which will help keep down the cost of a family holiday. *9 carrefour de l'Odéon, 75006 • Map L4 • 01 43 29 12 05• www.hotel-paris-relais-saint-germain.com • hotelrsg@wanadoo.fr • No disabled access • €€€€*

3 Relais du Louvre

Right by the Louvre and therefore with easy access to many of the city's main sights, several rooms can be combined, and some suites too. Decor varies from traditional to bright and modern, so state which you prefer. *19 rue des Prêtres-Saint-Germain-l'Auxerrois, 75001 • Map M2 • 01 40 41 96 42• www.relaisdulouvre.com • contact@relaisdulouvre.com • No disabled access • €€€*

4 Fleurie

Children under-12 stay free in this smart but lively St-Germain hotel, and those over 12 can have an extra bed in their parents' room for a small charge. Satellite TV and PC connections in each room, and a huge buffet breakfast. *32–4 rue Grégoire de Tours, 75006 • Map L4 • 01 53 73 70 00 • www.fleurie-hotel-paris.com • bonjour@hotel-de-fleurie.fr • No disabled access • €€€*

5 Méridien Montparnasse

Facilities here are what you would expect from a large chain hotel. Children's entertainment is laid on during Sunday brunch. *19 rue du Commandant René Mouchotte, 75014 • Map D6 • 01 44 36 44 36 • www.lemeridien-montparnasse.com • €€€*

6 Hôtel de l'Université

In this 17th-century St-Germain mansion, there is a discount for children sharing a room with their parents. *22 rue de l'Université, 75007 • Map K3 • 01 42 61 09 39 • www.hoteluniversite.com • hoteluniversite@wanadoo.fr • No disabled access • €€€*

7 Hôtel des Arts

A good choice for families on a budget, with triple rooms and cots available. The hotel is in one of Paris's *passages (see p50). 7 Cité Bergère, 6 rue du Faubourg Montmartre, 75009 • Map F2 • 01 42 46 73 30 • www.hoteldesarts.fr • contact@hoteldesarts.fr • No air conditioning • No disabled access • €*

8 Hôtel St-Jacques

Numerous Left Bank attractions are near this comfortable hotel with family rooms and cots available. Almost all rooms are en-suite and have TV. *35 rue des Écoles, 75005 • Map N5 • 01 44 07 45 45 • www.hotel-saintjacques.com • hotelsaintjacques@wanadoo.fr • No air conditioning • No disabled access • €€*

9 Résidence Hôtel Malesherbes

A collection of intriguing studios makes up for the slightly out-of-centre location. Parc Monceau and a good market are nearby. *129 rue Cardinet, 75017 • Map D1 • 01 44 15 85 00 • www.hotelparis17.com • hotel@hotel-romance.com • No air conditioning • No disabled access • €*

10 Hotel Ibis Bastille Opéra

Right in the heart of the Bastille district, this no-frills hotel may be a chain but it's handy for some of the city's best markets. Rooms are cheaper at weekends. *15 rue Breguet, 75011 • Map H5 • 01 49 29 20 20 • www.ibishotel.com • €*

For Paris for children **See pp60–61**

General Index

Acknowledgements

Authors
Donna Dailey and Mike Gerrard are award-winning journalists, specializing in travel, food and wine, and have written more than 30 guidebooks between them. Mike Gerrard's *Time for Food* guide to Paris for Thomas Cook won the Benjamin Franklin Award for best new guidebook in 2001. Their work has appeared in international publications such as the *Times*, *Washington Post* and *Global Adventure*.

Produced by Book Creation Services Ltd, London

Project Editor Zoë Ross
Art Editor Alison Verity
Designer Anne Fisher
Picture Research Monica Allende
Proofreader Stewart J Wild
Index Hilary Bird
Design and Editorial Assistance
Sonal Bhatt, Anna Brooke, Simon Davis, Nicola Erdpresser, Fay Franklin, Victoria Heyworth-Dunne, Conrad van Dyk, Paul Hines, Delphine Lawrance, Carly Madden, Sam Merrell, Jane Oliver-Jedrzejak, Helen Partington, Quadrum Solutions, Tamiko Rex, Philippa Richmond, Laura de Selincourt, Beatriz Waller, Sophie Warne, Dora Whitaker.

Additional Contributor Rosa Jackson
Main Photographer Peter Wilson
Additional Photography
Max Alexander, Michael Crockett, Robert O'Dea, Britta Jaschinski, Oliver Knight, Neil Lukas, Eric Meacher, Tony Souter, Steven Wooster

Illustrator Chris Orr & Associates

Cartography Dominic Beddow, Simonetta Giori (Draughtsman Ltd)
At Dorling Kindersley:

Senior Editor Marcus Hardy
Senior Art Editor Marisa Renzullo
Cartography Co-ordinator Casper Morris
Senior DTP Designer Jason Little
Production Joanna Bull, Marie Ingledew
Publishing Manager Kate Poole
Senior Publishing Manager Louise Bostock Lang
Director of Publishing Gillian Allan

Special Assistance
The authors would like to thank Eurostar and Room Service for help with their travel arrangements.

Picture Credits
t-top; tc-top centre; tr-top right; cla-centre left above; ca-centre above; cra-centre right above; cl-centre left; c-centre; cr-centre right; clb-centre left below; cb-centre below; crb-centre right below; bl-below left; bc below centre; br below right.

Works of art on the pages detailed have been reproduced with the permission of the following copyright holders:

Sculpture Palais Royale Courtyard Pol Bury @ADAGP, Paris and DACS, London 2006 96b; *Espace Montmartre* Salvador Dali © Kingdom of Spain, Gaia - Salvador Dali Foundation, DACS, London 2006 140tc; *Sculpture* Salvador Dali © Kingdom of Spain, Gaia - Salvador Dali Foundation, DACS, London 2006 144tl; *Lip Sofa* Salvador Dali © Kingdom of Spain, Gaia - Salvador Dali Foundation, DACS, London 2006 37c; *L'Ecoute* Henri de Miller ©ADAGP, Paris and DACS, London 2006 78tr; *Stravinsky Fountain* Niki de Saint Phalle and Jean Tinguely ©ADAGP, Paris and DACS, London 2006 27tr, 39r, 74tl.
The publishers would like to thank the following individuals, companies and picture libraries for permission to reproduce their photographs:

AFP, London: 56tl, 56b, 88tr; AKG, London:17tr, 20tl, 21tr, 29cr, 44tl, 44tr, 45t, 45c, 47c, 47b, 58b, 63t, 63b,128tc,135t, *Mona Lisa* by Leonardo da Vinci 6ca, 11t, 34tl, *The Raft of the Medusa* by Theodore Gericault 9t, *Leonardo da Vinci portrait* 11c, *Picnic on the Grass* by Manet 12b, *Empress Josephine* by Pierre Paul Prud'hon 20tc, *Capture* by Anton von Werner 23cr, *Tableau de Guerre Interprete* by Vallotton 114b, Erich Lessing: 10t, 10b,107tl, *The Lace-Maker* by Vermeer 9c, *Van Gogh Bedroom in Arles* by Van Gogh 12-13c, 36tl, *Statues of Dancers* by Degas 13t, *Cafe des Hauteurs* by Toulouse-Lautrec 13cr, *Blue Waterlilies* by Monet 13b, *Charles I* by workshop of Anthonis van Dyck 20tr, © Succession H Matisse/DACS, London 2006 *Sorrow of the King* by Matisse 27cr, 36b,

ALAMY IMAGES: Chad Ehlers 135tr, Matthew Richardson 171tc; MAX ALEXANDER: 4-5; ART ARCHIVE: Musée Carnavalet Paris/ Dagli Orti *Interior of Pantheon Church Paris* by Boilly 28-29c, Musee d'Orsay, Paris/ Dagli Orti *Blue Dancers* by Degas 14tl, *La Belle Angela* by Gaugin 14tr, *Cathedral at Rouen* by Monet 15t, *Dance at Moulin de la Galette* by Renoir 15b, 144b, *General Ferdinand Foch* 111b; L'ATELIER DE JOEL ROBUCHON: Gerard Bedeau 65cr; L'ATELIER MAITRE ALBERT: Eric Brissaud 127tr; AVIATIC HOTEL: 174c.

HOTEL BANVILLE: 176tr; BARRIO LATINO: 92tl; BRIDGEMAN ART LIBRARY: 26–27c, 45b, 46tr, 47t, Musee d'Armee, Paris 114tr, Lauros-Giraudon 128tr, *The Succession of Louis XIII* by Gianni 44b, Roger Viollet, Paris 114tl.

CAVEAU DE LA HUCHETTE Gary Wiggins performing 62b; CHRISTOPHE CAZARRE: 165 tr; CINEAQUA: 134TC; CORBIS: 33t.

RONALD GRANT ARCHIVE: 59t, 59c, 59b.

LA HALLE SAINT PIERRE: *Untitled* Stavroula Feleggakis 145tl.

LE JULES VERNE: Eric Laignel 64tc.

MUSEE NATIONALE DE LA MODE ET DU TEXTILE: Diego Zitelli 94tr.

MUSEE DU QUAI BRANLY: 112b.

SENDERENS: Roberto Frankenburg 99tl; LE SOUS-BOCK: Tarek Nini 79tc.

TOPHAM PICTUREPOINT: 21b, 46t, 56tr,57b,144tc,144b, 150cr, 154tl, 154 tr, 162tl, J.Brinon/STR 107tr, Daniel Frasnay 63b.

All other images are © DK. For further information see www.dkimages.com.

Phrase Book

In Emergency

Help!	**Au secours!**	*oh sekoor*
Stop!	**Arrêtez!**	*aret-ay*
Call a doctor!	**Appelez un médecin!**	*apuh-lay uñ medsañ*
Call an ambulance!	**Appelez une ambulance!**	*apuh-lay oon oñboo-loñs*
Call the police!	**Appelez la police!**	*apuh-lay lah poh-lees*
Call the fire brigade!	**Appelez les pompiers!**	*apuh-lay leh poñ-peeyay*

Communication Essentials

Yes/No	**Oui/Non**	*wee/noñ*
Please	**S'il vous plaît**	*seel voo play*
Thank you	**Merci**	*mer-see*
Excuse me	**Excusez-moi**	*exkoo-zay mwah*
Hello	**Bonjour**	*boñzhoor*
Goodbye	**Au revoir**	*oh ruh-vwar*
Good night	**Bonsoir**	*boñ-swar*
What?	**Quel, quelle?**	*kel, kel*
When?	**Quand?**	*koñ*
Why?	**Pourquoi?**	*poor-kwah*
Where?	**Où?**	*oo*

Useful Phrases

How are you?	**Comment allez-vous?**	*kom-moñ talay voo*
Very well,	**Très bien,**	*treh byañ*
Pleased to meet you.	**Enchanté de faire votre connaissance.**	*oñshoñ-tay duh fehr votr kon-ay-sans*
Where is/are…?	**Où est/sont…?**	*oo ay/soñ*
Which way to…?	**Quelle est la direction pour…?**	*kel ay lah deer-ek-syoñ poor*
Do you speak English?	**Parlez-vous anglais?**	*par-lay voo oñg-lay*
I don't understand.	**Je ne comprends pas.**	*zhuh nuh kom-proñ pah*
I'm sorry.	**Excusez-moi.**	*exkoo-zay mwah*

Useful Words

big	**grand**	*groñ*
small	**petit**	*puh-tee*
hot	**chaud**	*show*
cold	**froid**	*frwah*
good	**bon**	*boñ*
bad	**mauvais**	*moh-veh*
open	**ouvert**	*oo-ver*
closed	**fermé**	*fer-meh*
left	**gauche**	*gohsh*
right	**droit**	*drwah*
entrance	**l'entrée**	*l'on-tray*
exit	**la sortie**	*sor-tee*
toilet	**les toilettes**	*twah-let*

Shopping

How much does this cost?	**C'est combien s'il vous plaît?**	*say kom-byañ seel voo play*
I would like …	**je voudrais…**	*zhuh voo-dray*
Do you have?	**Est-ce que vous avez?**	*es-kuh voo zavay*
Do you take credit cards?	**Est-ce que vous acceptez les cartes de crédit?**	*es-kuh voo zaksept-ay leh kart duh kreh-dee*
What time do you open?	**A quelle heure êtes-vous ouvert?**	*ah kel urr voo zet oo-ver*
What time do you close?	**A quelle heure êtes-vous fermé?**	*ah kel urr voo zet fer-may*
This one.	**Celui-ci.**	*suhl-wee-see*
That one.	**Celui-là.**	*suhl-wee-lah*
expensive	**cher**	*shehr*
cheap	**pas cher, bon marché,**	*pah shehr, boñ mar-shay*
size, clothes	**la taille**	*tye*
size, shoes	**la pointure**	*pwañ-tur*
white	**blanc**	*bloñ*
black	**noir**	*nwahr*
red	**rouge**	*roozh*
yellow	**jaune**	*zhohwn*
green	**vert**	*vehr*
blue	**bleu**	*bluh*

Types of Shop

antique shop	**le magasin d'antiquités**	*maga-zañ d'oñteekee-tay*
bakery	**la boulangerie**	*booloñ-zhuree*
bank	**la banque**	*boñk*
bookshop	**la librairie**	*lee-brehree*
cake shop	**la pâtisserie**	*patee-sree*
cheese shop	**la fromagerie**	*fromazh-ree*
chemist	**la pharmacie**	*farmah-see*
department store	**le grand magasin**	*groñ maga-zañ*
delicatessen	**la charcuterie**	*sharkoot-ree*
gift shop	**le magasin de cadeaux**	*maga-zañ duh kadoh*
greengrocer	**le marchand de légumes**	*mar-shoñ duh lay-goom*
grocery	**l'alimentation**	*alee-moñta-syoñ*
market	**le marché**	*marsh-ay*
newsagent	**le magasin de journaux**	*maga-zañ duh zhoor-no*
post office	**la poste, le bureau de poste, le PTT**	*pohst, booroh duh pohst, peh-teh-teh*
supermarket	**le supermarché**	*soo pehr-marshay*
tobacconist	**le tabac**	*tabah*
travel agent	**l'agence de voyages**	*l'azhoñs duh vwayazh*

Sightseeing

abbey	**l'abbaye**	*l'abay-ee*
art gallery	**la galerie d'art**	*galer-ree dart*
bus station	**la gare routière**	*gahr roo-tee-yehr*
cathedral	**la cathédrale**	*katay-dral*
church	**l'église**	*l'aygleez*
garden	**le jardin**	*zhar-dañ*
library	**la bibliothèque**	*beebleeo-tek*
museum	**le musée**	*moo-zay*
railway station	**la gare (SNCF)**	*gahr (es-en-say-ef)*
tourist information office	**renseignements touristiques, le syndicat d'initiative**	*roñsayn-moñ toorees-teek, sandee-ka d'eenee-syateev*
town hall	**l'hôtel de ville**	*l'ohtel duh veel*

Staying in a Hotel

Do you have a vacant room?	**Est-ce que vous avez une chambre?**	*es-kuh voo-zavay oon shambr*
double room,	**la chambre à deux**	*shambr ah duh*

with double bed	**personnes, avec un grand lit**	*pehr-son avek un gronñ lee*
twin room	**la chambre à deux lits**	*shambr ah duh lee*
single room	**la chambre à une personne**	*shambr ah oon pehr-son*
room with a bath, shower	**la chambre avec salle de bains, une douche**	*shambr avek sal duh bañ, oon doosh*
I have a réservation.	**J'ai fait une reservation.**	*zhay fay oon rayzehrva-syoñ*

Eating Out

Have you got a table?	**Avez-vous une table libre?**	*avay-voo oon tahbl duh leebr*
I want to reserve a table.	**Je voudrais réserver une table.**	*zhuh voo-dray rayzehr-vay oon tahbl*
The bill please.	**L'addition s'il vous plaît.**	*l'adee-syoñ seel voo play*
Waitress/ waiter	**Madame, Mademoiselle/ Monsieur**	*mah-dam, mah-demwahzel/ muh-syuh*
menu	**le menu, la carte**	*men-oo, kart*
fixed-price menu	**le menu à prix fixe**	*men-oo ah pree feeks*
cover charge	**le couvert**	*koo-vehr*
wine list	**la carte des vins**	*kart-deh vañ*
glass	**le verre**	*vehr*
bottle	**la bouteille**	*boo-tay*
knife	**le couteau**	*koo-toh*
fork	**la fourchette**	*for-shet*
spoon	**la cuillère**	*kwee-yehr*
breakfast	**le petit déjeuner**	*puh-tee deh-zhuh-nay*
lunch	**le déjeuner**	*deh-zhuh-nay*
dinner	**le dîner**	*dee-nay*
main course	**le plat principal**	*plah prañsee-pal*
starter, first course	**l'entrée, le hors d'oeuvre**	*l'oñ-tray, or-duhvr*
dish of the day	**le plat du jour**	*plah doo zhoor*
wine bar	**le bar à vin**	*bar ah vañ*
café	**le café**	*ka-fay*

Menu Decoder

baked	**cuit au four**	*kweet oh foor*
beef	**le boeuf**	*buhf*
beer	**la bière**	*bee-yehr*
boiled	**bouilli**	*boo-yee*
bread	**le pain**	*pan*
butter	**le beurre**	*burr*
cake	**le gâteau**	*gah-toh*
cheese	**le fromage**	*from-azh*
chicken	**le poulet**	*poo-lay*
chips	**les frites**	*freet*
chocolate	**le chocolat**	*shoko-lah*
coffee	**le café**	*kah-fay*
dessert	**le dessert**	*deh-ser*
duck	**le canard**	*kanar*
egg	**l'oeuf**	*l'uf*
fish	**le poisson**	*pwah-ssoñ*
fresh fruit	**le fruit frais**	*frwee freh*
garlic	**l'ail**	*l'eye*
grilled	**grillé**	*gree-yay*
ham	**le jambon**	*zhoñ-boñ*
ice, ice cream	**la glace**	*glas*
lamb	**l'agneau**	*l'anyoh*
lemon	**le citron**	*see-troñ*
meat	**la viande**	*vee-yand*
milk	**le lait**	*leh*
mineral water	**l'eau minérale**	*l'oh meeney-ral*
oil	**l'huile**	*l'weel*
onions	**les oignons**	*leh zonyoñ*
fresh orange juice	**l'orange pressée**	*l'oroñzh press-eh*
fresh lemon juice	**le citron pressé**	*see-troñ press-eh*
pepper	**le poivre**	*pwavr*
pork	**le porc**	*por*
potatoes	**les pommes de terre**	*pom-duh tehr*
rice	**le riz**	*ree*
roast	**rôti**	*row-tee*
salt	**le sel**	*sel*
sausage, fresh	**la saucisse**	*sohsees*
seafood	**les fruits de mer**	*frwee duh mer*
snails	**les escargots**	*leh zes-kar-goh*
soup	**la soupe, le potage**	*soop, poh-tazh*
steak	**le bifteck, le steack**	*beef-tek, stek*
sugar	**le sucre**	*sookr*
tea	**le thé**	*tay*
vegetables	**les légumes**	*lay-goom*
vinegar	**le vinaigre**	*veenaygr*
water	**l'eau**	*l'oh*
red wine	**le vin rouge**	*vañ roozh*
white wine	**le vin blanc**	*vañ bloñ*

Numbers

0	**zéro**	*zeh-roh*
1	**un, une**	*uñ, oon*
2	**deux**	*duh*
3	**trois**	*trwah*
4	**quatre**	*katr*
5	**cinq**	*sañk*
6	**six**	*sees*
7	**sept**	*set*
8	**huit**	*weet*
9	**neuf**	*nerf*
10	**dix**	*dees*
11	**onze**	*oñz*
12	**douze**	*dooz*
13	**treize**	*trehz*
14	**quatorze**	*katorz*
15	**quinze**	*kañz*
16	**seize**	*sehz*
17	**dix-sept**	*dees-set*
18	**dix-huit**	*dees-weet*
19	**dix-neuf**	*dees-nerf*
20	**vingt**	*vañ*
30	**trente**	*tront*
40	**quarante**	*karoñt*
50	**cinquante**	*sañkoñt*
60	**soixante**	*swasoñt*
70	**soixante-dix**	*swasoñt-dees*
80	**quatre-vingts**	*katr-vañ*
90	**quatre-vingt-dix**	*katr-vañ-dees*
100	**cent**	*soñ*
1,000	**mille**	*meel*

Time

one minute	**une minute**	*oon mee-noot*
one hour	**une heure**	*oon urr*
half an hour	**une demi-heure**	*urr duh-me urr*
one day	**un jour**	*urr zhorr*
Monday	**lundi**	*luñ-dee*
Tuesday	**mardi**	*mar-dee*
Wednesday	**mercredi**	*mehrkruh-dee*
Thursday	**jeudi**	*zhuh-dee*
Friday	**vendredi**	*voñdruh-dee*
Saturday	**samedi**	*sam-dee*
Sunday	**dimanche**	*dee-moñsh*

Index of Main Streets